MASTERING THE GEORGIA

5TH GRADE

CRCT

IN

SOCIAL STUDIES

Developed to the Georgia Performance Standards

Kindred Howard
Katie Herman
Amy Fletcher
Cindy L. Rex
Elaine E. Schneider

American Book Company
PO Box 2638
Woodstock, GA 30188-1383
Toll Free: 1 (888) 264-5877 Phone: (770) 928-2834
Fax: (770) 928-7483 Toll Free Fax: 1 (866) 827-3240
www.americanbookcompany.com

Acknowledgements

The authors would like to gratefully acknowledge the formatting and technical contributions of Marsha Torrens and Yvonne Benson.

We also want to thank Charisse Johnson and Eric Field for developing the graphics for this book.

This product/publication includes images from CorelDRAW 9 and 11 which are protected by the copyright laws of the United States, Canada, and elsewhere. Used under license.

by American Book Company
PO Box 2638
Woodstock, GA 30188-1318

Printed in the United States of America

08/08 01/09 04/10

Table of Contents

Chapter 2 Historical Understandings: The Turn of the Century, World War I, and the 1920s 35

Chapter 3 Historical Understandings: The Great Depression and World War II 55

PREFACE

Mastering the Georgia 5th Grade CRCT in Social Studies will help students who are learning or reviewing material for the CRCT. The materials in this book are based on the testing standards as published by the Georgia Department of Education.

This book contains several sections. These sections are as follows: 1) general information about the book; 2) a diagnostic test; 3) an evaluation chart; 4) chapters that teach the concepts and skills that improve graduation readiness; 5) two practice tests. Answers to the tests and exercises are in a separate manual. The answer manual also contains a Chart of Standards for teachers to make a more precise diagnosis of student needs and assignments.

We welcome comments and suggestions about the book. Please contact the author at

American Book Company
PO Box 2638
Woodstock, GA 30188-1383

Toll Free: 1 (888) 264-5877
Phone: (770) 928-2834
Fax: (770) 928-7483
Web site: www.americanbookcompany.com

ABOUT THE AUTHORS

Lead Author:

Kindred Howard is a 1991 alumnus of the University of North Carolina at Chapel Hill, where he graduated with a B.S. in Criminal Justice and national honors in Political Science. In addition to two years as a probation and parole officer in North Carolina, he has served for over twelve years as a teacher and writer in the fields of religion and social studies. His experience includes teaching students at both the college and high school level, as well as speaking at numerous seminars. He is the author of several books on U.S. history, American government, and economics. His books are currently used by public schools in Georgia, the Carolinas, Louisiana, and Maryland. In 2005, Mr. Howard received a national recognition of excellence for scoring in the top fifteen percent, all time, on the national Praxis II exam for social studies. He currently serves as the social studies coordinator for American Book Company and is completing a M.A. in history at Georgia State University. Mr. Howard lives in Kennesaw, Georgia, with his wife and three children.

Katie Herman is a graduate of Kennesaw State University, where she received a B.A. in English. She is the co-author of several books on history and social studies, which are currently being used by public schools in Georgia and Louisiana. Ms. Herman currently works as a researcher and writer for American Book Company and plans to pursue a M.A. in professional writing. She lives in Woodstock, Georgia.

Amy Fletcher is a 2001 graduate of Brewton-Parker College in Mt. Vernon, Georgia, where she graduated with a B.S. in Early Childhood Education. She spent three years teaching elementary school before becoming an educational writer and stay-at-home mom. Her experience also includes directing and speaking at leadership conferences. She has authored children's fiction for magazine publication, and works with educational materials for grades K-8. Mrs. Fletcher lives in West Green, Georgia, with her husband and three children.

Cindy L. Rex is a 1984 alumnus of the University of Michigan-Flint. She graduated with a B.S. in Social Studies and Education and is a member of the education honor society, Kappa Delta Pi. In addition to a M.A. from Marygrove College, Detroit, she has thirty graduate credits from Eastern Michigan University in English. Her experience includes twenty-four years as a teacher and six years as a volleyball coach at Lakeville Middle School in Otisville, MI. She is also Head Teacher of the middle school building and the grade level Lead Teacher. She has been a constituent of the Michigan Educational Assessment Program as a team review member and the Item Writing Team (IWT), and was awarded a Fulbright Teacher Exchange for the 2008 – 2009 school year. Cindy lives in Birch Run, MI.

Elaine E. Schneider is a teacher and published author of several articles. As a freelance curriculum writer, she has worked with several major educational companies and is the managing editor of Lesson Tutor, an educational Web site.

Mastering the Georgia 5th Grade CRCT in SS Diagnostic Test

The purpose of this diagnostic test is to measure your knowledge in social studies. This test is based on the GPS-based Georgia CRCT in Social Studies and adheres to the sample question format provided by the Georgia Department of Education.

General Directions:

1. Read all directions carefully.
2. Read each question or sample. Then choose the best answer.
3. Choose only one answer for each question. If you change an answer, be sure to erase your original answer completely.
4. After taking the test, you or your instructor should score it using the evaluation chart following the test. Circle any questions you did not get correct and review those chapters.

1. The Twenty-sixth Amendment guarantees a U.S. citizen's right to vote at what age? SS5CG3

A. twenty-one

B. eighteen

C. sixteen

D. twenty-five

2. How did *Uncle Tom's Cabin* affect the abolitionist movement? SS5H1

A. It made abolitionists angry and even more determined to end slavery.

B. It created protests by Southern whites that ended the abolitionist movement.

C. It showed the importance of slavery and many abolitionists became slave owners.

D. It did not affect the abolitionist movement at all.

Read the quote below, and answer the following question.

> I'm an Oklahoma farmer, and my crops are not doing well. The Midwest is experiencing a horrible drought, making the soil very dry. Windstorms are ravaging the area, carrying the soil high into the air. Some of these storms are so big that they bury entire homes.

3. What is the quote above MOST LIKELY describing? SS5H5

A. stock market crash

B. Pearl Harbor

C. the great drought

D. the Dust Bowl

4. The line dividing Eastern and Western Europe after World War II was known as the SS5H7

A. Communist shield.

B. Great Divide.

C. iron curtain.

D. Berlin Wall.

5. Rebecca makes about $2500 a month. She pays $800 a month in rent and at least $1000 a month on other things. The remaining $700 a month goes in the bank. Which of the following statements is MOST accurate? SS5E4

A. Rebecca saves over half of her income.

B. Rebecca's expenses equal about $1800 a month.

C. Rebecca spends more than she makes.

D. Rebecca's expenses equal $2500 a month.

6. Which of the following is the BEST example of citizen participation in government? SS5CG1

A. attending a school

B. driving a car

C. owning a business

D. running for elected office

7. After the Civil War, tobacco and cotton became important industries in the SS5G2

A. North.

B. Midwest.

C. South.

D. East.

Use the map below to answer question number 8.

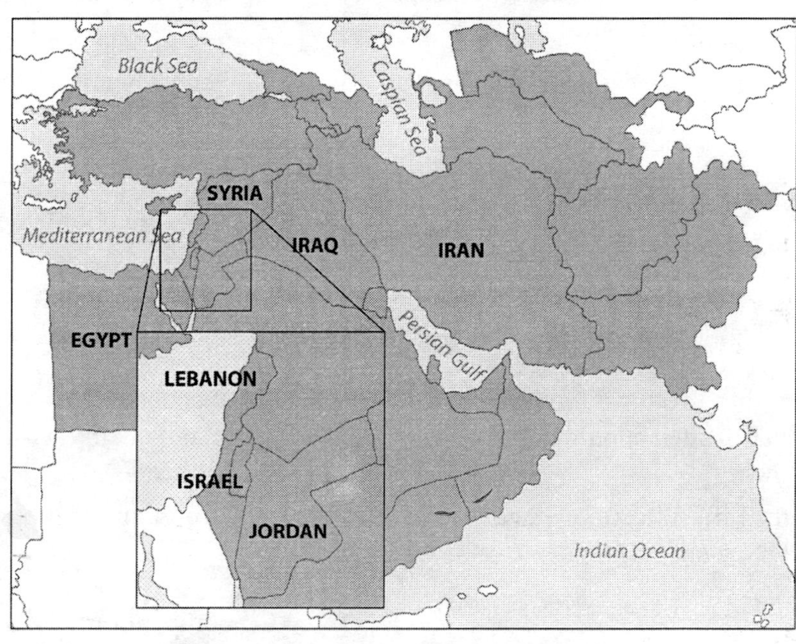

8. The entire region depicted in the map is often referred to as SS5H9

   A. Palestine.
   B. the Middle East.
   C. al Qaeda.
   D. the Persian Gulf.

9. Jake is trying to decide between a summer job as a camp counselor or as a farm laborer. The farm labor pays much better, but the work is more demanding with less time off. If Jake takes the job as a farm laborer, what would his opportunity cost be? SS5E1

   A. He would have more time off.
   B. He would make less money.
   C. He would have to work with children.
   D. There is no opportunity cost.

10. Which of the following BEST describes the United States' role in the formation of the United Nations? SS5H6

    A. The United States was very involved, hosting several meetings and becoming one of permanent members of the UN Security Council.
    B. The United States discussed the possibilities of an organization but never showed after World War II ended.
    C. The United States had no involvement in the formation of the United Nations.
    D. The United States refused to join the United Nations.

11. The three major institutions in the U.S. economy are SS5E2

A. corporations, taxes, and national parks.

B. private businesses, banks, and governments.

C. citizens, banks, and specialized industries.

D. businesses, taxes, and citizens.

12. A woman in the early 1900s who believed she should have the right to vote would have been MOST excited about which of the following? SS5CG3

A. the Fifteenth Amendment to the U.S. Constitution

B. the ideas of due process of law

C. the establishment of the Electoral College

D. the Nineteenth Amendment to the U.S. Constitution

13. Jim was an African American living in South Carolina in1865. He was uneducated and had no money or land. Which of the following would Jim MOST LIKELY have depended on? SS5H2

A. the Freedman's Bureau

B. the Compromise of 1877

C. the United Nations

D. black codes

14. During World War I, what did Germany use to attack ships? SS5H4

A. paratroopers

B. secret planes

C. U-boats

D. nuclear weapons

15. What do Gettysburg and Pittsburgh have in common? SS5G1

A. They are both in the East.

B. They are both located in Pennsylvania.

C. They are equal in size and population.

D. They are both famous for inventions.

16. Wal-Mart and Target sell many of the same items. Consumers must choose where to shop based on price and quality. What is this an example of? SS5E3

A. opportunity cost

B. government businesses

C. competition

D. fiscal policy

17. Which of the following is LEAST accurate about Martin Luther King, Jr.? SS5H8

A. He helped organize and lead the Montgomery bus boycott.

B. He often used violence to promote equality for African Americans.

C. He became the recognized leader of the civil rights movement.

D. One of his most famous speeches is known for the words "I have a dream."

18. Which of the following can lead to a new amendment to the Constitution? SS5CG2

A. jury duty

B. constitutional convention

C. campaign volunteering

D. due process

19. Suddenly, people were able to work at night. They could also eat later and enjoy activities normally reserved for daytime hours. Whose invention made these things possible? SS5H3
    A. Thomas Edison
    B. Alexander Graham Bell
    C. Jesse Owens
    D. Theodore Roosevelt

Read the list below and answer the following question.

- the economy prospered
- manufacturing and industries grew
- more jobs became available

20. What is the BEST heading for the list above? SS5H1
    A. Effects of the Civil War on the North
    B. Effects of the Civil War on the South
    C. Reasons the Civil War Ended
    D. Causes for the Start of the Civil War

21. Mark is arrested for a serious crime and sent to prison. After reviewing his case, the court realizes that the rules of the Constitution were not followed during Mark's trial. The court rules that the state SS5CG1
    A. violated Mark's right to due process.
    B. violated the principle of *E pluribus unum.*
    C. violated the Twenty-fourth Amendment.
    D. failed to fulfill its civic responsibility.

22. After World War II, tension between the United States and the Soviet Union escalated. Many feared this could lead to a nuclear war. What was this period called? SS5H7
    A. the Soviet scare
    B. the cold war
    C. the world crisis
    D. the War on Terror

23. G8 nations work together to maintain trade and peace. For instance, when Japan sells products in the United States, it helps the economies of both countries. What is this an example of? SS5E1
    A. voluntary exchange
    B. increased competition
    C. monetary policy
    D. fiscal policy

24. Which of the following was created by the flow of the Colorado River? SS5G1
    A. the Mojave Desert
    B. the Chisholm Trail
    C. the Grand Canyon
    D. the Salton Sea

25. Which of the following would have been MOST supportive of Jim Crow laws? SS5H2
    A. a Southern politician
    B. Abraham Lincoln
    C. an African American
    D. Ulysses S. Grant

Use the map below to answer the following question.

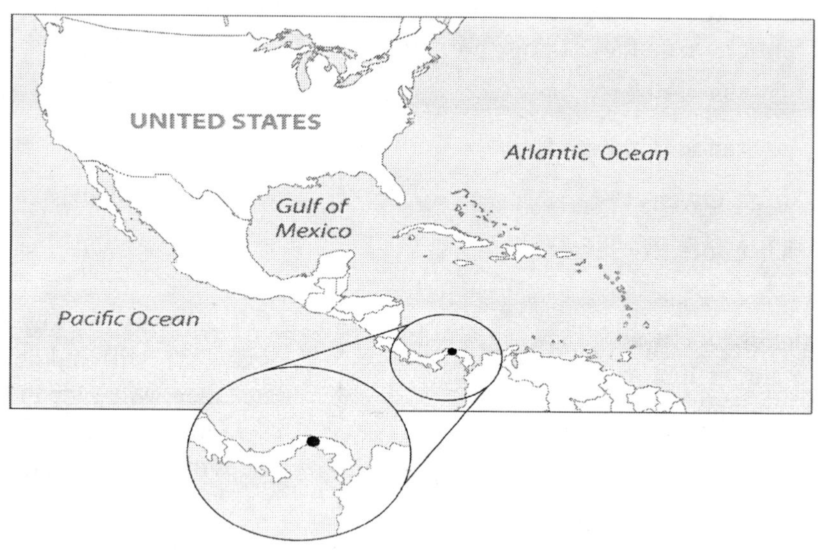

26. What does the image above MOST LIKELY represent? SS5H3

   A. Suez Canal
   B. Panama Canal
   C. Great Lakes Waterway
   D. Industrial Canal

27. The Montgomery bus boycott occurred in 1955. Which of the following was a direct outcome of this event? SS5H8

   A. Rosa Parks was murdered by members of the Ku Klux Klan.
   B. The Supreme Court ruled that any African Americans refusing to give up their bus seats would be arrested.
   C. The Supreme Court ruled that Montgomery could no longer segregate its buses.
   D. Martin Luther King Jr. became leader of the Black Panthers.

28. How did the development of railroads impact industrialization? SS5G2

   A. It led to the establishment of the first U.S. city.
   B. Railroads did not impact industrialization at all.
   C. Transportation to more areas became easier and industry expanded.
   D. Railroads led to the discovery of California.

Read the radio announcement that is listed below, and answer the following question.

> It's the bottom of the third inning. He smacks the ball high in the air, and it's sailing towards right field. It's out of the park! This is the first home run in All-Star game history. The fans are going wild! This is one of those magic moments in baseball when time stands still and the crowd is filled with a sense of greatness.

29. What American hero of the 1920s is the announcement MOST LIKELY referring to? SS5H4
    A. Hank Aaron
    B. Henry Ford
    C. Babe Ruth
    D. Chipper Jones

30. How did the 1929 stock market crash affect the United States economy? SS5H5
    A. Unemployment reached its highest level in United States history.
    B. Stock prices were higher than investors could afford.
    C. Congress voted to reject New Deal policies.
    D. Agriculture replaced manufacturing as the primary industry.

31. The money that workers receive for their labor is called SS5E3
    A. taxes.
    B. income.
    C. price.
    D. monetary policy.

32. What major event happened on September 11, 2001? SS5H9
    A. U.S.soldiers bombed Lebanon
    B. the Soviet Union collapsed
    C. the Persian Gulf War began
    D. terrorists attacked the United States

33. Which of the following states that delegates to the Electoral College vote separately for the offices of president and vice president of the United States? SS5CG3
    A. Twelfth Amendment
    B. Fifteenth Amendment
    C. Seventeenth Amendment
    D. Twenty-fourth Amendment

34. What is the BEST heading for the list below? SS5E4
    - Education
    - People could lose their jobs
    - Financial challenges

    A. Reasons to Save Money
    B. Reasons People Go into Debt
    C. Causes for Increased Income
    D. Reasons to Spend Money

35. What is the MAIN purpose of the amendment process? SS5CG2
    A. to elect delegates to the Electoral College
    B. to deny any changes to the U.S. Constitution
    C. to make sure the Constitution remains current
    D. to ensure due process is always followed

Use the timeline below to answer the following question.

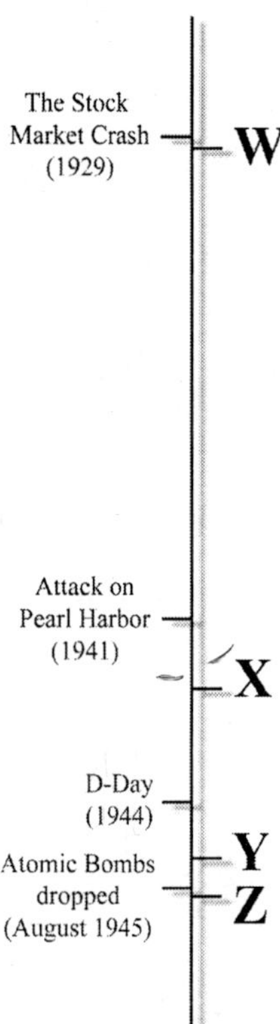

36. On the timeline above, where should VE-Day be listed? SS5H6
    A. letter W
    B. letter X
    C. letter Y
    D. letter Z

37. Why was slavery MOST important to plantation owners? SS5H1
    A. It created a need for a public education system.
    B. It provided protection from Union soldiers.
    C. It supported the abolitionist movement.
    D. It provided cheap labor.

38. Kelly owes the government seven hundred dollars in taxes. She pays the government the money she owes. Kelly is SS5CG1
    A. obeying the Seventh Amendment.
    B. fulfilling a civic role.
    C. having her civil rights violated.
    D. protecting herself from *double jeopardy.*

39. Danielle wants to buy a house, but she does not have enough money. Which of the following institutions would MOST LIKELY lend Danielle the money? SS5E2
    A. Wal-Mart
    B. Bank of America
    C. Target
    D. International Department of Revenue

40. Stalin wanted the western allies out of Berlin. His army surrounded West Berlin and would not let any supplies in or out. How did the United States continue to get supplies across Soviet lines? SS5H7
    A. the Iron Curtain
    B. the Berlin airlift
    C. the Berlin bomber
    D. the Marshall Plan

41. All of the following made it more difficult for African Americans to be politically active EXCEPT SS5CG3
    A. the Fifteenth Amendment.
    B. poll taxes.
    C. literacy tests.
    D. racial violence.

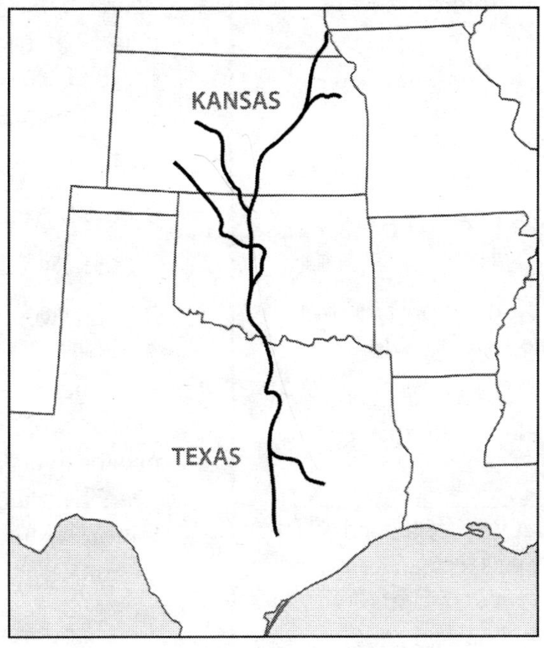

42. What does the image above represent? SS5G1

A. the first airplane flight

B. the Chisholm Trail

C. the march to Gettysburg

D. the Great Divide

43. How did the raid on Harpers Ferry influence the Civil War? SS5H1

A. It led slaveholders to fear Northern abolitionists and seek peace rather than war.

B. It led many slaveholders to believe that it would take bloodshed to protect the South's way of life.

C. It angered Northerners and led them to request harsher punishment for abolitionists.

D. It created violent protests in the North.

44. Which of the following DID NOT contribute to the U.S. becoming a world power after World War I? SS5G2

A. A lot of fighting took place on U.S. soil.

B. European industries were destroyed or badly damaged.

C. Many foreign nations were trying to recover.

D. U.S. production increased and U.S. industries thrived.

45. Why did President Truman decide to drop an atomic bomb on Hiroshima? SS5H6

A. Japan was about to win the war.

B. Japan refused to surrender unconditionally.

C. Japan had just bombed Pearl Harbor.

D. The United Nations ordered him to, during the Korean War .

Read the passage below, and answer the following question.

On May 7, 1915, it was torpedoed without warning by a German U-boat. The ship sank within eighteen minutes. Over one thousand people died. The sinking turned public opinion against Germany and most people in the U.S. began to favor war.

46. What is the passage MOST LIKELY referring to? SS5H4

A. the *Titanic*

B. the *Lusitania*

C. Pearl Harbor

D. the *USS Maine*

47. Mary Jane wants to go shopping for new shoes. She hears about a sale at a local store and decides to go there first. What encourages her to do this? SS5E1

A. specialization

B. price incentive

C. opportunity cost

D. name-brand incentive

48. Arthur lives in Georgia in the year 1924. Arthur goes to his county office to vote on a candidate for the U.S. senate. Which amendment made this possible? SS5CG3

A. the Fifteenth Amendment

B. the Seventeenth Amendment

C. the Twelfth Amendment

D. the Twenty-third Amendment

49. A farmer in South Carolina plants sweet potatoes and pecans every other year. The other years he plants cotton. Whose contribution has this farmer benefited from? SS5H3

A. Woodrow Wilson

B. Theodore Roosevelt

C. William McKinley

D. George Washington Carver

50. Which of the following is Thurgood Marshall MOST remembered for? SS5H8

A. winning the *Brown v. Board of Education* case

B. being the first African American to run for president

C. the assassination of John F. Kennedy

D. being the first man on the moon

51. During the 1950s, which U.S. senator became convinced that Communists were trying to gain control of the U.S. government? SS5H7

A. John F. Kennedy

B. Joseph McCarthy

C. Harry Truman

D. Nikita Khrushchev

Use the map below to answer question number 52.

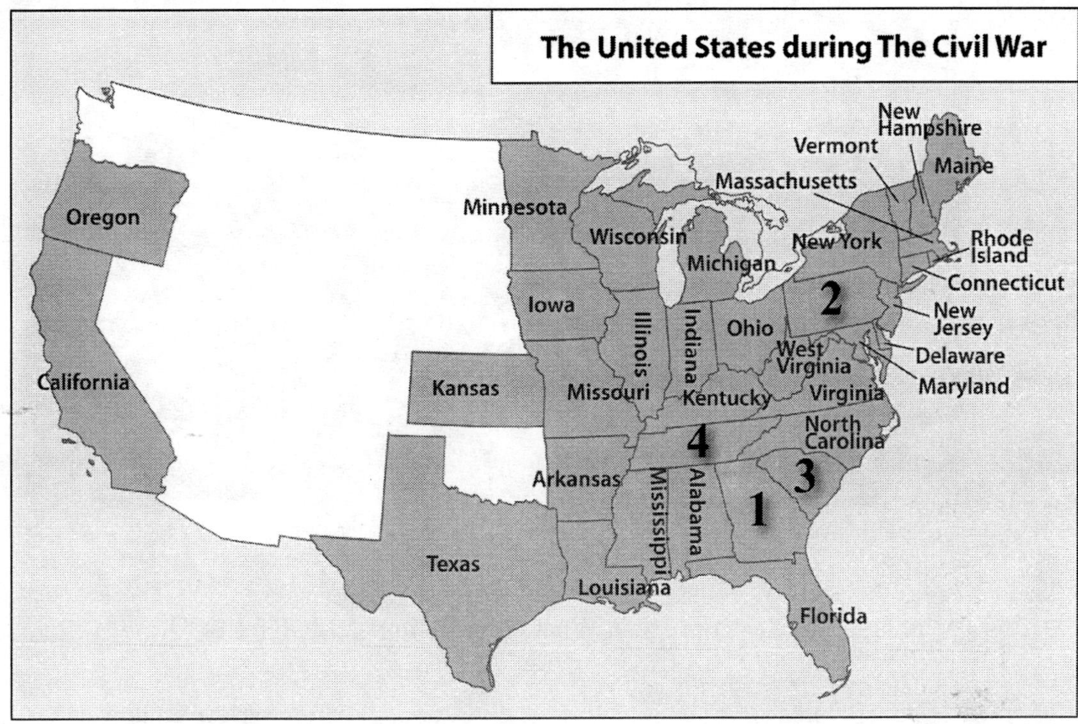

52. Where did the Battle of Gettysburg occur? SS5H1

A. 1 B. 2 C. 3 D. 4

53. It was 1865, and Tom was an African American citizen. He was very poor and had no money, but he wanted to vote on Election Day. What MOST LIKELY prevented Tom from being able to vote? SS5H2

A. a grandfather clause

B. black codes

C. poll tax

D. threats from a white male

54. What event lasted only forty-two days and resulted in Iraq's withdrawal from Kuwait? SS5H9

A. Camp David Accords

B. War on Terror

C. Persian Gulf War

D. al-Qaeda

Use the image below to answer question number 55.

55. The image above is from 1867. What does the image MOST LIKELY represent? SS5H2

A. sharecropping

B. immigration

C. African American landowners

D. industrialization

56. Voluntary exchange tends to help SS5E1

A. sellers.

B. buyers.

C. neither sellers or buyers.

D. both sellers and buyers.

57. Someone who moved from China to the United States in 1901 would have been considered a(n) SS5H3

A. immigrant.

B. expansionist.

C. nativist.

D. imperialist.

58. During the early twentieth century, who became famous for his poems and stories about black life in America? SS5H4

A. Louis Armstrong

B. Arthur Zimmerman

C. Langston Hughes

D. Martin Luther King Jr.

59. Who wrote the best-selling novel *Gone with the Wind*? SS5H5

A. Pearl Buck

B. Margaret Mitchell

C. Sinclair Lewis

D. Jesse Owens

60. The study of how specific physical characteristics define a region is called SS5G1

A. man-made geography.

B. physical geography.

C. industrialization.

D. economic development.

61. Brian lives in Atlanta, GA. He stands on a corner and preaches against the war in Iraq. He wears a shirt that reads, "Peace not War." Brian is practicing his SS5CG1

A. First-Amendment rights.

B. Second-Amendment rights.

C. Nineteenth-Amendment rights.

D. Twelfth-Amendment rights.

62. In August of 1963, more than 200,000 civil rights supporters stood together in the nation's capital. Martin Luther King Jr. gave his famous "I have a dream" speech. What was this event called? SS5H8

A. Washington boycott

B. civil disobedience meeting

C. march on Washington

D. Civil rights movement

63. The largest salt lake in California is SS5G1

A. the Salton Sea.

B. the Great Salt Lake.

C. Lake Arrowhead.

D. the Dead Sea.

Below is the Fourth Amendment to the United States Constitution. Review it, and answer the following question.

> "The right of the people to be secure in their persons, houses, papers, and effects, against unreasonable searches and seizures, shall not be violated, and no warrants shall issue, but upon probable cause, supported by Oath or affirmation, and particularly describing the place to be searched, and the persons or things to be seized."

64. Based on the Fourth Amendment, which of the following is MOST accurate? SS5CG1

A. Citizens may not be searched without a warrant or probable cause.

B. Law enforcement officers may search a citizen's house anytime they choose.

C. An accused person is entitled to a lawyer.

D. A person who is found "not guilty" may not be charged with the same crime again.

65. How did the Twenty-third Amendment affect presidential elections? SS5CG3

A. It made Washington, D.C. a state.

B. It allows electors from Washington, D.C. to participate in the Electoral College.

C. It replaced the Electoral College with a popular vote.

D. It limits presidents to only two terms.

66. What was the MAIN purpose of the Civilian Conservation Corps? SS5H5

A. It provided employment for young, unmarried men during the Depression.

B. It gave money to single women with children.

C. It provided aid to freed slaves after the Civil War.

D. It organized peaceful protests during the civil rights movement.

67. Which of the following is the largest salt lake in the Western Hemisphere? SS5G1

A. the Salton Sea

B. the Great Salt Lake

C. the Persian Gulf

D. Lake Mojave

68. Jack is hungry and thirsty. He only has enough money for chips or a drink. He can not buy both. If Jack buys the drink, what is his opportunity cost? SS5E1

A. quenching his thirst

B. spending all his money

C. satisfying his hunger

D. stealing the chips

69. What do Pearl Harbor and Gettysburg have in common? SS5G1

A. They are both located in Pennsylvania.

B. They are both desert regions.

C. They are both natural geographical features.

D. They are both sites where historic battles took place.

70. In 1861, the firing on Fort Sumter by Confederate troops forced President Abraham Lincoln to take action. What did he choose to do? SS5H1

A. ask people in the South to overthrow their leaders

B. surrender Fort Sumter and raise an army for battle

C. meet with Confederate leaders to find a settlement

D. surrender Fort Sumter, hoping that would end the fighting.

Evaluation Chart for Georgia Grade 5 CRCT in Social Studies

Directions: On the following chart, circle the question numbers that you answered incorrectly and evaluate the results. These questions are based on the Georgia Competency Standards. Then turn to the appropriate topics (listed by chapters), read the explanations, and complete the exercises. Review other chapters as needed. Finally, complete the practice test(s) to assess your progress and further prepare you for the **Georgia Grade 5 Social Studies Test**.

Note: Some question numbers will appear under multiple chapters because those questions require demonstration of multiple skills.

Chapter	Diagnostic Test Question
1. Historical Understandings: The Civil War and Reconstruction	2, 13, 20, 25, 37, 43, 52, 53, 55, 70
2. Historical Understandings: The Turn of the Century, World War I, and the 1920s	14, 19, 26, 29, 46, 49, 57, 58
3. Historical Understandings: The Great Depression and World War II	3, 10, 30, 36, 45, 59, 66
4. Historical Understandings: The Cold War and U.S. Society from 1950 to 1975	4, 17, 22, 27, 40, 50, 51, 62
5. The United States Since 1975	8, 32, 54
6. Geographical Understandings	7, 15, 24, 28, 42, 44, 60, 63, 67, 69
7. Government and Civics	1, 6, 12, 18, 21, 33, 35, 38, 41, 48, 61, 64, 65
8. Economic Understanding	5, 9, 11, 16, 23, 31, 34, 39, 47, 56, 68

Chapter 1
Historical Understandings: The Civil War and Reconstruction

This chapter addresses the following competencies.

SS5H1	The student will explain the causes, major events, and consequences of the Civil War.
SS5H2	The student will analyze the effects of Reconstruction on American Life.

1.1 Causes of the Civil War

Slavery

American colonists began buying African slaves in 1619. Under **slavery**, black Africans were captured, sold, and owned like property. Many African slaves died from diseases and abuse as they sailed on slave ships across the Atlantic. The slaves that survived lived very hard lives. They worked long hours. Their masters often beat them if they did not obey or worked too slow. Slave families were often separated. Husbands and wives were sold away from one another. Slave traders (people who sold slaves) took children away from their parents. Some slaves were able to buy their freedom or escape. Most blacks, however, born in the seventeenth, eighteenth, and early nineteenth centuries lived all their lives as slaves.

Colonial Slavery

Plantations

Southern Cotton Plantation

At first, all of the American colonies had slaves. After the United States won its independence in 1776, things slowly began to change. Over time, northern states relied less on slaves. The North started to develop more manufacturing and industry. The South, however, relied on **cash crops**. These were crops grown in large amounts that provided most of the region's wealth. Tobacco, rice, indigo, and sugar were important southern cash crops. In the 1790s, a man named Eli Whitney invented the **cotton gin**. This machine made processing cotton much faster. **Cotton** became the South's most important cash crop and made many large landowners wealthy.

The huge farms on which large landowners raised their cash crops were called **plantations**. Plantations required lots of labor. Plantation owners relied on slaves to work the fields and harvest crops. They also used slaves for many other tasks, such as cooking, cleaning, and helping to run the plantation. By the middle of the nineteenth century, many northern states had **abolished** (done away with) slavery. Some northerners felt slavery gave the South an unfair advantage because it provided cheap labor. Others felt it was morally wrong. As the United States expanded west and gained new territories, the fight over slavery grew. Southern leaders wanted new states to allow slavery. Northern leaders did not want slavery in new states. For a few years, politicians on both sides were able to compromise to maintain peace. Most new southern states became **slave states,** while new northern states became **free states**.

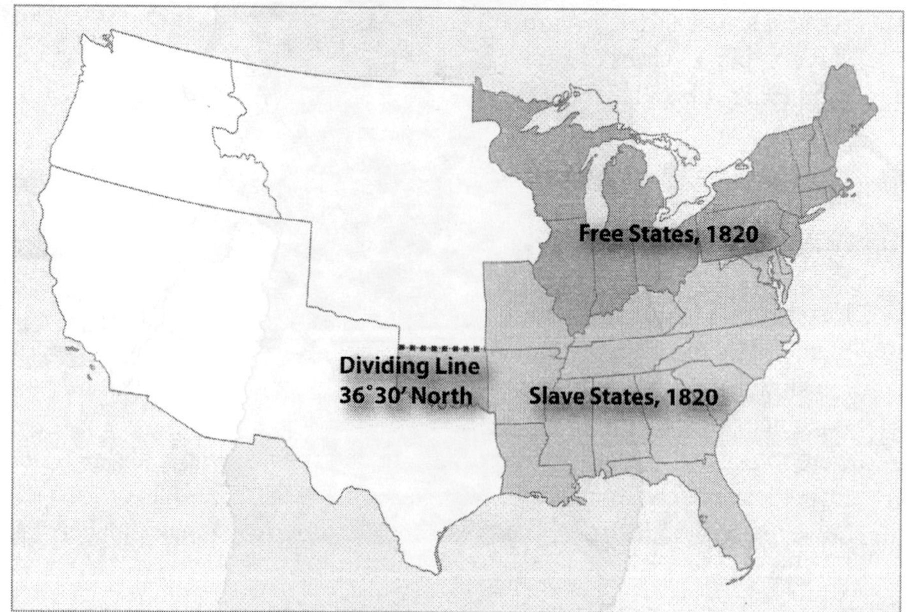

Free and Slave States

The Missouri Compromise

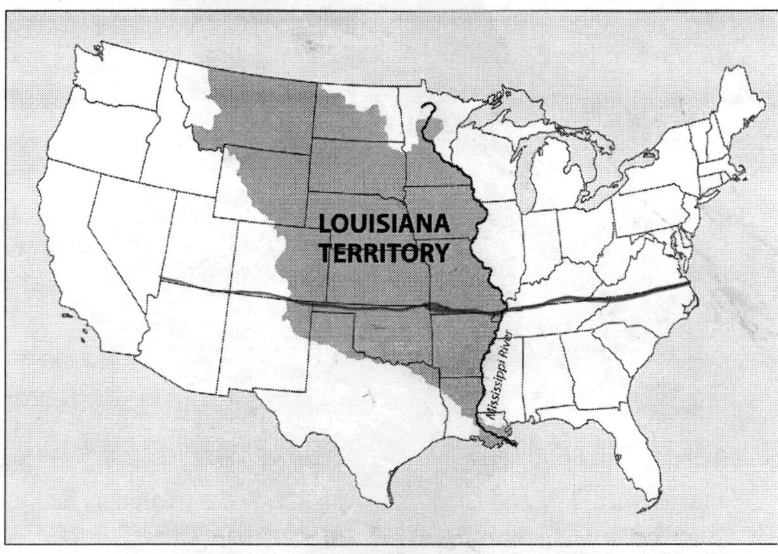

Louisiana Territory and the Mississippi River

In 1803, President Thomas Jefferson bought the Louisiana Territory from France. The purchase opened up new lands for white settlement. Before the Louisiana Purchase, the United States only stretched as far west as the Mississippi River. Following the Louisiana Purchase, the nation had to decide whether or not to allow slavery further west. In 1820, Missouri (a territory west of the Mississippi) applied to become a state. Southerners wanted it admitted as a slave state. Northerners wanted it to be a free state. The **Missouri Compromise** allowed Missouri to enter the Union as a slave state while Maine entered as a free state. It also stated that all future states north of Missouri's southern border would be free states. All those south of the same border would be slave states. The Missouri Compromise helped keep peace between those who opposed slavery and those who supported it.

The Compromise of 1850

Slavery also became a big issue when California became a state in 1850. Senator Henry Clay of Kentucky helped work out another important compromise. The **Compromise of 1850** allowed California to enter the Union as a free state. It also let people in the Utah and New Mexico territories decide the issue by **popular sovereignty**. People in these territories would be allowed to vote on whether or not to allow slavery. In order to get southerners to agree, the compromise included the **Fugitive Slave Law**. It stated that northerners must return runaway slaves to their southern masters. Many northerners did not like the law and did not obey it.

THE ABOLITIONIST MOVEMENT AND *UNCLE TOM'S CABIN*

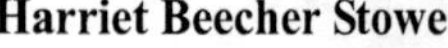
Harriet Beecher Stowe

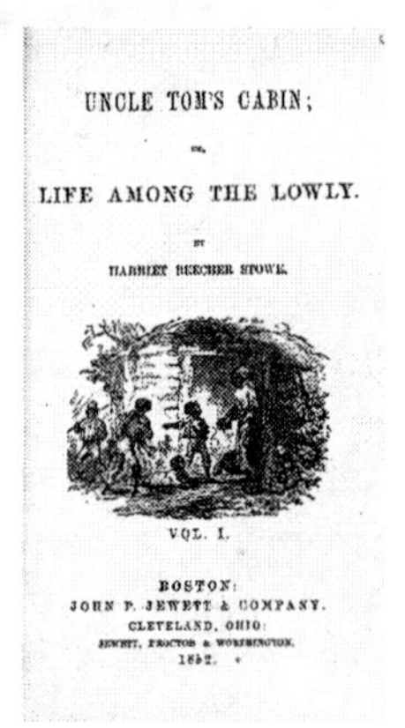
UNCLE TOM'S CABIN;
OR,
LIFE AMONG THE LOWLY.
BY
HARRIET BEECHER STOWE.
VOL. I.
BOSTON:
JOHN P. JEWETT & COMPANY.
CLEVELAND, OHIO:
JEWETT, PROCTOR & WORTHINGTON.
1852.

Stowe's *Uncle Tom's Cabin*

By the 1850s, a strong **abolitionist movement** existed in the North. Abolitionists wanted to end slavery. Both whites and blacks took part. One of the most famous abolitionists was **Harriet Beecher Stowe**. In 1852, Stowe published a book called ***Uncle Tom's Cabin***. It was a fictional story that showed the cruelty of slavery. The story made many people angry. Abolitionists became even more determined to end slavery. They believed that all slaves were treated as badly as those in *Uncle Tom's Cabin*. Slaveowners, on the other hand, believed that *Uncle Tom's Cabin* did not present the truth. They were angry and argued that not all slaves were treated cruelly.

BLEEDING KANSAS

In 1854, Congress passed a law called the **Kansas-Nebraska Act**. The law said that people in the Kansas and Nebraska territories could decide by popular sovereignty whether or not to have slaves. This upset a lot of people because, under the Missouri Compromise, these territories were supposed to be free. Soon after the law was passed, Kansans who supported slavery and those who were against it began fighting. The violence was so bad that the territory became known as **Bleeding Kansas**. The Kansas-Nebraska Act only increased the tension between the North and South.

Portrait of "Bleeding Kansas"

THE DRED SCOTT DECISION

Dred Scott

After his master died, a slave named Dred Scott sued for his freedom. The United States Supreme Court ruled against him. It stated that Scott was not a citizen and had no right to sue. The Court also said that slave masters cannot be denied of their "property" (their slaves) without due process. The decision meant that a slave master could keep his or her slaves even if they entered a free state. Abolitionists were furious! The **Dred Scott decision** also upset people who supported popular sovereignty because it interfered with the right of states to decide their own slave laws. Many people in the South, however, were very pleased with the decision.

John Brown's Raid

John Brown

John Brown's raid took place in 1859. John Brown was a white abolitionist. He thought the only way to end slavery was by force. One October night, he and his followers raided the United States arsenal at Harpers Ferry, Virginia. (An arsenal is a place where weapons are kept.) Brown wanted to give the weapons to slaves who could use them to fight for freedom. The plan failed when army troops surrounded the arsenal. The soldiers killed some of the raiders and captured Brown. The government hanged John Brown just a few days later. Many Northerners called Brown a hero. Southern slave owners thought he was an example of how dangerous abolitionists had become.

States' Rights versus Federal Power

Southern leaders defended slavery by arguing for **states' rights**. Those who preached states' rights believed that the federal government could not tell states what to do. They believed that the Founding Fathers wanted the states to have most of the governing power, not the central government.

Abraham Lincoln and the Election of 1860

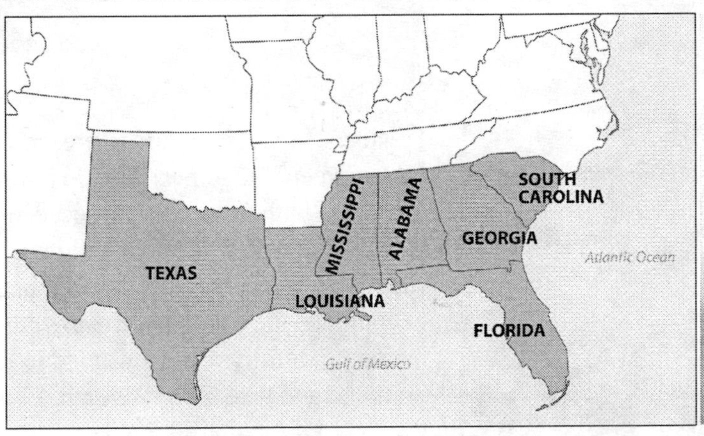

Confederate States of America

Abraham Lincoln

Southern leaders argued that each state had the right to decide for itself whether or not to allow slavery. Slavery became the main issue in the **presidential election of 1860**. The Democratic Party split. Northern Democrats supported Stephen Douglas, who favored popular sovereignty. Southern Democrats wanted a pro-slavery candidate. Republicans hoped to stop the spread of slavery into new territories. Some of them were even abolitionists. They supported **Abraham Lincoln**. Southerners did not want Lincoln as president because they feared he would try to end slavery. Shortly after Lincoln won the election, South Carolina seceded (left) the Union. Mississippi, Alabama, Georgia, Florida, Louisiana, and Texas soon seceded also. Together, these states declared themselves a new nation: the **Confederate States of America**.

Practice 1.1: Causes of the Civil War

1. Slavery was most popular in

   A. the North. B. the South. C. California. D. Kansas.

2. Slavery became important to plantation owners because it

   A. provided labor.
   B. allowed popular sovereignty.
   C. supported the abolitionist movement.
   D. decreased the need for cash crops.

3. What happened during John Brown's raid? How did it affect the debate over slavery?

4. Who was Harriet Beecher Stowe? What did she do to increase the debate over slavery?

5. What did someone who supported states' rights believe?

1.2 The Civil War

Fort Sumter

Fort Sumter

President Lincoln wanted to preserve the Union (keep it together). He did not like the fact that Southern states had seceded. However, many in the North did not want a war. Most northerners wanted the president to convince the South to remain with the Union peacefully. Others wanted to let the South go and take slavery with it. Even if he wanted to, Lincoln did not have enough support to use force against the South. If there was going to be a war, the South would have to start it.

In 1861, the Union still had troops at **Fort Sumter**, South Carolina. The South decided that it wanted the Union forces gone. The Confederates opened fire on the fort, forcing the Union troops to surrender and leave. The South felt great pride after its victory. However, by attacking Fort Sumter, the Confederacy also made many northerners angry. They now viewed the Union as under attack. Suddenly, Lincoln had the support that he needed for war. The **Civil War** between the states had begun. Lincoln called for 75,000 volunteers to fight for the Union. The Confederacy called for volunteers as well. Slave states that had not yet seceded had to decide which side to support. Kentucky,

Maryland, Missouri, and the western portions of Virginia voted to stay with the Union. (This western portion of Virginia later became the state of West Virginia.) North Carolina, Arkansas, Tennessee, and most of Virginia joined the Confederacy.

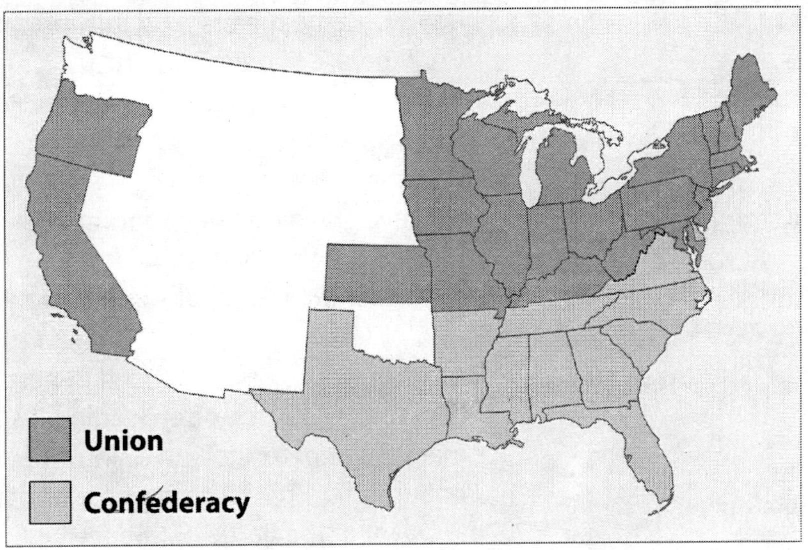

Union and Confederacy after Fort Sumter

Key Union Figures of the Civil War	
Abraham Lincoln	Lincoln was the president of the United States during the Civil War
Ulysses S. Grant	Grant served as overall commander of the Union Army during the final months of the war. He accepted Lee's surrender at Appomattox Courthouse.
William T. Sherman	Sherman was a Union general who captured Atlanta in 1864. He burned and destroyed cities, farms, and industries in Georgia as he marched from Atlanta to Savannah.

Key Confederate Figures of the Civil War	
Jefferson Davis	Davis became the first and only president of the Confederate States of America.
Robert E. Lee	Robert E. Lee was a gifted general. He commanded the Confederacy's Army of Northern Virginia and won many battles in which he was outnumbered. However, he didn't have enough men or resources to keep fighting General Grant's large army. He surrendered to Grant at Appomattox Courthouse in April, 1865.
Thomas "Stonewall" Jackson	Jackson was Lee's most gifted general. He helped Lee win key battles, often leading his troops to cover many miles of territory in a single day. He died of pneumonia after his own troops shot him by accident at the Battle of Chancellorsville.

Major Battles and Campaigns

First Bull Run

Most Northerners expected to win the war quickly. The Union had more people, more industries to produce weapons and supplies, more railroads, and a larger, better-trained army. The South, however, began the war with better generals (at least in the East) and determined leaders. Northerners saw the war as a fight to preserve the Union. Many Southerners saw it as a war to defend their homeland and their way of life.

The first major battle between the two armies happened in Virginia near Bull Run Creek in 1861. The **First Battle of Bull Run** (also called the First Battle of Manassas, after the nearest town) was a surprising loss for the Union. The Confederacy defeated the Union Army and could have invaded Washington, D.C. if its troops had been better trained. First Bull Run showed both sides that the war would not be so short after all.

ANTIETAM

Battle of Antietam

Robert E. Lee

In the fall of 1862, Confederate General **Robert E. Lee** tried to invade the North. He did a good job of keeping his invasion a secret, until Union soldiers found a copy of his plans in an abandoned camp. The two armies met in Maryland and fought the **Battle of Antietam**. Antietam was the bloodiest single day of the war. The Union stopped Lee's invasion, forcing the Confederates to retreat into Virginia. The victory gave Lincoln the support he needed to issue the **Emancipation Proclamation**. This executive order declared the slaves in the Confederate states free. It did not grant freedom to slaves in states loyal to the Union. That was because Lincoln still needed the support of these states to win the war. Once the Emancipation Proclamation became known, many African Americans volunteered to fight in the Union military.

The Emancipation Proclamation

GETTYSBURG

The Battle of Gettysburg

In early July 1863, Lee's Confederate Army met the army of Union General George Meade. The battle occurred over several days just outside Gettysburg, Pennsylvania. The **Battle of Gettysburg** was the bloodiest battle of the entire war. Roughly 50,000 men died or were wounded. The Union won the battle, ending Lee's last attempt to invade the North. Four months after the battle, President Lincoln stood on the battlefield and gave a speech known as the **Gettysburg Address**. Lincoln honored the men who had died there, and expressed his hope that the war would soon end.

THE ATLANTA CAMPAIGN AND SHERMAN'S MARCH TO THE SEA

Casualties of the Battle of Gettysburg

In 1864, Lincoln appointed **Ulysses S. Grant** overall commander of the Union army. Grant put his most trusted general, **William T. Sherman**, in charge of his western forces. In May, Sherman marched into Georgia. He wanted to reach Atlanta because of its importance as a railroad hub. If Sherman took Atlanta, he could hurt the South's ability to ship supplies and men. The Confederate Army did its best to stop Sherman, but it was not strong enough. Sherman finally took Atlanta in September. His successful **Atlanta Campaign** placed the city under Union control. It also increased support for President Lincoln in the North. Before Atlanta, many Northerners wanted to replace Lincoln with a president who would negotiate with the South and end the war. After Sherman's success, Northerners believed the war could be won and re-elected Lincoln.

After taking Atlanta, Sherman ordered much of the city burned. He then began a march from Atlanta to Savannah that became known as his **march to the sea**. On its way to the coast, Sherman's army burned buildings, destroyed rail lines, set fire to factories, and demolished bridges. Sherman hoped to end the South's ability to make and ship supplies. Without supplies, the South would have to surrender. People in Savannah were so scared by news of the destruction that they surrendered to Sherman without a fight.

William T. Sherman

Ulysses S. Grant

The War Ends

Surrender at Appomattox

General Grant knew he had more men than General Lee. He decided to force Lee to face him in head-to-head battles. Grant's army pushed south and fought Lee's in a number of bloody fights. In just a few months, over sixty thousand of Grant's soldiers were dead or wounded. Still, because Lee had far less men, it was the Confederates who retreated. When Grant's troops surrounded the Confederate Army in Virginia, General Lee elected to surrender. On April 9, 1865, Robert E. Lee surrendered to Ulysses S. Grant at **Appomattox Courthouse**.

Effects of the War

The Civil War had **major effects** on the North and the South. Thousands of young men from both regions died or were wounded during the war. Many returned home missing legs, arms, or bearing other scars from the fighting. Both sides experienced great human suffering.

Economically, however, the two regions were affected differently. The North prospered. Its manufacturing and industries grew. More people were employed as the Union worked to support its war effort. The Southern economy, on the other hand, suffered. The South had depended on cash crops. The end of slavery meant that it no longer had its main source of labor. Since most of the fighting took place in the South, many of the region's farms, railroads, and industries had been destroyed. At the end of the war, the North had grown stronger. The South faced an uncertain future.

Practice 1.2: The Civil War

1. Of the following, who was a gifted general who commanded the Confederate Army at both Antietam and Gettysburg?

   A. Thomas Jackson
   C. Robert E. Lee
   B. George Meade
   D. Ulysses S. Grant

2. William T. Sherman is MOST remembered for his

   A. Emancipation Proclamation.
   C. victory at Appomattox.
   B. march to the sea.
   D. defeat at Gettysburg.

3. How did the war affect the economies of the North and South differently?

1.3 Reconstruction

Radical versus Presidential Reconstruction

Andrew Johnson
Lincoln's Successor

Thaddeus Stevens,
a Radical Republican

Following the war, President Lincoln wanted to rebuild the South. He wanted the Union to be strong and include the states that had seceded. Sadly, he did not live long after Lee's surrender. Just a few days after Appomattox, an assassin named John Wilkes Booth shot and killed the president. Vice President **Andrew Johnson** became president after Lincoln died. He wanted to make it easy for the South to rejoin the Union. He soon ran into resistance. A group of Congressmen, known as the **Radical Republicans,** wanted to force the South to accept strict conditions. They also wanted to protect the rights of newly freed African Americans in the southern states. The process of rebuilding the South after the Civil War was known as **Reconstruction**.

Key Constitutional Amendments

In 1865, Congress and the states ratified the **Thirteenth Amendment**. It made slavery illegal throughout the United States. Eventually, the Radical Republicans won control of Reconstruction and passed two other key amendments. The **Fourteenth Amendment** made African Americans citizens. The **Fifteenth Amendment** guaranteed African American men the right to vote (women still could not vote, no matter their race). Among other things, the Radical Republicans forced Southern states to ratify these amendments. They also placed military rule over Southern states until they complied with all the conditions of Reconstruction.

THE FREEDMEN'S BUREAU

The federal government established the **Freedmen's Bureau** to help freedmen (newly freed slaves) adjust to life after slavery. It was the first federal relief agency in U.S. history. The Freedmen's Bureau provided clothes, medical attention, food, education, and even land to African Americans coming out of slavery. Lacking support, it ended in 1869. However, during its brief time, it helped many freed African Americans throughout the South.

The Freedmen's Bureau

RESISTANCE TO RECONSTRUCTION

BLACK CODES AND SHARECROPPING

Although slavery was over, most white Southerners were not ready to accept African Americans as equals. Freedmen did not own land or have much money. White landowners took advantage of freedmen's poverty to keep them serving whites. Before the Radical Republicans gained control of Reconstruction, many southern states passed **black codes**. These were laws that made it illegal for African Americans to live or work in certain areas. They also allowed whites to arrest African Americans who were not working. Once arrested, these African Americans could be forced to work for white landowners. Black codes kept African Americans living like slaves by keeping them on the plantations. These codes were later outlawed under Radical Reconstruction.

African American Sharecropper

Another system that oppressed blacks was **sharecropping**. African American sharecroppers farmed land owned by white landowners. In exchange, they were given a place to live and part of the crop. Dishonest landlords often cheated them and treated them like slaves. Unable to pay their debts, sharecroppers remained forced to provide labor for white landowners.

The Ku Klux Klan

The KKK in the 1800s

After Radical Reconstruction outlawed black codes, many Southern whites continued to resist giving African Americans equal rights. Some even used violence. One violent group was the **Ku Klux Klan**. The Klan was a secretive organization that dressed in hooded white robes. It used threats, violence, and murder to intimidate blacks and those who helped them. The Klan often practiced lynchings (mob-initiated killings in which the victim is kidnapped and murdered).

Jim Crow Laws, Poll Taxes, and Literacy Tests

Rutherford Hayes

The presidential election of 1876 resulted in a political compromise known as the **Compromise of 1877**. Democrats agreed to allow the Republican, Rutherford Hayes, to become president. In exchange, the Republicans agreed to end Reconstruction. This allowed Southern states to have more self-rule. Southern states soon passed **Jim Crow laws**. These laws legalized **segregation** (separation of races) by requiring whites and blacks to use separate facilities. Southern whites also wanted to keep African Americans from voting. Since the Constitution guaranteed African Americans the right to vote under the Fifteenth Amendment, southern lawmakers thought of creative ways to **disfranchise** blacks. (*Disfranchise* means to keep from voting). They established **poll taxes**. Poll taxes required people to pay to vote. Since most African Americans were poor, many of them could not afford to pay the tax. Southern states also used **literacy tests**. Voters had to prove they could read and write. African Americans were often uneducated and had a hard time passing these tests. Finally, Southern states often passed **grandfather clauses**. Grandfather clauses stated that men whose ancestors had voted before or served in the Confederate military could vote without having to pass a literacy test or pay a poll tax. Since it was usually only whites who met these conditions, grandfather clauses allowed poor, illiterate whites to vote while still keeping most blacks from voting. African Americans who tried to vote or challenged these laws often became victims of violence.

Practice 1.3: Reconstruction

1. The process of rebuilding and transforming the South after the Civil War was called
   - A. Reconstruction.
   - B. disenfranchisment.
   - C. segregation.
   - D. sharecropping.

2. Which of the following ended slavery in the United States?
   - A. the Emancipation Proclamation
   - B. Thirteenth Amendment
   - C. Fourteenth Amendment
   - D. Fifteenth Amendment

3. Which of the following made African Americans citizens?
   - A. Thirteenth Amendment
   - B. Fourteenth Amendment
   - C. grandfather clauses
   - D. black codes

4. What were some of the methods used by white Southerners to keep free African Americans from exercising their rights after the Civil War?

5. What was the Freedmen's Bureau? What was it created to do?

Chapter 1 Review

Key People, Terms, and Concepts

slavery
cash crops
cotton gin
cotton
plantations
abolition
slave states
free states
Missouri Compromise
Compromise of 1850
popular sovereignty
Harriet Beecher Stowe
Uncle Tom's Cabin
Kansas-Nebraska Act
Bleeding Kansas
Fugitive Slave Law
Dred Scott decision
John Brown's raid
states' rights
election of 1860
Abraham Lincoln
Confederate States of America
Fort Sumter
Civil War
Ulysses S. Grant
William T. Sherman
Jefferson Davis
Robert E. Lee
Thomas "Stonewall" Jackson
First Battle of Bull Run
Antietam
Emancipation Proclamation
Gettysburg
Gettysburg Address
Atlanta Campaign
march to the sea
Appomattox Courthouse
effects of the war
Andrew Johnson
Radical Republicans
Reconstruction
Thirteenth Amendment
Fourteenth Amendment
Fifteenth Amendment
Freedmen's Bureau
black codes
sharecropping
Ku Klux Klan
Compromise of 1877
Jim Crow laws
segregation
disfranchise
poll taxes
literacy tests
grandfather clauses

Multiple Choice Questions

1. Cotton was important because it was
   A. the basis of the Northern economy.
   B. a key cash crop in free states.
   C. a source of wealth that relied on slavery.
   D. a product that funded the Union's war effort.

2. The Missouri Compromise and the Compromise of 1850 were both meant to
   A. stop the spread of slavery.
   B. settle the issue of slavery west of the Mississippi.
   C. allow slave states east of the Mississippi.
   D. make popular sovereignty legal in new U.S. territories.

Look at the map below, and answer the following question.

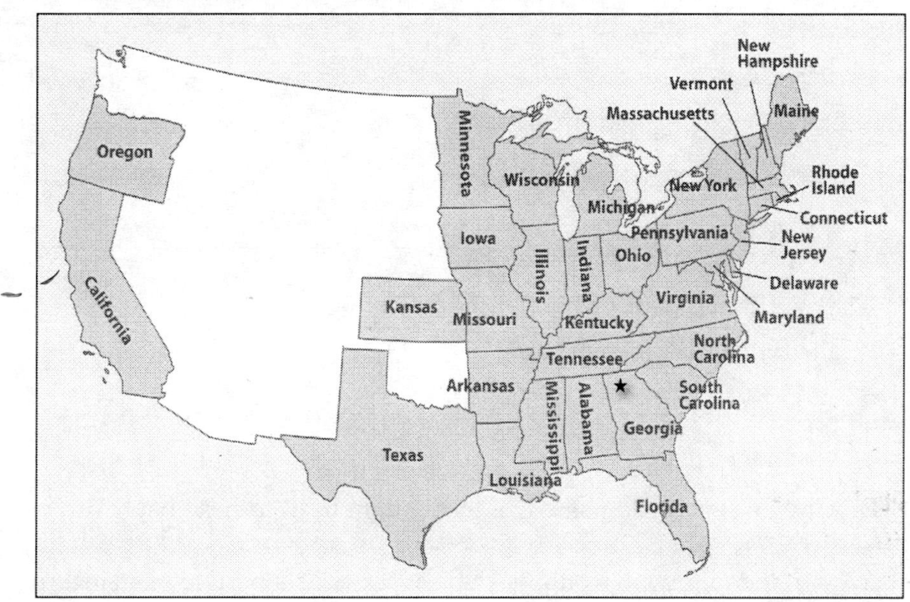

3. Assume that the star on the map represents a city. In 1862, this city would have been part of
   A. the Confederacy.
   B. the Union.
   C. Reconstruction.
   D. a state in which pro-slavery and anti-slavery forces battled for control.

4. Who of the following was a radical abolitionist whose actions struck anger and fear into the heart of southern slave owners?
   A. Harriet Beecher Stowe
   B. Abraham Lincoln
   C. Ulysses S. Grant
   D. John Brown

5. It was the bloodiest battle of the Civil War and ended Lee's last attempt to invade the North. Which battle was it?
   A. First Bull Run
   B. Antietam
   C. Gettysburg
   D. Appomattox

Look at the map below, and answer the following question.

6. The map above shows which of the following?
   A. the Battle of Antietam
   B. Reconstruction
   C. Sherman's march to the sea
   D. Grant's strategy to make Lee face him in head-to-head battles

7. Who of the following would have been MOST supportive of states' rights?
   A. a Radical Republican
   B. Jefferson Davis
   C. a congressman from New York
   D. Abraham Lincoln

8. Who of the following would have been MOST thankful for the Freedmen's Bureau?
   A. white Southern leaders during Reconstruction
   B. Southern African Americans following the Civil War
   C. supporters of states' rights before the Civil War
   D. supporters of the Dred Scott decision

9. Slavery is illegal in the United States because of
   A. Reconstruction.
   B. the Emancipation Proclamation.
   C. the Thirteenth Amendment.
   D. Jim Crow laws.

10. Poll taxes and literacy tests were creative ways whites tried to deny African Americans the rights guaranteed them by the
    A. Emancipation Proclamation.
    B. Thirteenth Amendment.
    C. Fourteenth Amendment.
    D. Fifteenth Amendment.

Chapter 2
Historical Understandings: The Turn of the Century, World War I, and the 1920s

This chapter addresses the following competencies.

SS5H3	The student will describe how life changed in America at the turn of the century.
SS5H4	The student will describe U.S. involvement in World War I and post-World War I America.

2.1 The Turn of the Century

Life in the West

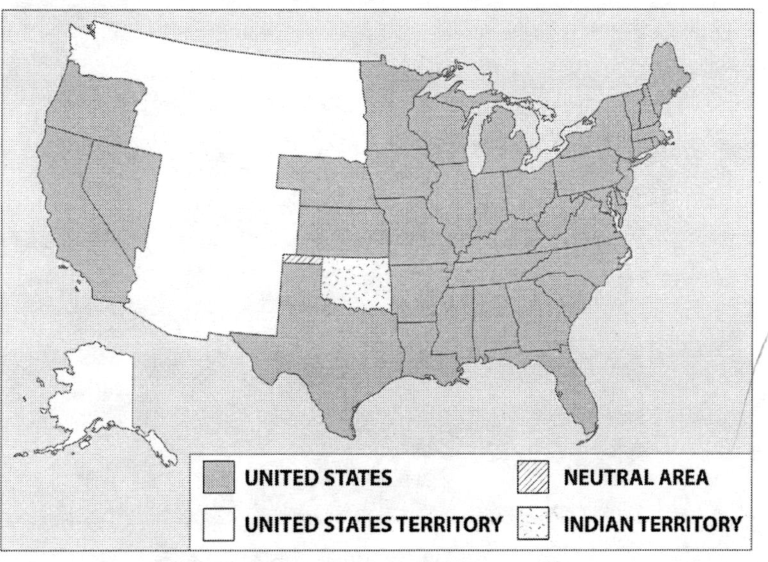

U.S. Territories After the Civil War

The end of the nineteenth century and the beginning of the twentieth marks a time known as the **turn of the century**. It was a time of great change in the United States. The western United States saw amazing growth. Following the Civil War, more and more people moved west to claim land and seek opportunities. As the United States government took more and more land away from Native Americans, territory became available for white settlers. Many settlers became farmers. They took advantage of new inventions like the steel plow, mechanical reaper, and windmill to farm the Great Plains and other parts of the Midwest. Others became miners. Following the discovery of gold in California and other parts of the West, many settlers moved to these regions hoping to strike it rich. A number of western settlers became ranchers. Ranchers owned herds of cattle. Available land and open plains allowed ranchers to raise large herds during the late 1800s.

Many of the Native American people who had lived in these regions for centuries suffered as the United States expanded. The U.S. government forced many of them to move to special areas called **reservations**. Each time settlers discovered gold or white citizens demanded more land, these same Native Americans were often forced to move again. The government broke promises to Native American tribes as it forced them to give up more and more territory. Sometimes Native Americans resisted. This caused several wars between the U.S. Army and Native Americans. Most of the time, the United States Army won because it was much stronger and had advanced weapons. Occasionally, however, Native Americans did win some victories. The largest Native American victory happened at the **Battle of Little Bighorn** in 1876. A U.S. commander named George Armstrong Custer thought he could surprise and defeat a band of Sioux warriors. Custer had only a few hundred men. He did not know that the Sioux had thousands. He and the men under his command rushed recklessly into battle. The Sioux quickly surrounded and killed them. The battle became known as **Custer's Last Stand**. It was the last major victory for Native Americans over U.S. forces. In the end, the U.S. government was too strong. By the end of the 1800s, the U.S. government controlled all the land between Mexico and Canada, stretching from the Atlantic to the Pacific Ocean.

Native Americans in the Late 1800s

Cowboys and Cattle Drives

African American Cowboy

Cowboys became legendary figures during the late 1800s. Cowboys drove large herds of cattle from ranches to towns and markets where they could be shipped and sold. These **cattle drives** (journeys taken to drive herds to market) could often take days or weeks. Many of these cowboys were African Americans. **Black cowboys** were common in places like Texas. Often, these black cowboys were freed slaves who made their way west following the Civil War.

Cattle Trails

A number of key **cattle trails** developed during the late 1800s. Cattle trails were known routes used by cowboys to drive cattle great distances. The **Chisholm Trail** ran from Texas, north through Oklahoma and into Kansas. Texas cowboys used it to drive herds to Kansas towns where the cattle could be loaded onto trains and shipped east to market. The **Great Western Cattle Trail** was another famous path used by cowboys. It also ran from Texas to Kansas, ending in Dodge City. Just like the Chisholm Trail, cowboys relied on the Great Western Cattle Trail to get their herds to railway stations so that the cattle could be transported by train.

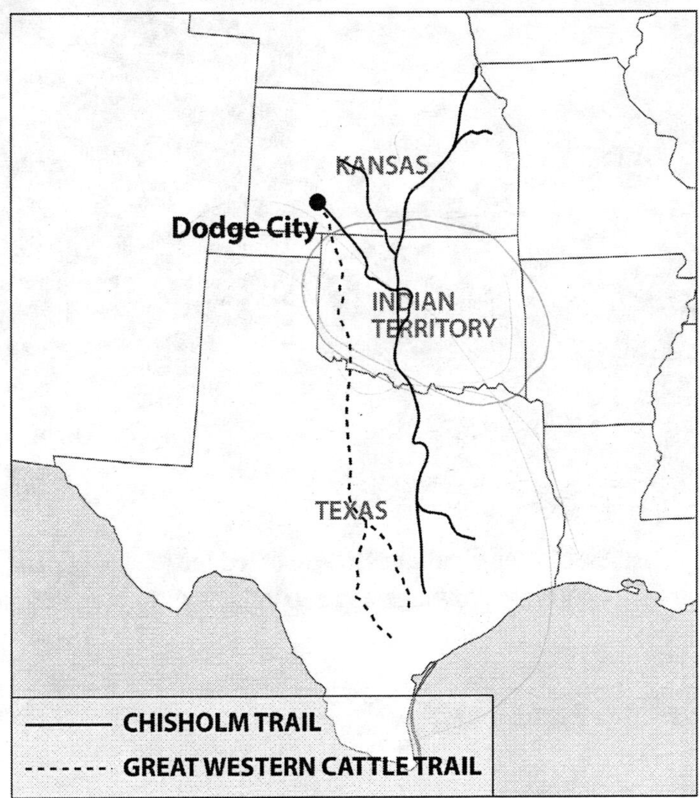

The Chisholm Trail and the Great Western Trail

THE END OF THE CATTLE DRIVES

By the end of the 1800s, landowners began using barbed wire to fence in their property. This made it hard to drive cattle because herds could no longer cross large open plains. Meanwhile, railroad owners constructed more and more railways. Ranchers did not have to rely on long cattle drives in order to get their cattle to train stations. By the early 1900s, the glory days of the cowboy were over.

Cattle Drive in the Late 1800s

INVENTIONS AND INNOVATIONS

THE WRIGHT BROTHERS

Two brothers, **Wilbur and Orville Wright**, built the world's first successful airplane. Orville piloted their first flight in 1903. It was short (only twelve seconds), but it marked the beginning of air travel. Just over a decade later, militaries in different countries used airplanes in World War I. Planes eventually made travel much easier and faster for everyday citizens.

First Flight in Kitty Hawk, NC

Orville Wilbur

The Wright Brothers

BELL AND EDISON

During the 1870s, **Alexander Graham Bell** invented the telephone. His telephone greatly improved communication by allowing people to talk to one another despite being separated by great distance.

Thomas Edison

Thomas Edison was an inventor who was interested in sound. He discovered how to record spoken words. Edison named his new invention the phonograph. Later, he invented the motion picture camera. Edison also invented the **electric light bulb**. The light bulb changed business and how people lived. Before Edison's light bulb, people could only work in the daytime or by the light of oil lamps. Oil lamps did not provide very much light. After the invention of the light bulb, however, factories could stay open later. More goods were produced. People could also enjoy more nighttime entertainment and stay up later. Edison came up with the idea of central power companies. These companies provided electricity to entire cities. Edison had his first company supplying most of New York City by 1882.

George Washington Carver

George Washington Carver was one of the first African Americans to make great contributions in science. While an instructor at the Tuskegee Institute, he developed his **crop rotation method**. Carver knew that southern farmers relied on cotton for most of their money. However, he also knew cotton used up many of the nutrients in the soil. Without nutrients, nothing would grow. Carver taught growers to plant crops that enriched the soil every other year. In between cotton crops, farmers planted peanuts, peas, soybeans, sweet potatoes, and pecans. To make sure that the farmers could sell their products, Carver discovered new uses for the crops they grew. Carver discovered more than three hundred new uses for peanuts.

George Washington Carver

Cotton Farmers in the Late 1800s

Practice 2.1: The Turn of the Century

1. The years marking the end of the nineteenth century and the beginning of the twentieth are often called the

   A. age of innovation.
   B. cattle trail era.
   C. turn of the century.
   D. old West.

2. Which of the following statements about cowboys is TRUE?

   A. They did not exist until the 1900s.
   B. Many of them were African Americans.
   C. Most cowboys were farmers.
   D. Cowboys became less important once cattle trails developed.

3. Thomas Edison is MOST remembered for his

   A. invention of the telephone.
   B. ability to build airplanes.
   C. use of electricity.
   D. development of crop rotation.

4. Who was George Washington Carver? What is one of the things he's remembered for?

2.2 America's Expanding Role in the World

William McKinley and the Spanish American War

President William McKinley

In 1897, **William McKinley** became the president of the United States. He entered office at a time when many U.S. citizens wanted the nation to expand. The West was conquered. A number of citizens and leaders now wanted the United States to conquer foreign territories as well. Some felt it was important to keep the nation strong. Others felt that the United States should civilize the rest of the world. Many favored expansion because they believed it would produce wealth. They wanted the resources of foreign territories and hoped to open up foreign markets in Asia and South America.

War Begins

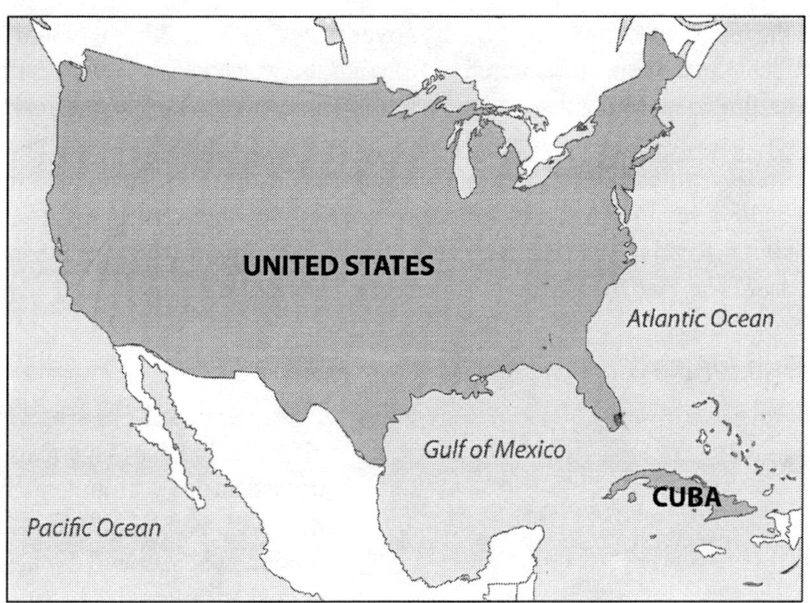

The United States and Cuba

The *USS Maine*

In the late 1890s, **Cuba** was ruled by Spain. However, the Cuban people wanted their independence. Many of them revolted. The Spanish responded with military force. Large numbers of Cubans were removed from their homes and put in prison camps. In the United States, many newspapers and political leaders called for war. They claimed that it was the duty of the United States to defend the Cuban people. In reality, many of these leaders and businessmen wanted Cuba's resources and markets more than they cared about Cuban citizens. Finally, when a U.S. ship called the ***USS Maine*** mysteriously exploded in a Cuban harbor, the United States blamed Spain and declared war. Historians (people who study history for a living) later declared that the explosion was probably an accident. The **Spanish-American War** began in 1898.

A "Splendid Little War"

The war quickly spread to other parts of the world. When a U.S. naval commander, Commodore George Dewey, learned Congress had declared war, he set sail for another Spanish colony, **the Philippines**. He easily defeated the Spanish navy and took control of the islands. Meanwhile, in Cuba, the U.S. forces defeated Spain in just a few months. Most people in the United States saw it as an easy victory. One U.S. official called the conflict a "splendid little war."

The Platt Amendment

Before the war began, the United States government promised that it would allow Cuba to be independent once Spain surrendered. Following the war, the United States kept this promise. However, President McKinley and others still wanted to protect U.S. interests. The United States kept part of its military in Cuba until the new government was in place. It also insisted that the **Platt Amendment** be part of Cuba's new constitution. The Platt Amendment gave the United States a say in how Cubans ran their country. It allowed the United States to take action in Cuba if it thought it was necessary and gave the nited States permanent control of two Cuban naval bases. The Platt Amendment stayed in effect until the 1930s.

The Philippines

The Philippines

Puerto Rico and Guam became U.S. territories after the Spanish-American War. No territory caused as much argument among Americans, however, as the Philippines. **Imperialists** (people who favored expansion) wanted to keep the Philippines because of its natural resources and location in Southeast Asia. They felt it would give U.S. businesses access to East Asian markets and provide a good base for the U.S. Navy. **Isolationists** (people who were against expansion) believed the United States should let the Philippines be an independent nation. They feared more wars. Many isolationists also believed it was morally wrong. The United States was supposed to stand for democracy and freedom. Those who supported the Philippines' independence did not think it was right for the United States to deny freedom to Filipinos (natives of the Philippines). Most Filipinos agreed. A war between Filipinos who wanted their freedom and the United States raged for two years. Finally, in 1901, U.S. forces captured the Filipino leader and ended the war. In 1902, the Philippines became an "unorganized territory" of the United States. In 1946, it became an independent nation.

THEODORE ROOSEVELT

Theodore Roosevelt

Rough Riders

One of the leaders favoring war with Spain was Assistant Secretary of the Navy **Theodore Roosevelt**. Roosevelt believed strongly in expansion. He also thought that a war with Spain would be good for the country. When the fighting started, he resigned from his position in Washington, D.C., and became the commander of a unit known as the **Rough Riders** that was fighting in Cuba. The Rough Riders' charge up San Juan Hill became famous and helped make Roosevelt a hero. In 1901, he became vice president of the United States. A few months later, he became the president, after an assassin shot and killed President William McKinley.

THE PANAMA CANAL

In order to protect U.S. interests, President Roosevelt wanted to build a canal (man-made waterway) across a portion of Panama. The canal would allow ships to travel back and forth between the Atlantic and Pacific Oceans without having to sail around South America. Unfortunately for Roosevelt, Colombia ruled Panama and would not lease him the land to build the canal. In 1903, however, the Panamanian people revolted. In exchange for Roosevelt's support, the Panamanians leased the United States the necessary territory once Panama won its independence. The **Panama Canal** officially opened in 1914.

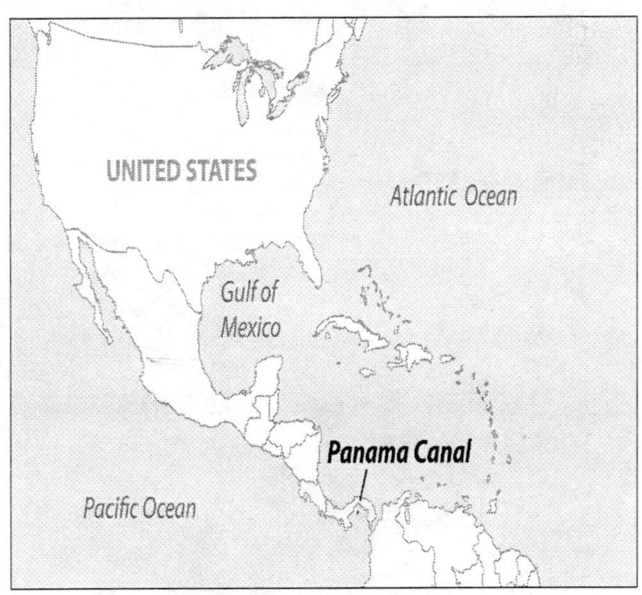

Map of the Panama Canal

The Panama Canal

THE ROOSEVELT COROLLARY

President Roosevelt also issued the **Roosevelt Corollary**. It was a policy that stated the United States had the right to keep European nations from occupying territories in Latin America. Its purpose was to protect the United States' economic interest, and keep it the dominant country in the Western Hemisphere.

IMMIGRATION

Immigrants Arriving in the Early 1900s

In the late 1800s, many in Europe and Asia were looking for a better life. They often faced poverty, disease, starvation, persecution, and the effects of wars in their homelands. Many fled to America, hoping it would be a land of opportunity. Between 1870 and 1900, more than twelve million **immigrants** (people who moved to the United States from a foreign land) arrived in the U.S.. People came from many places. They brought with them "strange" languages, unfamiliar religions, and different customs. Many Jews made their way to the United States to escape persecution. Most immigrants settled in large cities like New York.

They provided labor for the new factories and industries that were developing. Thanks to immigrants, the U.S. urban population (number of people who live in cities) grew greatly around the turn of the century.

TENEMENTS, GHETTOES, AND NATIVISTS

Tenement Housing

Urban Ghettoes

Most immigrants were poor. They worked long hours in city factories for little pay. Many lived in tenements. **Tenements** were cheap, dirty, overcrowded apartments. They often housed more than one family. Immigrants commonly lived in urban ghettoes. **Ghettoes** were neighborhoods where immigrants from the same country lived because of the similarities they shared. The ghettoes featured poor sanitation, unclean air, and disease.

Some people did not welcome foreigners. **Nativists** were people born in the United States who disliked immigrants. Nativists feared that people from other countries would take their jobs. They also did not trust the foreign customs that immigrants had. Nativists were prejudiced against those who looked different, talked differently, and practiced different religions. The government limited the number of immigrants who could come from certain countries during the late 1800s and early twentieth century.

AMERICAN CITIZENS!

A PAPER ENTITLED THE

AMERICAN PATRIOT.

CONSTITUTION AND LAWS

IN FAVOR OF

The protection of American Mechanics against Foreign Pauper Labor.
Foreigners having a residence in the country of 21 years before voting.
Our present Free School System.
Carrying out the laws of the State, as regards sending back Foreign Paupers and Criminals.

OPPOSED TO

Papal Aggression & Roman Catholicism.
Foreigners holding office.
Raising Foreign Military Companies in the United States.
Nunneries and the Jesuits.
To being taxed for the support of Foreign paupers millions of dollars yearly.
To secret Foreign Orders in the U. S.

We are burdened with enormous taxes by foreigners. We are corrupted in the morals of our youth. We are interfered with in our government. We are forced into collisions with other nations. We are tampered with in our religion. We are injured in our labor. We are assailed in our freedom of speech.

The PATRIOT is Published by J. E. Farwell & Co., 32 Congress St., Boston, And for Sale at the Periodical Depots in this place. Single copies 4 Cents.

Nativist Newspaper

Practice 2.2: America's Expanding Role in the World

1. What country did the United States go to war with while William McKinley was president?

   A. Cuba B. Spain C. England D. Russia

2. Theodore Roosevelt can BEST be described as a/an

   A. imperialist. B. isolationist. C. immigrant. D. Filipino.

3. What is an immigrant? Who were nativists? How did nativists feel about immigrants, and why?

2.3 World War I and the 1920s

Europe Goes to War

World War I Fighting

During the early years of the twentieth century, many European nations formed **alliances**. In an alliance, countries agree to help each other if one of them is attacked. In 1914, Archduke Francis Ferdinand was the heir to the throne of Austria-Hungary. While he visited the territory of Bosnia, Serbian nationalists (Serbians who wanted Bosnia to be part of Serbia, not Austria-Hungary) assassinated him. Austria-Hungary blamed Serbia and threatened war. Russia, Serbia's ally, promised to defend Serbia if Austria-Hungary attacked. Germany quickly vowed to fight on the side of Austria-Hungary. Soon all of Europe was at war. Germany and Austria-Hungary formed an alliance called the Central Powers. Russia, Great Britain, and France became the leaders of an alliance known as the Triple Entente. The conflict eventually involved nations around the world. It later became known as **World War I**.

The United States Joins the Fighting

At first, most U.S. citizens wanted to stay out of the war. They believed it was Europe's fight, not the United States'. President **Woodrow Wilson** won re-election in 1916 vowing not to get the U.S. involved in the fighting. Over time, however, a number of things happened that led the United States to enter the war.

Woodrow Wilson

U-Boats and the *Lusitania*

During World War I, Germany used **U-boats**. U-boats were submarines (ships that sail under water). They could stay hidden beneath the surface of the water as they fired torpedoes that sank ships. German U-Boats fired on not only enemy ships, but also on ships from other countries. Germany believed these ships were actually carrying goods meant to help the nations it was fighting. Some of these ships carried U.S. citizens. In May of 1915, German submarines sank a passenger ship called the ***Lusitania***. Over a hundred U.S. passengers died. People in the United States were furious! In reality, the U.S. government was secretly using the *Lusitania* and other passenger ships to sneak military supplies to Great Britain and its allies. To most people, however, Germany's actions looked like an evil attack against innocent civilians. Public opinion started to change. More people in the United States began to favor war.

The *Lusitania* Sinks

THE ZIMMERMANN TELEGRAM

Arthur Zimmermann

Another event that caused outrage in the United States was the **Zimmermann Telegram**. Germany's foreign minister, Arthur Zimmermann, sent a secret telegram to Mexico City. It asked Mexico to attack the United States if the United States ever went to war with Germany. In return, Germany promised to help Mexico win back parts of North America it had lost to the U.S. during the 1800s. Mexico did not agree to the deal, but when people in the U.S. learned of the offer, they were alarmed. The Zimmerman nTelegram led more citizens to support the idea of going to war.

U.S. INVOLVEMENT AND VICTORY IN EUROPE

U.S. Soldiers in WWI

The first U.S. soldiers reached Europe in 1918. They arrived just in time to help turn back Germany's attack against Paris. By the time U.S. forces arrived, millions of Europeans were already dead. Many homes and cities had been destroyed. The presence of the Americans made it clear to Germany that it could not hope to win. It signed an **armistice** (agreement to stop fighting) in November 1918. President Wilson and the other Allied leaders drafted a treaty ending the war. Although Wilson did not want to punish Germany, the other countries did. Their nations had fought much longer and suffered more death and destruction than the United States. The **Treaty of Versailles** forced Germany to take total blame for the war. It also made Germany pay for the war and greatly decrease the size of its military. Many of the German people grew very bitter because of the treaty. Meanwhile, many in the United States feared that the treaty would lead the U.S. into alliances with foreign countries. The Senate refused to ratify it, claiming it feared the Treaty of Versailles could lead to future wars.

President Wilson Meets With Other Allied Leaders

The Roaring Twenties

Building an army to fight in World War I meant that the nation needed weapons and supplies. Such production created jobs and high demand for products. As production and jobs increased, so did prosperity. After the war ended, most citizens just wanted to return to normal and enjoy the new wealth. The decade that followed the war became known as the *Roaring Twenties.*

Jazz and the Harlem Renaissance

The Jazz Age

The first years of the 1920s were called the **Jazz Age**. Jazz was a new form of music that made its way from New Orleans to northern cities early in the decade. African American musicians created it. It is a style of music in which performers use brass, woodwind, and percussion instruments to improvise (play without looking at notes) rather than rely on sheet music. The fast and spirited beat of jazz made it popular with both blacks and whites. Jazz led to the creation of several new dances during the 1920s. Trumpeter **Louis Armstrong** became one of the most famous jazz musicians in history during this period.

Louis Armstrong

The Harlem Renaissance

Langston Hughes

Another important movement among the African American community was the **Harlem Renaissance**. It involved black writers and artists. It was named for Harlem, New York, the mostly black community where it began. **Langston Hughes** became famous for his poems and stories about black life in America. Other writers, including women like **Zora Neale Hurston**, also published noted works during this time.

Zora Neale Hurston

Henry Ford and the Automobile

Henry Ford

Ford's Model T

Early in the twentieth century, only a few people owned automobiles. Only the rich could afford to buy them. Then, a man named **Henry Ford** introduced the idea of **mass producing** cars. He wanted to make so many cars that he could afford to sell them much cheaper and still make a profit. This would make Ford a lot of money and make it possible for common people to own an automobile. Ford introduced a new kind of **assembly line**. An assembly line allows workers to focus on one task rather than trying to assemble the whole product. Each of Ford's workers was responsible for assembling one part of each car. Earlier assembly lines required workers to walk from station to station. Ford's brought the parts to the workers. His employees could stand in one spot, while the parts came to them. This made the work much faster and increased production. Ford paid his employees $5 a day (a good salary back then) so that they could also afford to buy his cars. Henry Ford's first mass-produced car was known as the Model T. It revolutionized the auto industry. Ford's ideas about mass production and his assembly line helped make other businesses better as well.

American Heroes

American heroes arose during the 1920s. One of the most popular was **Babe Ruth**. Ruth was a great baseball player. He played most of his career with the New York Yankees. Ruth became famous for his powerful hitting. Before he left the game, he became the all-time home run leader. His 714 home runs stood as a record until 1974, when an Atlanta Brave named Hank Aaron finally broke it. Babe Ruth still ranks third on the all-time home run leaders list.

Babe Ruth

Charles Lindbergh

Charles Lindbergh also became a hero during this period. Lindbergh became the first person in history to fly a solo flight nonstop across the Atlantic Ocean. He flew from the United States to Paris, France, in 1927. Today, Lindbergh's plane hangs from the ceiling of the National Air and Space Museum in Washington, D.C.

Practice 2.3: World War I and the 1920s

1. Which of the following is a reason that the United States entered World War I?
   A. The United States was angry that an archduke had been assassinated.
   B. Mexico and Germany attacked the United States.
   C. President Wilson hated Germany and wanted to punish it.
   D. German submarines were attacking U.S. ships.

2. Louis Armstrong was a
   A. famous African American writer.
   B. great jazz musician.
   C. baseball hero of the 1920s.
   D. heroic pilot.

3. How did Henry Ford change the car industry?

CHAPTER 2 REVIEW

Key Terms, People, and Concepts

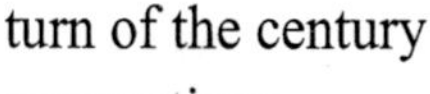

turn of the century
reservations
Battle of Little Bighorn
Custer's last stand
cattle drives
black cowboys
cattle trails
Chisholm Trail
Great Western Cattle Trail
Wilbur and Orville Wright
Alexander Graham Bell
Thomas Edison
electric light bulb
George Washington Carver
crop rotation method
William McKinley
Cuba
USS Maine
Spanish-American War
the Philippines
Platt Amendment
imperialists
isolationists
Theodore Roosevelt
Rough Riders
Panama Canal
Roosevelt Corollary
immigrants
tenements
ghettoes
nativists
alliances
World War I
Woodrow Wilson
U-boats
Lusitania
Zimmermann Telegram
armistice
Treaty of Versailles
Jazz Age
Louis Armstrong
Harlem Renaissance
Langston Hughes
Zora Neale Hurston
Henry Ford
mass production
assembly line
Babe Ruth
Charles Lindbergh

Multiple Choice Questions

1. Long journeys on which cowboys would move herds of cattle across the plains to western towns were known as
   - A. cattle trails.
   - B. reservations.
   - C. cattle drives.
   - D. cattle rides.

2. It was common for cowboys, jazz musicians, and artists of the Harlem Renaissance to be
   - A. nativists.
   - B. immigrants.
   - C. African Americans.
   - D. Native Americans.

3. An event that occurred sometime between 1899 and 1902 could be said to have happened
   - A. during the Jazz Age.
   - B. after World War II.
   - C. during the Spanish-American War.
   - D. around the turn of the century.

4. What did Orville Wright and Charles Lindbergh have in common?
   - A. Both had major impact on air travel.
   - B. Both were heroes of World War I.
   - C. Both immigrated to the United States.
   - D. Both supported the Zimmermann Telegram.

5. A factory owner is producing more than he ever dreamed of because his workers can work late into the night. This factory owner is probably MOST grateful for
   - A. Woodrow Wilson's ability to keep the United States out of war.
   - B. Thomas Edison.
   - C. the Wright Brothers.
   - D. the Harlem Renaissance.

6. A Georgia farmer plants cotton only every other year. The other years he plants peanuts and soybeans. This farmer has been influenced by
   - A. Theodore Roosevelt.
   - B. Charles Lindbergh.
   - C. Langston Hughes.
   - D. George Washington Carver.

7. Who was president when the Spanish-American War began?
   - A. William McKinley
   - B. Theodore Roosevelt
   - C. Woodrow Wilson
   - D. George Washington Carver

8. What do Cuba, the Philippines, Guam, and Puerto Rico all have in common?
   A. They each fought against the United States during World War I.
   B. Millions of people emigrated from all four nations around the turn of the century.
   C. All four were territories involved in the Spanish-American War.
   D. All four became U.S. territories as part of the Platt Amendment.

9. What was important about the *Lusitania*?
   A. It was a German U-boat that attacked U.S. ships.
   B. It was a ship that Germany sank, leading to U.S. involvement in World War I.
   C. It was a ship that mysteriously blew up in a Cuban harbor and led to the start of the Spanish-American War.
   D. It was a plane that Charles Lindbergh successfully flew across the Atlantic Ocean in 1927.

10. Someone who moved from Poland to New York City in 1903 would have been considered
    A. a nativist.
    B. an immigrant.
    C. an isolationist.
    D. an expansionist.

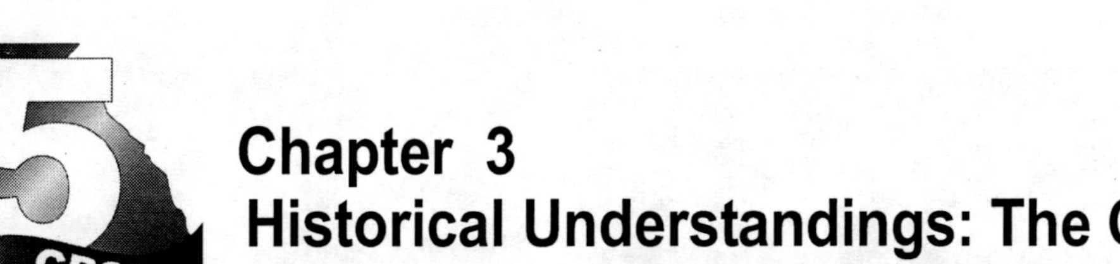

Chapter 3 Historical Understandings: The Great Depression and World War II

This chapter addresses the following competencies.

SS5H5	The student will explain how the Great Depression and New Deal affected the lives of millions of Americans.
SS5H6	The student will explain the reasons for America's involvement in World War II.

3.1 THE GREAT DEPRESSION AND THE NEW DEAL

THE STOCK MARKET CRASH

The decades leading up to 1929 were exciting and prosperous. Women took on new roles and gained the right to vote. African Americans received praise for works of art, literature, music, and contributions to society. Businesses thrived. Other than farmers who suffered from falling agricultural prices, most of the U.S. economy seemed strong. Then, in 1929, the stock market crashed! (Stocks are investments in companies.) During the 1920s, many people bought stock expecting companies to make money. When stock prices fell, many of these investors lost everything! The crash caused others to panic and sell off the stock they had. Soon banks were recalling loans (making people pay back loans earlier than expected). When people couldn't pay, a number of banks closed. Many citizens who had put their money in banks lost their life savings. The **stock market crash of 1929** marked the start of the **Great Depression**. It was the worst economic crisis in U.S. history. Many had to rely on **soup kitchens**, which gave out free food to the

Wall Street, 1929

poor, to survive. **Hoovervilles** (communities made of shacks where poor, homeless people lived) popped up in cities. They were named after **Herbert Hoover**. Hoover was president when the Great Depression struck. Most citizens blamed Hoover for the crisis.

Soup Kitchen

Hooverville

Herbert Hoover

THE DUST BOWL

The Dust Bowl

Even before the Depression, farmers had struggled. The Depression only made things worse. One episode that devastated farmers in the Midwest was the **Dust Bowl**. During World War I, farmers did well. The war created a demand for farm produce and raised farm prices. Farmers raised a lot of crops during this period. Unfortunately, many of them did not understand the importance of crop rotation. They kept raising crops that used up many of the nutrients in the soil. Their methods left much of the farmland dry, useless, and uncovered by crops. During the early '30s, the Midwest also experienced a horrible drought (lack of rain), making the soil even drier. The Dust Bowl was a series of windstorms that carried the soil high into the air. These storms created massive dark clouds of dust. Some of these storms were so big that they buried entire homes and blanketed cities. The Dust Bowl forced many Midwest farmers to leave their farms and move to other parts of the country in hopes of starting over.

FRANKLIN ROOSEVELT AND THE NEW DEAL

Franklin D Roosevelt

In 1932, U.S. voters elected a new president: **Franklin D. Roosevelt**. Known to many as FDR, Roosevelt was very positive and offered hope to hurting Americans. He was also prepared to try new things to deal with the Depression. He introduced the **New Deal**. It was a set of government programs that relied on **deficit spending**. The government went into debt, spending borrowed money, in hopes that its programs would get people back to work and the economy headed in the right direction.

CIVILIAN CONSERVATION CORPS (CCC)

Poster Promoting the Civilian Conservation Corps

One New Deal program was the **Civilian Conservation Corps**. The CCC provided jobs for young, unmarried men. These young men worked in the national parks installing electric lines, building fire towers, and planting new trees.

TENNESSEE VALLEY AUTHORITY (TVA)

Roosevelt pushed Congress to create the **Tennessee Valley Authority** in 1933. The TVA built hydroelectric dams. It created jobs and supplied cheap electricity to parts of the South that had never had electric power before. The southern Appalachians were one of the poorest areas in the nation. With the help of the TVA, this region prospered as never before.

Appalachian Mountains During the 1930s

Works Progress Administration (WPA)

Congress established the **Works Progress Administration** in 1935. It was part of a second group of New Deal programs, sometimes called the Second New Deal. It provided jobs for unskilled workers. The WPA hired people to build government buildings, roads, and other public projects. It also provided money for the arts.

Social Security

The New Deal also introduced a program to help people who retired or who were out of work. **Social Security** promised government money to the unemployed and those over sixty-five years of age. Social Security is the only New Deal program that still exists today.

The CCC, TVA, and WPA were just three of several New Deal programs introduced during the 1930s. Most historians agree that the New Deal did not end the Depression. It wasn't until World War II that the U.S. economy drastically improved. But the New Deal did supply some relief to help people get through one of the darkest economic times in U.S. history.

Practice 3.1: The Great Depression and the New Deal

1. In 1933, a farmer with a family of five in Oklahoma would have been MOST DIRECTLY affected by the

   A. CCC.
   B. Dust Bowl.
   C. TVA.
   D. stock market crash.

2. Which of the following BEST describes President Franklin Roosevelt's New Deal?

   A. a company in which investors buy stock
   B. government programs designed to ease economic hardship
   C. a power company supplying much of southern Appalachia with electricity
   D. strategy for improving national parks and forests

3. What was the Great Depression? When did it start? What effects did it have?

4. What was the New Deal? What did Roosevelt hope it would do?

3.2 IMPORTANT CULTURAL ELEMENTS OF THE 1930S

MOVIES AND SINGERS

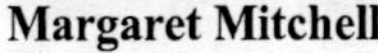

Margaret Mitchell

Scene from "Gone with the Wind"

Movies became more popular during the Great Depression. Fred Astaire and Ginger Rogers danced their way into the hearts of millions on the big screen. Child star Shirley Temple became an American sweetheart as she danced and sang in popular films. One of the most sensational movies of the era was the 1939 film *The Wizard of Oz*. Another classic movie of the period was based on **Margaret Mitchell's** best-selling novel, ***Gone with the Wind***. It depicted life on a Southern plantation during the Civil War. Published in 1936, it became a movie in 1939 and won more Academy Awards than any other film up to that time.

MUSICIANS AND ARTISTS

Duke Ellington

In music, Bing Crosby and Billie Holiday became popular singers. Meanwhile, talented musicians like **Duke Ellington** increased the popularity of jazz and big band music. Ellington assembled one of the most talented jazz orchestras in history. He recorded many jazz classics and appeared in movies. **Sinclair Lewis** was a novelist who became the first American in history to win the Nobel Prize in Literature. A few years later, **Pearl Buck** became the first U.S. woman to win the honor.

SPORTS HEROES

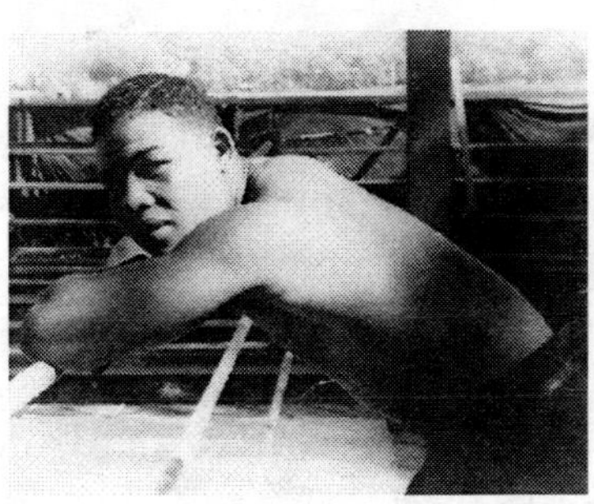

Joe Lewis

Great athletes competed in the 1930s. One of the most famous was heavyweight boxing champion **Joe Louis**. Nicknamed "The Brown Bomber," Louis became known for his powerful punches. In 1938, Louis (an African American) won a famous fight against German boxer Max Schmeling. The Nazi Party that ruled Germany was racist. It taught that white people were naturally superior to other races. Pointing out that Schmeling had already beaten Louis in an earlier match,

German officials claimed that there was no way a black fighter could beat a white fighter. In front of more than seventy thousand people at Yankee Stadium in New York, Louis proved them wrong. He knocked out Schmeling in less than three minutes.

Jesse Owens

Another great athlete was **Jesse Owens**. Owens was also an African American. He won four gold medals in track and field at the 1936 Olympic Games. His victories were even more significant because the games took place in Berlin, Germany. Owens defeated a host of white athletes as Nazi leader Adolf Hitler looked on.

Practice 3.2: Important Cultural Elements of the 1930s

1. Duke Ellington is remembered for his accomplishments in
   A. track and field.
   B. boxing.
   C. acting.
   D. jazz.

2. What is Margaret Mitchell most remembered for?

3. What did Jesse Owens accomplish in 1936? What made his accomplishment especially significant?

3.3 World War II

Germany and Japan

Hitler's Aggression

Adolf Hitler

After World War I, many Germans were bitter about the Treaty of Versailles. The Treaty forced **Germany** to pay for the war and caused Germany's economy to suffer. The worldwide depression hit Germany hard. (The Great Depression affected countries around the world, not just the United States.) Many Germans blamed other European nations and German Jews for their hardships. They wanted new leadership. **Adolf Hitler** took advantage of the unhappiness to lead his Nazi Party to power. Hitler preached hatred of the Jews and promised to return Germany to greatness. By 1933, he was firmly in power.

Hitler wanted to expand his empire, which he called the **Third Reich**. He invaded the Rhineland, Austria, and parts of Czechoslovakia. Since other European nations did not want another war, they did little to stop him. Instead, they chose **appeasement**. Appeasement is the belief that it is best to let an aggressive nation have what it wants. The hope is that this will satisfy its leaders and stop the aggression. But Hitler had no intention of stopping. He signed an alliance with two other aggressive nations: Italy and Japan. In 1939, Germany invaded Poland, starting **World War II** in Europe. By the end of 1940, Hitler's forces conquered other European nations, including France. They had also attacked Great Britain and were preparing to invade the Soviet Union.

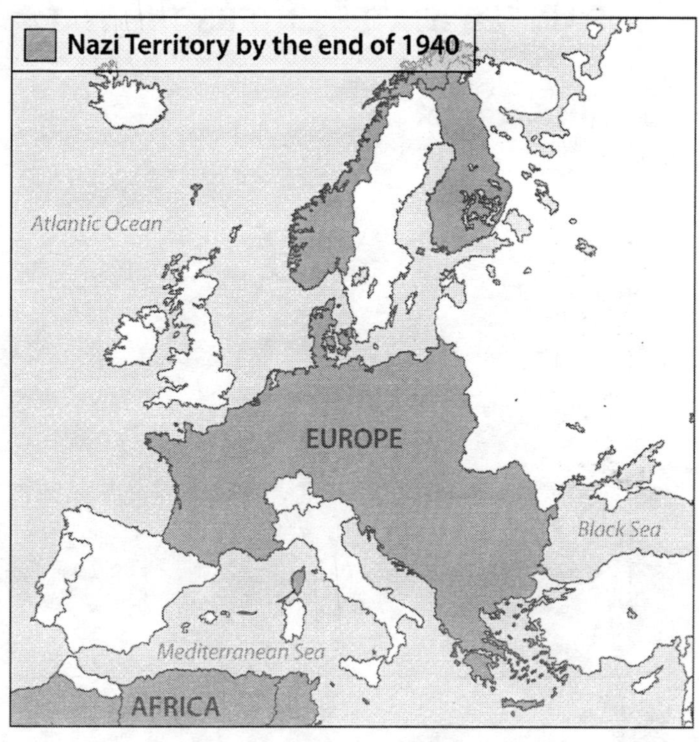

Nazi Territory, 1940

Japan's Aggression

Beginning in the 1920s, **Japan** decided to expand its territory in Southeast Asia. The young **Emperor Hirohito** did not desire war, but he did not possess most of the power in Japan. Instead, the government fell under the control of the military. As a tiny island nation, Japan lacked natural resources. Many in the military saw the invasion of other territories as the best way to solve this problem. By the late 1930s, Japan controlled most of the Chinese coast and was determined to conquer other territories as well.

Emperor Hirohito

The United States Enters the War

Pearl Harbor

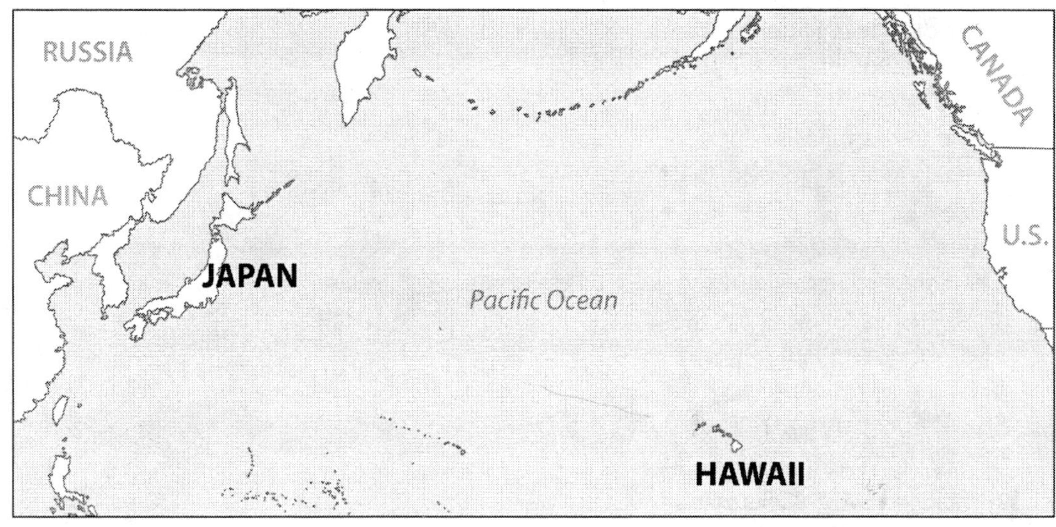

Japan and Hawaii

The Attack on Pearl Harbor

The United States was very concerned about Germany and Japan. Still, many citizens did not want the United States to go to war. Then, in late 1941, everything changed. Japanese leaders believed that the U.S. Pacific Fleet at **Pearl Harbor**, Hawaii, was anchored too close to Japan. They felt it threatened Japan's expansion. On December 7, 1941, Japanese planes launched a surprise attack on Pearl Harbor. It was intended to destroy the Pacific Fleet and keep it from interfering with Japan's plans. The attack destroyed U.S. ships and planes. It also killed or wounded nearly three thousand people. The next day, President Roosevelt asked Congress to declare war. Congress agreed. Because Germany and Japan were partners in war, the United States soon found itself at war with Germany as well. The United States had entered World War II.

The War at Home

While U.S. soldiers were away fighting in Europe and the Pacific, citizens at home did their part to support the war effort. The military needed weapons and supplies. Production increased and the economy boomed. Citizens began looking for ways to conserve goods so that more could go to the soldiers. People planted **victory gardens** in which they raised their own vegetables. Some voluntarily decided not to eat meat on certain days of the week. Citizens collected rubber, copper, steel, and other goods to be recycled. The government acted as well. It used **rationing** to limit how much citizens could buy. Rationing forced people to conserve certain goods.

THE ROLE OF WOMEN

Women's role in society changed during the war. Over 275,000 women served in the United States military. The largest military division of women was the **WAC (Women's Army Corps)**. Military women served in nearly every role except combat. Meanwhile, civilian women played an important part in the war effort at home. Many of the nation's men left their jobs to go fight. The country, however, still needed workers to produce goods. Thousands of women filled the gap by working in the nation's factories and industries. **Rosie the Riveter** became the symbol of such women. It was the title of a song about a woman who went to work as a riveter while her husband went off to war. Posters of "Rosie" encouraged women to go to work and help production.

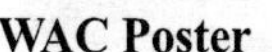

WAC Poster

Rosie the Riveter Poster

MINORITIES

The 442nd Regiment

The Tuskegee Airmen

Minorities also played an important role. Many African Americans, Hispanic Americans, Native Americans, and other minorities went to work on farms and in factories to help with the wartime production. Many of them also joined the armed forces. The **Tuskegee Airmen** were African American fighter pilots. As a squadron, they successfully protected every U.S. bomber they escorted during the war. A group of Native American Marines became known as **code**

talkers. The Marine Corps developed a coded radio language based on the Navajo language (the Navajo are a Native American tribe). Code talkers played an important role in secret communications. The code proved very effective. The Japanese never figured it out. Perhaps most impressive was an army infantry regiment known as the **442nd**. It was made up totally of Japanese American soldiers. The 442nd fought in Europe and became the most decorated unit in U.S. history.

THE WAR AND RACISM

Although they served honorably, African American soldiers remained segregated from white soldiers. They served in all-black units under the command of white officers. On navy ships and army posts, African Americans were usually assigned menial tasks like cooking. Many African Americans resented that the government expected them to fight for a country that did not give them equal rights. African American soldiers returned home no longer willing to accept inequality. Many of them helped lead a new **civil rights movement** that challenged Americans' view of race.

Japanese Internment Camp

One of the most tragic events of World War II was the **internment of Japanese Americans**. After Pearl Harbor, many in the U.S. government feared that Japanese Americans would help Japan. In an effort to avoid spying and sabotage, President Roosevelt signed an executive order. (Sabotage is when someone damages weapons or machines on purpose.) The executive order called for the government to relocate thousands of Japanese Americans to internment camps (government camps). Many Japanese Americans had to leave their homes. Some lost their jobs or their own businesses. Although some German and Italian Americans were interned as well, these groups did not face nearly as much racism or suspicion as Japanese Americans.

The War in Europe

North Africa and Italy

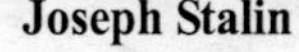
Joseph Stalin

Winston Churchill

In June 1941, Germany invaded the Soviet Union (USSR). After Pearl Harbor, the United States, Great Britain, the USSR, and a number of other nations fought together as the **Allies**. Germany, Italy, and Japan formed the **Axis Powers**. Although the Soviet Union's leader, **Joseph Stalin**, urged the United States and Great Britain to invade Western Europe, President Roosevelt and Britain's Prime Minister **Winston Churchill** decided to attack in North Africa first. North Africa was important because of the Suez Canal. The canal allowed ships to travel back and forth between the Mediterranean and Red Sea without having to sail around Africa. Following their victory in North Africa, the British and U.S. forces invaded and conquered southern Italy. Italy's Axis leader, **Benito Mussolini**, escaped to the north. There he became the leader of a puppet government under Adolf Hitler. (A puppet government is one that rules a country but answers to a stronger foreign government).

D-Day

D-Day Invasion

Following a meeting between Stalin, Churchill, and Roosevelt, the Allies agreed that the time had come for an invasion of Western Europe. U.S. General **Dwight D. Eisenhower** commanded the invasion. On June 6, 1944, Allied troops launched a surprise attack on Northern France. The invasion became known as **D-Day**. It was a huge success. As the Soviets marched towards Berlin from the east, the western Allies liberated France and other countries as they advanced from the west.

VICTORY IN EUROPE AND THE HOLOCAUST

In April 1945, Hitler realized he had lost. As Soviet troops surrounded Berlin, Hitler committed suicide rather than be captured. In May, Germany surrendered. The Allies celebrated **V-E Day** (Victory in Europe Day). President Roosevelt did not see the day of victory. He died earlier that same month at his vacation home in Warm Springs, Georgia. **Harry Truman** became the new president.

Victims of the Holocaust

Nuremberg Trials

As the Allies advanced through Europe, they made a horrifying discovery. They found **concentration camps** housing thousands of starving and tortured prisoners. Most of these prisoners were Jewish. At first, Hitler's government simply passed laws discriminating against Jews. After he invaded the Soviet Union, however, Hitler tried to exterminate the Jewish people. He also sought to kill other people the Nazis felt were unfit to live. Among these groups were Slavs, the mentally ill, gypsies, homosexuals, and Jehovah's Witnesses. But no group suffered as much as the Jews. Jewish people of all ages were arrested. Many were executed immediately or shipped to camps where they were killed upon arrival. Others were forced to work or were tortured in the camps before finally being murdered. Over six million Jewish people perished. This horrible period became known as the **Holocaust**. After the war, a number of German leaders stood trial for these crimes. Most were found guilty. Some received long prison sentences. Others were hanged.

THE WAR IN THE PACIFIC

MIDWAY

The Japanese badly damaged the U.S. Pacific Fleet during the attack on Pearl Harbor. Not long after, they scored another big victory. Japanese forces invaded the Philippines, taking the islands and capturing thousands of Allied troops. Unfortunately for Japan, however, things changed at the **Battle of Midway**. Midway was a tiny island in the Pacific Ocean. The United States considered it important because it helped protect Hawaii and the west coast of the United States. Japan's leading admiral hoped he could force the United States

Battle of Midway

to fight Japan at Midway. He planned to attack while the U.S. fleet was still weak. Japan succeeded in forcing a fight, but its naval commanders failed to win the battle. The United States defeated Japan and turned the tide of the war in the Pacific.

ISLAND HOPPING

The U.S. military then used a strategy called **island hopping**. U.S. forces conquered one set of islands after another as they fought their way towards Japan. Forces under the command of Admiral Chester Nimitz advanced across the Central Pacific. Meanwhile, General Douglas MacArthur and Admiral William Halsey commanded forces that attacked from the south and retook the Philippines.

Iwo Jima

One of the fiercest battles occurred on the island of **Iwo Jima**. It took more than one hundred thousand U.S. soldiers nearly a month to defeat a Japanese force of twenty-five thousand. Japanese soldiers often believed it was more honorable to fight to the death rather than surrender. One of the most famous images of the war was that of U.S. Marines raising an American flag over Iwo Jima.

THE ATOMIC BOMB

Following Germany's surrender, President Truman met with Churchill and Stalin in Potsdam, Germany (Churchill was later replaced at the conference by a new Prime Minister, Clement Attlee). There they issued the **Potsdam Declaration**. It restated the Allies' policy of **unconditional surrender**. Unconditional surrender meant that the Allies would set all the rules for Japan's surrender; Japan would have no say. In truth, Japan was ready to surrender. The Japanese had suffered greatly from the war. They knew that they could not keep the Allies from reaching Japan. Japan's leaders, however, would not accept unconditional surrender. They wanted a guarantee that Japan would still have an emperor after the war. The Allies refused to listen to Japan's request.

Attlee, Truman, and Stalin at the Potsdam Conference

During the war, the United States developed the **atomic bomb**. It was the world's first nuclear weapon. It was far more powerful than any weapon ever invented. When Japan refused to surrender unconditionally, Truman ordered the bomb dropped on the Japanese city of **Hiroshima**. On August 6, 1945, a U.S. plane called the *Enola Gay* dropped the bomb. It destroyed Hiroshima. Thousands of Japanese people were killed. Thousands more died later from radiation caused by the explosion. When Japan still delayed in surrendering, the president ordered a second atomic bomb dropped on **Nagasaki**. The death and destruction caused by these horrifying weapons forced Japan to surrender. People in the United States celebrated **V-J Day** (Victory over Japan Day). After the war, the Allies allowed Japan to keep its emperor. Hirohito remained the emperor of Japan until his death in 1986.

Hiroshima After the Atomic Bomb

Hiroshima in the Mid-1980s

THE UNITED NATIONS

The UN Building in New York City

After World War I, countries established the League of Nations. They hoped the League would encourage peace and avoid future wars. The League had no power to enforce its decisions, however. Most countries saw World War II as evidence that the League did not work. After WWII, the United States and its allies led the way in establishing a new organization. In 1944, the United States hosted meetings to come up with a plan for the organization. In April 1945, leaders from fifty countries met in San Francisco to draft a charter. In October, the **United Nations (UN)** was formed. Its purpose was to maintain peace between countries, make sure nations obeyed international law, and protect human rights. Although nations from around the world sent representatives, most of the decision-making power fell to five permanent members of the **UN Security Council**: the United States, Soviet Union, China, Great Britain, and France. In order for the UN to take any military action to enforce its decisions, all five of the permanent members had to agree. Today, the Soviet Union no longer exists. Its former seat belongs to Russia. The UN continues to seek peaceful solutions to international problems while providing relief to human suffering around the world.

Practice 3.3: World War II

1. The United States entered World War II in response to
   A. Hitler seizing power in Germany.
   B. Hitler's troops invading Poland.
   C. Japan's attack on Pearl Harbor.
   D. Japan and Germany signing an alliance.

2. Joseph Stalin was the leader of
   A. Germany.
   B. Italy.
   C. Great Britain.
   D. the Soviet Union.

3. Rosie the Riveter symbolized
   A. women in the armed forces during WWII.
   B. rationing.
   C. women who went to work to support the war effort.
   D. the suffering of U.S. citizens forced to live in internment camps.

4. What was rationing? What was it intended to accomplish?

5. Why did the Japanese attack Pearl Harbor?

6. Why did President Truman decide to drop the atomic bomb?

7. What is the United Nations, and why was it founded?

CHAPTER 3 REVIEW

Key Terms, People, and Concepts

stock market crash of 1929
Great Depression
soup kitchens
Hoovervilles
Herbert Hoover
Dust Bowl
Franklin D. Roosevelt
New Deal
deficit spending
Civilian Conservation Corps
Tennessee Valley Authority
Works Progress Administration
Social Security
Margaret Mitchell
Gone with the Wind
Duke Ellington
Sinclair Lewis
Pearl Buck
Joe Louis
Jesse Owens
Germany
Adolf Hitler
Third Reich
appeasement
World War II
Japan
Emperor Hirohito
Pearl Harbor
victory gardens
rationing
WAC
Rosie the Riveter
Tuskegee Airmen
code talkers
442nd infantry regiment
civil rights movement
Japanese American internment
Allies
Axis Powers
Joseph Stalin
Winston Churchill
Benito Mussolini
Dwight D. Eisenhower
D-Day
V-E Day
Harry Truman
concentration camps
the Holocaust
Battle of Midway
island hopping
Iwo Jima
Postdam Declaration
unconditional surrender
atomic bomb
Hiroshima
Nagasaki
V-J Day
United Nations
UN Security Council

Multiple Choice Questions

1. Who wrote the book *Gone with the Wind*?
   A. Sinclair Lewis
   B. Pearl Buck
   C. Margaret Mitchell
   D. Mildred Didrikson

2. Who won four gold medals in track at the 1936 Olympics?
   A. Joe Louis
   B. Sinclair Lewis
   C. Pearl Buck
   D. Jesse Owens

3. Who was Italy's leader during World War II?
   A. Joseph Stalin
   B. Benito Mussolini
   C. Leonardo da Vinci
   D. Hirohito

4. What organization replaced the League of Nations in 1945?
   A. the National League
   B. the Allied Powers
   C. the Axis Powers
   D. the United Nations

5. What event happened in 1929 that signaled the start of the Great Depression?
   A. World War II ended.
   B. Pearl Habor wasattacked.
   C. The stock market crashed.
   D. Roosevelt began deficit spending.

Read the quote below, and answer the following question.

> "It's all covered. As far as the eye can see… all there is is dirt and destitution. Only a few roofs and the occasional fence post can be seen. No crops will grow here. No life left here."
>
> – North Texas farmer, 1932

6. The farmer quoted above is MOST LIKELY talking about
   A. life in a Hooverville.
   B. the stock market crash.
   C. the New Deal.
   D. the Dust Bowl.

7. The CCC, TVA, and WPA were all part of
   A. Roosevelt's New Deal.
   B. Hoover's plan to deal with the Depression.
   C. the war effort.
   D. the Tennessee Valley Authority.

8. Margaret Mitchell and Pearl Buck were both
   A. notable writers.
   B. women whose novels became Academy Award-winning films.
   C. female jazz musicians.
   D. great athletes of the 1930s.

9. Look at the list of events below. Which answer correctly lists them in the order in which they happened?
   1. attack on Pearl Harbor
   2. V-E Day
   3. D-Day
   4. the Great Depression
   5. Japanese American internment
   6. Atomic bombs dropped
   7. V-J Day

   A. 3, 1, 6, 2, 7, 4, 5
   B. 1, 4, 2, 5, 3, 7, 6
   C. 4, 1, 5, 3, 2, 6, 7
   D. 1, 6, 4, 3, 2, 7, 5

10. What did the Tuskegee Airmen, 442nd infantry regiment, and code talkers have in common with one another?
   A. They were each examples of how minorities worked in factories to support the war effort.
   B. They were each examples of the important role played by African Americans during WWII.
   C. They each were groups that fought at the Battle of Midway.
   D. They each showed the important contribution of minorities in the military.

Chapter 4
Historical Understandings: The Cold War and U.S. Society from 1950 to 1975

This chapter addresses the following competencies.

SS5H7	The student will discuss the origins and consequences of the cold war.
SS5H8	The student will describe the importance of key people, events, and developments between 1950 – 1975.

4.1 The Cold War

The Cold War in Europe

Stalin

Truman

The United States and the Soviet Union were very different. As a **capitalist democracy**, the United States allowed citizens and businesses to own private property, determine economic production, and pursue profits. Its Constitution also guaranteed basic human rights and allowed citizens to have a role in their government. The Soviet Union, on the other hand, was a **Communist dictatorship**. Its dictator, Joseph Stalin, commonly ordered the imprisonment or execution of anyone who opposed his rule. Communism meant that the state, not citizens or businesses, owned nearly all the property and determined production. After the war, these differences led the two sides to distrust one another. Stalin feared that the United States and Great Britain would invade the USSR while they still had their armies in Germany. He decided not to give up the territories his army had conquered during the war. Instead, he made them part of the Soviet Union or set up new Communist governments that answered to him. Meanwhile, the United States and Great Britain believed that Stalin wanted to invade Western Europe. They believed he wanted to spread Communism to the rest of the continent. They saw Stalin's refusal to give up Eastern Europe as proof that they were right. This period marked the start of the **cold war**. It was a time when people around the world feared the tension between the United States and USSR would eventually lead to war.

THE IRON CURTAIN

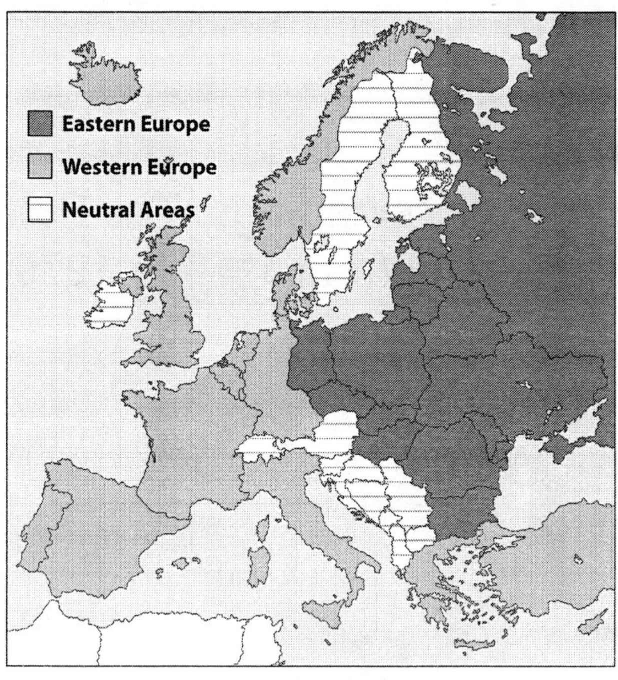

The Iron Curtain

Following Germany's defeat, the Allies divided the country. The United States, Great Britain, and France governed sections of western Germany. The USSR governed eastern Germany. The Allies also divided the German capital of **Berlin**. Even though Berlin was in the Soviet sector of Germany, each of the allied powers governed a portion of the city. The United States, Great Britain, and France believed this arrangement was temporary. They thought Germany would soon be a free democracy. Stalin, however, would not give up East Germany. Eventually, Germany became two separate nations. West Germany became a capitalist democracy. East Germany became a Communist state. Former British Prime Minister Winston Churchill described Europe as being divided by an "**iron curtain**." On the west side of the "curtain" were the democracies of Western Europe. On the east side were the Communist nations of Eastern Europe.

CONTAINMENT POLICY AND THE TRUMAN DOCTRINE

Gen. George Marshall

The United States decided that it could not remove Communism from Eastern Europe without war. Since no one wanted another war, President Truman adopted a **containment policy**. Containment meant that the United States would not attempt to remove Communism from places where it already existed. However, it would do all it could to make sure that Communism didn't spread to other parts of the world. Truman's vow to help other nations resist Communism became known as the **Truman Doctrine**. In Europe, the Truman Doctrine led to the **Marshall Plan**. This plan involved the U.S. government giving money to European nations. The money helped them rebuild after the war. By helping nations rebuild, the United States believed it would prevent the spread of Communism.

THE BERLIN AIRLIFT

Stalin wanted the western Allies out of Berlin. His army surrounded West Berlin and would not let any supplies in or out. Truman responded with the **Berlin airlift**. For several months in 1948 and '49, the United States and its allies flew planes delivering supplies across the Soviet lines and into West Berlin. Not wanting a war, Stalin finally gave up. But the Berlin airlift only made the two sides angrier with one another.

Berlin Airlift

NATO

Just before the end of the Berlin airlift, the United States signed a treaty with Canada and several European nations. Each nation vowed to help the others if the Soviets attacked. They also formed **NATO (the North Atlantic Treaty Organization)**. NATO would provide a combined military force to fight against any attack from Eastern Europe.

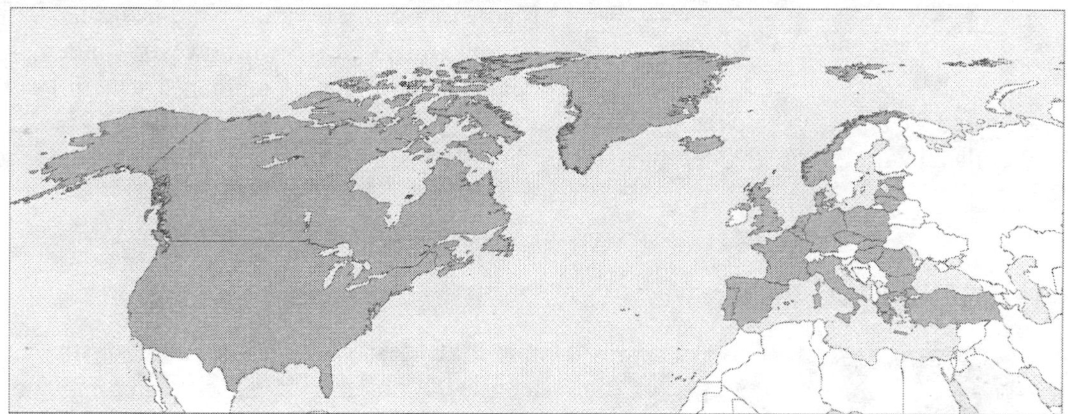

Nato Nations

THE ARMS RACE

Within a few years of the United States dropping its first atomic bomb, the Soviet Union developed its own nuclear weapons. A few years later, both nations developed hydrogen bombs that were thousands of times more powerful than the bombs dropped on Hiroshima and Nagasaki. A **nuclear arms race** developed between the United States and the USSR. Both nations created more and more nuclear weapons. Soon both sides had nuclear missiles that could travel thousands of miles in minutes and destroy cities on the other side of the world. People lived in fear of a nuclear war that would destroy the entire planet.

THE KOREAN WAR

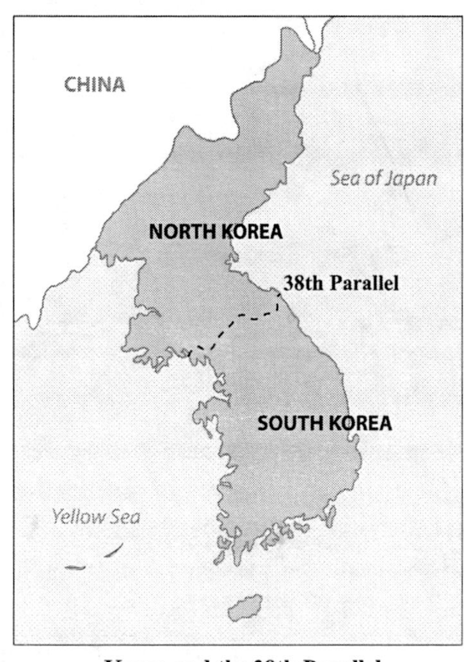

Korea and the 38th Parallel

U.S. Troops during the Korean War

After World War II, the Allies split the East Asian nation of Korea in half. North Korea became a Communist state. South Korea became a capitalist democracy. The **38th parallel** served as a dividing line between the two nations. In 1950, North Korean troops crossed the 38th parallel and quickly conquered much of South Korea. The United Nations elected to send troops to stop the invasion. President Harry Truman put General Douglas MacArthur in charge. MacArthur drove back the North Koreans. Before he could fully defeat them, however, Chinese troops (China had become a Communist state in 1949) crossed the border to help the North Koreans. The **Korean War** continued until 1953. It resulted in a cease-fire that left the country divided at almost the same place as before the war began.

JOSEPH MCCARTHY

Senator Joseph McCarthy

Joseph McCarthy was a U.S. senator from the state of Wisconsin. During the 1950s, he became convinced that Communists were trying to gain control of the U.S. government. He vowed to find these Communists and drive them out. At first, many U.S. citizens backed McCarthy despite the fact that he had very little evidence to support his claims. Eventually, however, McCarthy went too far. He accused high-ranking military officers of being Communists. When McCarthy tried to make his case on television during a series of congressional hearings, most people thought he came off looking cruel, paranoid, and perhaps crazy. The hearings ruined McCarthy's political career.

The Cuban Missile Crisis

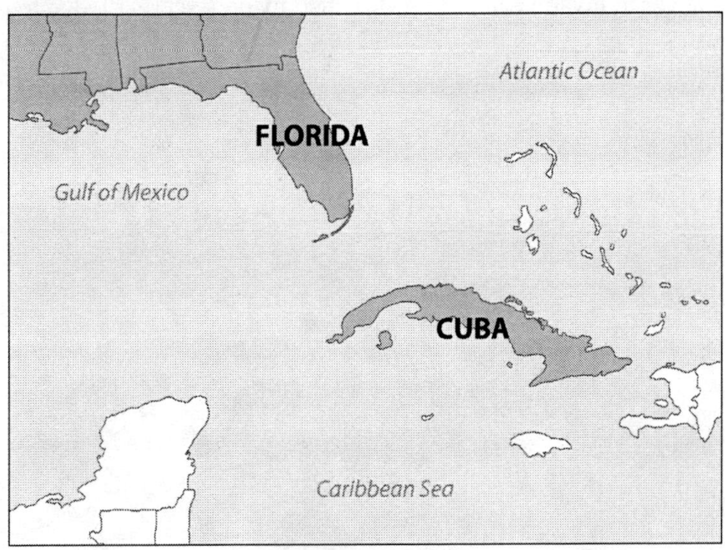

Florida and Cuba

John F. Kennedy

Nikita Khrushchev

Cuba is a small island nation less than a hundred miles off the coast of Florida. In 1959, Communist rebels under the leadership of Fidel Castro overthrew the government and took control of the country. The United States quickly grew concerned. Shortly after **John F. Kennedy** became president in 1961, he approved an attempt to overthrow Castro's government. The plan failed and increased Castro's fear that the United States might try to invade Cuba. Castro struck a deal with the Soviet Union and its leader **Nikita Khrushchev**. Khrushchev had taken over as First Secretary of the USSR's Communist Party after Stalin died in 1953. Although the Soviet government was no longer a dictatorship under Khrushchev, the new leader was still a tough politician who distrusted the United States. On one occasion, while addressing representatives from capitalist nations, he pounded his shoe on a table and vowed, "We will bury you!" He also tried to bully the United States and its allies into leaving West Berlin in 1958. He eventually backed down when President Eisenhower strengthened NATO's armed forces there.

Cuba allowed the Soviets to place nuclear missiles in Cuba in 1962. When President Kennedy learned of the missiles, he called on Khrushchev to remove them and ordered a blockade of the island. (A blockade is when naval ships prevent any other ships from leaving or docking in a country's ports). For thirteen days, the world watched and feared that the **Cuban Missile Crisis** might lead to nuclear war. Finally, the Soviets agreed to remove the missiles and the U.S. promised never to invade Cuba. The U.S. also made a secret pledge to remove missiles it had in Turkey.

VIETNAM

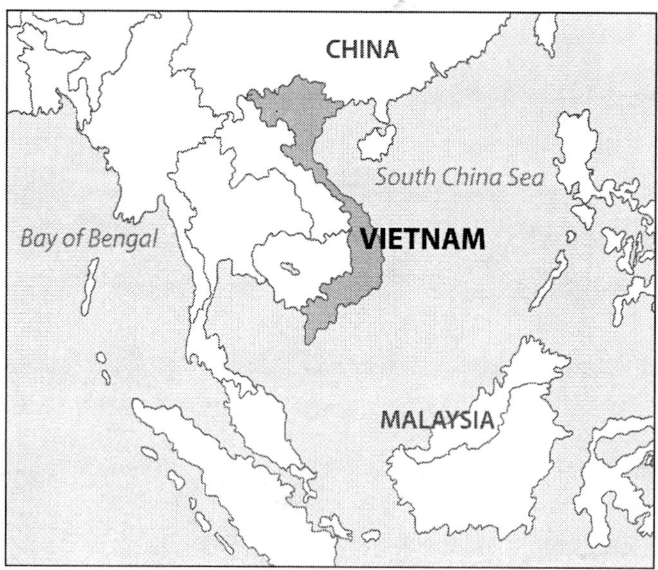

Map of Vietnam

Ho Chi Minh

In 1954, an international treaty divided the tiny Southeast Asian country of Vietnam. Communists ruled North Vietnam. A pro-U.S. government ruled South Vietnam. Soon, the two sides were at war. Because the southern leader was corrupt, many peasants in South Vietnam formed a rebel army called the Vietcong and fought alongside the North Vietnamese. The United States did not want South Vietnam to fall to Communism. First, it sent military advisors who only gave advice to the South Vietnamese. When that was not effective, President Lyndon Johnson ordered bombings and began sending thousands of troops. The **Vietnam War** escalated in the 1960s and was unlike any war the United States had ever fought. Even though the U.S. military was much stronger, the Vietcong struck quickly and unexpectedly. After killing or wounding as many U.S. soldiers as they could, Vietcong fighters would then retreat back into the thick jungle. The Vietcong did not try to win battles as much as they tried to make the United States tired of fighting. The U.S. military grew frustrated because it could not keep the Vietcong engaged in a battle long enough to totally defeat them.

Over time, people in the United States got tired of the war. Many protested against it and demanded that the troops return home. Finally, in 1973, the United States signed a peace agreement that pulled U.S. troops out of Vietnam. Soon, however, war erupted again between North and South Vietnam. In 1975, the Communists took the South Vietnamese capital. After a long and bloody war, the Communists finally controlled the entire country.

What was Different about Vietnam?

Television in the '60s

The Vietnam War was different from previous wars in many ways. It was the first war to occur during the age of **television.** In previous wars, citizens had to rely on radio, newspapers, or edited news reels to receive word of the fighting. Vietnam was the first war in which citizens could actually see much of the death and destruction from their own living rooms. Such scenes led many citizens to have strong opinions about the war. Many questioned the way their government was fighting the war. Others opposed the war completely.

Vietnam also occurred during a time in which more young citizens were attending colleges than ever before. During the 1960s, many college students began to question traditional values and authority figures, including their own government. A huge **antiwar movement** arose on many campuses. It spread to other parts of society. Unlike World War II and Korea, the nation became divided over Vietnam.

War Protest

Finally, Vietnam was different because the United States lost. Vietnam fell to Communism despite the United States' best efforts. Many U.S. soldiers returned home feeling forgotten or hated rather than like heroes. Some suffered lasting health and mental problems caused by the war. A few had to face the fact that they had committed horrible acts against civilians while in Vietnam. Even today, memories of Vietnam affect U.S. politics and society.

Practice 4.1: The Cold War

1. The imaginary line that separated free Western Europe from Communist Eastern Europe was known as the

   A. Communist shield.
   B. Capitalist-Communist divide.
   C. iron curtain.
   D. steel door.

2. The tension between the United States and the Soviet Union that many feared could lead to a nuclear war was called the

   A. cold war.
   B. arms race.
   C. iron curtain.
   D. Berlin airlift.

3. The Korean War began when
   A. Joseph Stalin decided to blockade Berlin.
   B. Castro allowed the Soviet Union to put missiles in his country.
   C. President Lyndon Johnson sent more troops to the region.
   D. Communist forces crossed the 38th parallel.

4. What is NATO? Why was it formed after WWII?

5. What happened during the Cuban Missile Crisis?

6. How was Vietnam different from other wars?

4.2 The Civil Rights Movement

Important Events and People

Following World War II, legalized segregation still existed in the South. African Americans had to remain separate from whites in public places. They had to use separate entrances, sit in different waiting rooms, and even use different bathrooms and water fountains. On public buses, blacks usually had to sit in the rear while whites sat up front. After World War II, many African Americans called for an end to segregation and injustice. Their protests helped give birth to the **civil rights movement**.

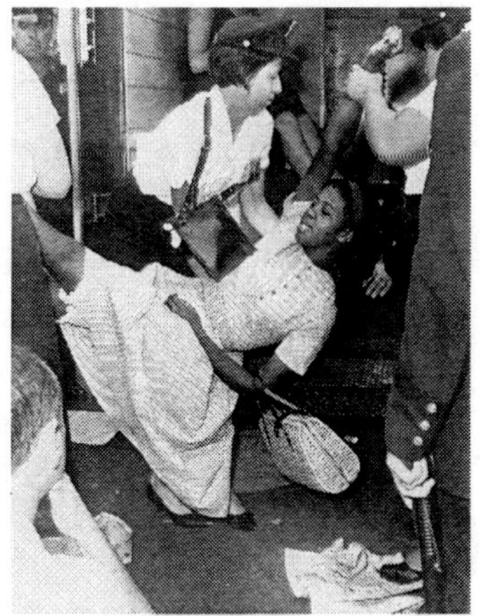

Civil Rights Protest

Brown v. Board of Education

Thurgood Marshall

In 1954, the **NAACP** (National Association for the Advancement of Colored People) challenged school segregation. The case arose after a Kansas school system did not allow an African American girl named Linda Brown to attend an all-white school. The NAACP argued in court that segregation violated the Constitution. It claimed segregation was unlawful because black schools were not equal to white schools. It wanted the courts to stop segregation in public education. The NAACP turned to a talented lawyer named **Thurgood Marshall** to argue its case. The NAACP won. The Supreme Court struck down school segregation in ***Brown v. Board of Education***. Thirteen years later, Thurgood Marshall became the first African American ever appointed to the United States Supreme Court.

MONTGOMERY BUS BOYCOTT

In 1955, the city government of Montgomery, Alabama, required blacks to sit in the rear of public buses. It also required African Americans to give up their seats to white passengers if the bus were full. City officials arrested an African American woman named **Rosa Parks** when she refused to give up her seat. Parks' arrest caused anger among the African American community. A young Baptist minister named **Martin Luther King Jr.** helped organize and lead the **Montgomery bus boycott**. African Americans refused to ride public buses. They walked or carpooled instead. The boycott cost the city a lot of money because many of the citizens who usually paid to ride the buses were black. The boycott ended after the Supreme Court ruled that Montgomery could no longer segregate its buses.

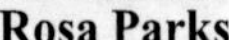

Rosa Parks

Martin Luther King Jr

DR. MARTIN LUTHER KING JR.

Protestors Being Beaten

March on Washington

Dr. King became the recognized leader of the civil rights movement. He believed in **nonviolence** (peaceful protests) and **civil disobedience** (peacefully disobeying unjust laws). Many African Americans adopted his methods. African Americans were arrested for sitting in all-white areas or assembling for civil rights protests and rallies. King, himself, was arrested a number of times and wrote one of his most famous letters from the jail in Birmingham, Alabama. King also used **television**. As people across the country watched news clips of peaceful civil rights protestors being beaten by police and insulted by racists, support for the movement grew. Soon, whites as well as blacks were traveling to the South to help the movement.

THE MARCH ON WASHINGTON

One of the most famous events of the civil rights movement was the 1963 **march on Washington**. In August, more than 200,000 civil rights supporters marched in the nation's capital. Dr. King gave perhaps his most famous speech standing in front of the Lincoln Memorial. Many know it as his "I have a dream" speech, because he spoke of his dream that, one day, all U.S. citizens would be judged by the "content of their character" rather than the color of their skin.

MILITANT MOVEMENTS

Not all African Americans thought that nonviolence was the best way to gain equality. **Militant movements** that believed it was okay to use violence also arose. Such movements attracted many younger, more radical blacks. The Nation of Islam and the Black Panthers were two of the most famous militant groups. Perhaps the most famous militant leader was **Malcolm X**. Malcolm became part of the Nation of Islam and preached distrust of all whites. He later left the "Nation" and, after going on a Muslim pilgrimage (religious journey), came to believe that some whites were good. He began preaching cooperation rather than hatred of all whites. Some blacks did not like Malcolm changing his message. On February 21, 1965, three African American men assassinated Malcolm X while he spoke at a rally in New York City.

Malcolm X

THE ASSASSINATION OF MARTIN LUTHER KING, JR.

King's Assassination

Despite his belief in nonviolence, Dr. King had enemies. Many government officials distrusted and feared him. Militant blacks felt he was too weak. White racists hated him for challenging their beliefs. On April 4, 1968, a white gunman **assassinated** (murdered) Dr. King as he stood on a hotel balcony in Memphis, Tennessee. African American communities in a number of U.S. cities erupted in violence. Riots broke out across the country. People as far away as South Africa mourned his death. Although King was dead, his dream and his cause lived on. The civil rights movement continued to win rights for African Americans.

Civil Rights Legislation

The civil rights movement led to passage of civil rights laws during the 1960s. The 1964 **Civil Rights Act** made segregation and discrimination illegal in many public places, such as hotels, restaurants, and theaters. The **Twenty-fourth Amendment** to the Constitution ended the poll tax and made it easier for African Americans to vote. The **Voting Rights Act** of 1965 gave the president power to outlaw literacy tests and send federal officials to make sure blacks got a fair chance to vote in elections.

Practice 4.2: The Civil Rights Movement

1. What did the court case known as *Brown v. Board of Education* establish?

   A. Public buses cannot discriminate.

   B. Public schools cannot segregate.

   C. Segregation is not legal in theaters and hotels.

   D. All-black schools must be equal to all-white schools.

2. Rosa Parks is most associated with

   A. militant movements.

   B. the march on Washington.

   C. the Montgomery bus boycott.

   D. *Brown v. Board of Education.*

3. Who was Dr. Martin Luther King, Jr.? What did he believe was the BEST way for blacks to gain their civil rights? How did television help his movement?

4. What was some of the key civil rights laws passed during the '60s? What changes did such legislation make?

4.3 Social Unrest

Social Movements of the '60s and '70s

The 1960s and '70s were a time of social unrest. People began to question traditional ways and call for change. Many wanted government to take a more active role in solving society's problems. Below is a table showing some of the movements that grew during the period.

SOCIAL MOVEMENTS OF THE '60s and '70s	
Civil Rights Movement	The civil rights movement sought equal rights for African Americans and other minorities. Many of the other movements that arose in the 1960s were inspired by the civil rights movement.
Women's Movement	Women who joined this movement called for an end to gender discrimination. They also wanted to change many of the old ideas about how women should act and what roles they should be limited to.
Environmental Movement	Environmentalists demanded that the government do more to protect the environment. They wanted laws governing business and restricting how industries got rid of waste.
Students for a Democratic Society (SDS)	SDS was a political and social movement that began on college campuses. Its members wanted government to act in radical ways to end poverty and social injustice. They also questioned many traditionally held values and called for an end to the war in Vietnam.
Youth Counter Culture	Many older teens and young adults became part of a youth counter culture. The counter culture rejected many of their parents' traditional values. Members of the counter culture often experimented with illegal drugs and behaved in ways many Americans viewed as immoral.

Pasrticipants at Woodstock, a 1969 Counterculture Youth Gathering

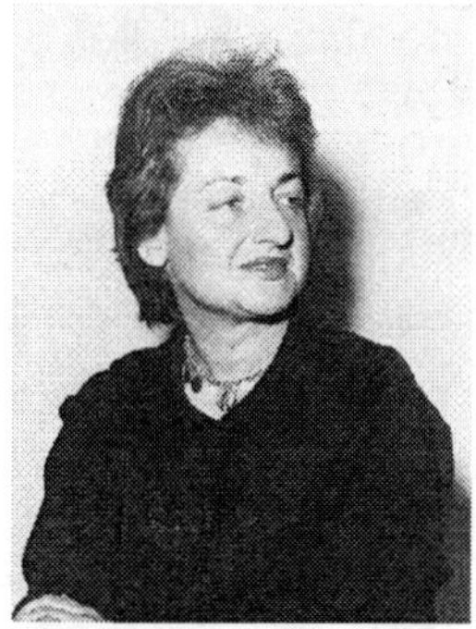

Betty Friedan, Leader of the Women's Movement

Students for a Democratic Society Rally

President John F. Kennedy

The Kennedy-Nixon Debate

In 1960, **John F. Kennedy** defeated Vice President Richard Nixon in one of the closest presidential races in history. It was the first time television played a major role in the election. In addition to both candidates' election ads, Kennedy and Nixon also met in the first **televised debate**. Most of the citizens who heard the debate on the radio thought that Nixon had won. But most of those who watched on television thought the younger, more confident looking Kennedy had. Many historians believe that television helped Kennedy win the election.

Kennedy became a very popular president. Only forty-three years old when he took office, he was the youngest man ever elected president. His skills as a communicator, good looks, and sense of humor only added to his popularity. After the Cuban Missile Crisis, many citizens also viewed him as a good leader.

Kennedy and Space Exploration

U.S. Space Program

Kennedy was a strong supporter of **space exploration**. During the 1950s, the Soviet Union successfully launched satellites and put a man in space. Kennedy and others feared that falling behind in the space race was dangerous. They were convinced the Soviets would use their space technology to build more powerful nuclear weapons. Kennedy challenged the U.S. space program to put a man on the moon by the end of the '60s. In 1969, U.S. Astronaut Neil Armstrong became the first human being to walk on the moon. Today, thanks to such early efforts, the United States often sends people into outer space. Meanwhile, **satellites** (machines that orbit the Earth providing communication signals and pictures) have greatly impacted the way people live. Satellites enable people to watch live events on the other side of the world, hear accurate weather forecasts on their local news network, and get instant traveling directions as they drive in their cars.

Kennedy and Civil Rights

At first, President Kennedy did not do a lot to back the civil rights movement. He believed in civil rights, but he also needed the support of southern politicians who opposed the movement. Eventually, as support for the movement grew, Kennedy introduced civil rights legislation to Congress. Some of his proposals became law under President Lyndon Johnson.

President John F. Kennedy

NOVEMBER 22, 1963

Lyndon Johnson Being Sworn In to Office

On November 22, 1963, when Lee Harvey Oswald **assassinated President Kennedy** in Dallas, Texas. The young president was loved by many citizens, and the entire nation mourned his death. Vice President Lyndon Johnson became president in his place. Historians often debate how history might have been different if Kennedy had lived. Some believe the Vietnam War never would have happened.

ROBERT KENNEDY

Robert Kennedy

Robert Kennedy was President Kennedy's younger brother. He served as President Kennedy's attorney general (the nation's highest law-enforcement officer) and played a key role in bringing a peaceful end to the Cuban Missile Crisis. He worked hard to battle organized crime and supported civil rights. He became an opponent of the Vietnam War and supported a number of social causes. In 1968, Robert Kennedy ran for president. Many thought he would win the Democratic Party's nomination, especially after his victory in the California primary. That same night, however, as Kennedy made his victory speech, an assassin shot him at close range. **Robert Kennedy's assassination** saddened many who had hoped he would end the war in Vietnam and deal with the country's social problems. A few months later, the Democratic convention erupted in a riot when the Democrats nominated Vice President Hubert Humphrey to be their party's presidential candidate. Humphrey lost the election to Richard Nixon. Nixon continued U.S. involvement in Vietnam until 1973. He also appointed judges he hoped would reverse some of the civil rights legislation of the 1960s.

Practice 4.3: Social Unrest

1. Describe how television impacted the presidential race of 1960.

2. Describe how the assassinations of John F. Kennedy and Robert Kennedy impacted the nation. How might they possibly have impacted history had they both lived?

CHAPTER 4 REVIEW

Key Terms, People, and Concepts

capitalist democracy
Communist dictatorship
cold war
Berlin
iron curtain
containment policy
Truman Doctrine
Marshall Plan
Berlin airlift
NATO
nuclear arms race
38th parallel
Korean War
Joseph McCarthy
John F. Kennedy
Nikita Khrushchev
Cuban Missile Crisis
Vietnam War
television's effect on the Vietnam War
antiwar movement
civil rights movement
NAACP
Thurgood Marshall
Brown v. Board of Education
Rosa Parks
Martin Luther King Jr.
Montgomery bus boycott
nonviolence
civil disobedience
television's effect on the Civil Rights Movement
march on Washington
militant movements
Malcolm X
effects of Martin Luther King's assassination
Civil Rights Act
Twenty-fourth Amendment
Voting Rights Act
John F. Kennedy
1960 televised debate
space exploration
satellites
effects of John F. Kennedy's assassination
Robert Kennedy
effects of Robert Kennedy's assassination

Multiple Choice Questions

1. What did Churchill call the imaginary wall that separated Western and Eastern Europe after World War II?
   A. the East-West wall argument
   B. the steel door
   C. the iron curtain
   D. the Berlin airlift

2. During what event did U.S. airplanes drop food and supplies to the people in West Berlin?
   A. Berlin airlift
   B. World War II
   C. British Air Raid
   D. Soviet Food Drive

3. What group of nations promised to support each other if attacked by the Soviet Union?
   A. NATO
   B. Allied Forces
   C. Berlin blockade
   D. internal security

4. What senator made lists of people he thought might be Communists?
   A. Douglas MacArthur
   B. Dwight Eisenhower
   C. Gary Powers
   D. Joseph McCarthy

5. Who was the attorney who won the *Brown v. Board of Education* case?
   A. Thurgood Marshall
   B. Robert Kennedy
   C. Malcolm X
   D. Martin Luther King, Jr.

6. Which of the following actions would Dr. Martin Luther King have MOST LIKELY supported?
   A. segregation in the U.S. military
   B. African Americans carrying guns in case they are attacked by white racists
   C. the arrest of Rosa Parks
   D. African Americans sitting at an all-white lunch counter asking to be served

Look at the map below, and answer question #7.

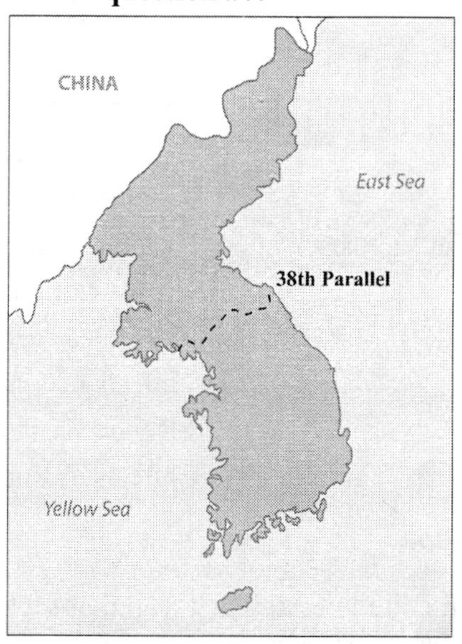

7. Which region is depicted on the map?
   A. Vietnam
   B. the Soviet Union
   C. Cuba
   D. Korea

8. Why were many of Robert Kennedy's supporters sad the morning after he won the California primary?
   A. Victory in California was still not enough to give him the nomination.
   B. Kennedy had been assassinated the night before.
   C. Kennedy dropped out of the race.
   D. Robert Kennedy continued to support the Vietnam War.

Chapter 5
The United States Since 1975

This chapter addresses the following competency.

SS5H9	The student will trace important developments in America since 1975.

5.1 U.S. Involvement in World Events

Pursuit of Peace in the Middle East

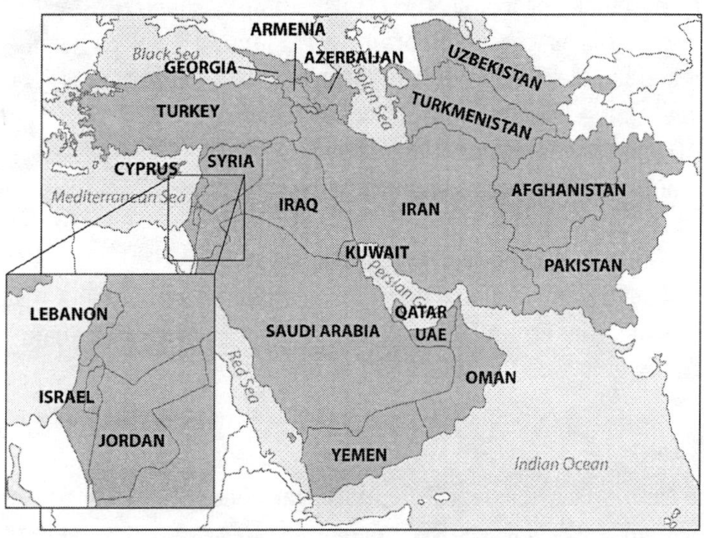

Middle Eastern Countries

The United States has tried to help maintain peace in the Middle East since the end of World War II. In 1948, the United Nations recognized **Israel** as an independent Jewish state. Many Arab nations still dislike Israel because it took land away from the **Palestinians** (Arabs who lived in the region before Israel became a nation). The Palestinians had long hoped for independence after living for decades under European authority. They believe that they, not Israelis, are entitled to

OPEC Meeting

the land that forms modern Israel. For over sixty years, the **Israeli-Palestinian Conflict** has resulted in much violence. The United States has traditionally supported Israel. Arab nations support the Palestinians and consider Israel an enemy. Some Arabs consider the United States an enemy as well.

Middle Eastern Oil Field

The United States and other countries want peace in the Middle East because it is an important region. The Mediterranean Sea, Red Sea, Persian Gulf, and Suez Canal are all important for trade and commerce. In addition, the Middle East is home to much of the world's **oil**. A number of Middle East countries rely on oil exports for most of their revenue. Wars and other conflicts can affect oil supplies, raise oil prices, and affect nations' economies.

The Camp David Accords

Camp David Accords

For years, Israel and Egypt were enemies. In 1977, Egyptian President Anwar Sadat visited Israel in an effort to make peace. U.S. President Jimmy Carter saw this as a great opportunity. He invited Sadat and Israel's Prime Minister Menachem Begin to Camp David (the president's private retreat). Carter helped negotiate a peace agreement between the two countries known as the **Camp David Accords**. Many applauded the three leaders. Some Arabs, however, were upset with Sadat. They felt he had sold out the Palestinian people by not insisting that they be given land in Palestine. The Camp David Accords improved Egyptian-Israeli relations, but it did little to end fighting between Israelis and Palestinians.

Lebanon

In the early '80s, President Ronald Reagan sent U.S. troops to **Lebanon**. The troops were part of a United Nations force. Reagan claimed that the troops were there to establish peace after fighting broke out between Israelis and Palestinians. Some Lebanese citizens welcomed the UN force. Others, however, saw it as a foreign army sent to support Israel. In October 1983, a suicide bomber drove a car full of explosives into a U.S. Marine barracks, killing over two hundred people. When the U.S. forces finally left, Lebanon was still an unstable country.

The Persian Gulf War

Saddam Hussein

Persian Gulf War

In 1990, Iraqi President **Saddam Hussein** ordered an invasion of the tiny neighboring country of Kuwait. Saddam argued that the territory of Kuwait actually belonged to Iraq. He also wanted Kuwait's abundant oil fields. The United States led an international UN force that invaded Kuwait in 1991. The **Persian Gulf War** lasted only forty-two days. It resulted in Iraq's withdrawal from Kuwait. Thousands of Iraqis died in the war, compared to just a few hundred of the UN forces. The success of the U.S. war effort made President George H.W. Bush very popular among U.S. citizens, until economic hardships led to his defeat in the 1992 election.

Current Peace Efforts

Today, the United States continues to seek stability in the Middle East. U.S. officials often try to mediate negotiations between Israel and Palestinians. They also try to keep peaceful relations with Arab nations like Saudi Arabia. It is sometimes difficult for the United States. Many countries in the region distrust the United States because of its history as an ally of Israel.

Secretary of State Condoleeza Rice Meeting with Israeli and Palestinian Leaders

The War on Terror

September 11, 2001, Terrorist Attack

Since 2001, many U.S. policies in the Middle East have centered around the **War on Terror**. On **September 11, 2001**, terrorists from the Middle East hijacked four U.S. commercial airplanes. Two of the planes flew into the World Trade Center towers in New York City. The nation watched in horror as the massive towers crashed to the ground, killing thousands. Meanwhile, a third plane crashed into the Pentagon in Washington, D.C. (The Pentagon is the United States' military headquarters.) The fourth plane crashed in a field in Pennsylvania, after the passengers revolted against the hijackers. In a single day, thousands of Americans died at the hands of terrorists. Citizens were shocked, sad, and angry. **President George W. Bush** (the oldest son of President George H.W. Bush) responded by declaring the War on Terror.

Afghanistan

Osama bin Laden

The United States soon determined that a terrorist group called **al Qaeda** carried out the attacks. President Bush was determined to capture al Qaeda's leader, **Osama bin Laden**. Bin Laden and his followers hid and trained in Afghanistan. When Afghanistan's leaders would not hand over the terrorists, President Bush organized an international force that invaded the country and overthrew the government. Bin Laden, however, got away. In 2010, international forces are still searching for him as they try to establish a new, stable government in Afghanistan.

Iraq

In 2003, President Bush, and several other world leaders proclaimed that Iraqi President Saddam Hussein had **weapons of mass destruction** (weapons capable of killing massive amounts of people, such as nuclear or chemical weapons). They based this claim on intelligence reports, Saddam's history of using chemical weapons, and Saddam's refusal to allow UN investigators into Iraq to see if such weapons existed. The United States also claimed Saddam had ties to al Qaeda. Despite not having UN support, the United States led an international force that invaded Iraq and, in just weeks, overthrew Saddam's government. The United States helped establish a new, democratic Iraqi government. The new government eventually tried Saddam following his capture and hanged him in December 2006.

President George W. Bush

Following the fall of Saddam, the United States and its allies faced serious problems in Iraq. No one was ever able to prove that Saddam had ties to al Qaeda. Even more serious, the United States could not find any weapons of mass destruction. Many in the United States criticized the war and accused Bush of lying. Others defended Bush's decision. Attacks from insurgent groups (anti-American groups in Iraq fighting against the United States and the new Iraqi government) have also kept the country unstable and killed thousands of U.S. soldiers. In 2010, U.S. forces still remain in Iraq.

Fall of Saddam Hussein

The War on Terror at Home

Airport Security After September 11

September 11 drastically changed life in the United States. President Bush established a new government department: the **Department of Homeland Security**. Its role is to combat terrorism at home. (It also provides aid to parts of the country hurt by natural disasters.) Security measures for airports and other public places became much stricter, causing passengers a great deal of inconvenience and making air travel more difficult. Congress also passed the **Patriot Act**, which gives law enforcement more power to listen in on citizens' phone calls, read emails, and conduct investigations without warrants. At times, the government has also arrested and held suspected terrorists without following traditional rules of due process. (See chapter 7, section 7.1, regarding due process.)

Practice 5.1: U.S. Involvement in World Events

Look at the map below, and answer the following question.

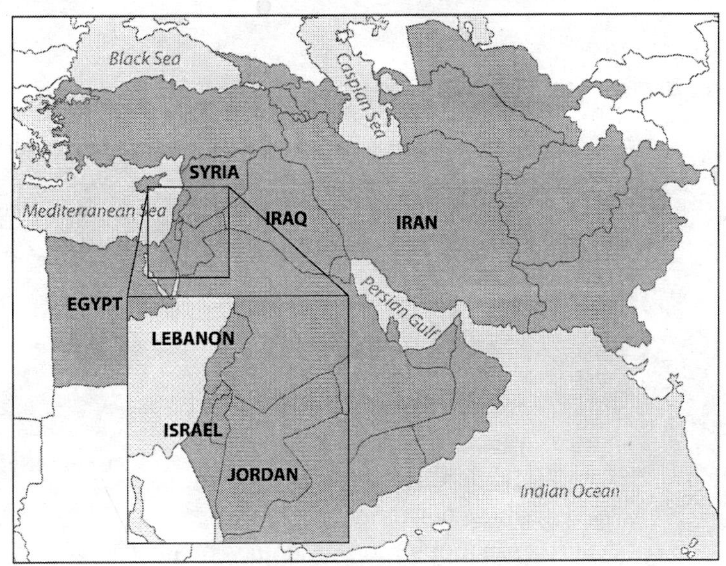

1. The region depicted in the map is commonly referred to as
   A. Palestine.
   B. the Middle East.
   C. Camp David.
   D. the Persian Gulf.

2. How did the United States respond to what happened on September 11, 2001?
   A. It sent troops to Lebanon.
   B. It signed the Camp David Accords.
   C. It declared the War on Terror.
   D. It negotiated Saddam Hussein's surrender with Afghanistan.

3. What are some of the problems the United States has faced in Iraq since 2003?

4. What are some of the changes that have occurred in the United States as a result of September 11, 2001?

5.2 End of the Cold War and Advent of Modern America

Collapse of the Soviet Union

Mikhail Gorbachev

Collapse of the Berlin Wall

In 1985, **Mikhail Gorbachev** became the leader of the Soviet Union. Gorbachev knew his country could not continue an arms race against the United States. The Soviet economy was in bad shape. Many Soviets were poor and hurting. The Soviet Union could not keep spending billions of dollars on nuclear weapons; it needed to spend more on improving production and providing basic needs for its citizens. Under Gorbachev, the USSR made changes that allowed more freedom and some capitalism. It also did not try to control Eastern Europe as much. Once the people in these countries got a taste of freedom, many of them did not want to remain citizens under Communist governments anymore. By the late '80s, Communist governments began to fall. Many Eastern European countries replaced their old Communist regimes with more democratic forms of government and allowed more capitalism. Germany became a unified country once again. Eventually, the Soviet Union dissolved in the early '90s. It broke into several independent countries. The collapse of the Soviet Union marked the end of the cold war and western fears about Communism in Europe.

Modern U.S. Society

U.S. society has changed a lot in the last thirty years. Many of these changes have been due to new technology. **Personal computers** have become very common. The first computers were developed during World War II. They were so large that they often took up entire rooms. Today, computers sit on desks, in laps, and even in pockets. In 2010, nearly every household in the United States has a personal computer. Many people have laptop computers that are portable and can be used from nearly anywhere. Today's computers can compute information in seconds and perform countless tasks. Computers allow businesses, governments, and citizens to work much faster and produce much more than in the past. Televisions, cell phones, cars, and many other devices are often equipped with advanced computers.

Internet Use

The development of the **Internet** has made computers even more effective. The Internet is a communication system people access using their computer. It links homes, businesses, libraries, government institutions, universities, and schools all over the world. By connecting their computers to the Internet, people can communicate with each other on the other side of the world right away. The Internet has changed the way students do research, study, practice for tests, and go to school. It enables companies to allow employees to work part, or even all, of their schedules from home. Citizens use the Internet to gather news, shop, or exchange information. Today, it is more common for U.S. citizens to exchange emails than to write letters. The Internet has impacted politics by allowing citizens to learn more and gather up-to-date information about political issues and candidates quickly.

Problems Presented by Computers and the Internet

The Internet and computers also present **new problems**. Sometimes, harmful, illegal, and/or dangerous information travels over the Internet. Criminals often use the Internet to access people's personal information in order to steal money and/or their identity. People who go online have to be careful about whom they interact with. Otherwise, they could become a victim of online predators (criminals who use the Internet to find victims).

Internet Problems

Practice 5.2: End of the Cold War and Advent of Modern America

1. Which of the following contributed the LEAST to the collapse of the Soviet Union?
   A. economic concerns
   B. the United States
   C. capitalism
   D. the Internet

2. Ray goes online and uses the Internet to check his credit. He discovers that someone has stolen his identity and opened an online charge account in his name. Ray is experiencing
   A. political changes caused by the Internet.
   B. runaway capitalism.
   C. a problem that accompanies technology.
   D. a harmful email.

3. Describe why the Soviet Union and Communism in Eastern Europe collapsed.

4. What are some of the ways computers and the Internet have changed U.S. society?

Chapter 5 Review

Key Terms, People, and Concepts

Israel
Palestinians
Israeli-Palestinian conflict
oil
Camp David Accords
Lebanon
Saddam Hussein
Persian Gulf War
War on Terror
September 11, 2001
al Qaeda
Osama bin Laden
weapons of mass destruction
Department of Homeland Security
Patriot Act
Mikhail Gorbachev
personal computers
Internet
Internet's impact on politics
new problems presented by the Internet

Multiple Choice Questions

Look at the map below ,and answer the following question.

1. Which of the following MOST concerns the territory depicted in the map?
   A. the Persian Gulf War
   B. the Israeli-Palestinian conflict
   C. the U.S. War on Terror
   D. the search for Osama bin Laden

2. Which of the following is one of the reasons that the United States wants peace in the Middle East?

   A. The United States is against the Camp David Accords.

   B. Peace will make it easier for Palestinians to control Israel.

   C. Peace and stability often make it easier to get oil.

   D. Ending war in the Middle East will end most of the crime that occurs over the Internet.

3. What was significant about September 11, 2001?

   A. It was the day terrorists attacked the United States.

   B. It was the day the Persian Gulf War began.

   C. It marked the beginning of the Camp David Accords.

   D. It was the day the Soviet Union collapsed.

Look at the map below, and answer the following question.

4. Which of the following conflicts involved President George H.W. Bush ordering U.S. troops into the region depicted on the map?

   A. the Israeli-Palestinian Conflict

   B. Lebanon

   C. the Persian Gulf War

   D. the War on Terror

5. Which of the following was NOT a reason given by President George W. Bush for invading Iraq?

   A. The U.S. wanted Iraq's oil.

   B. Saddam Hussein supported terrorists.

   C. Iraq had weapons of mass destruction.

   D. Iraq was dangerous.

6. The Department of Homeland Security and the Patriot Act are both
   A. meant to end the Israeli-Palestinian Conflict.
   B. plans to rebuild Eastern Europe following the USSR's collapse.
   C. intended to protect the United States from terrorist attacks.
   D. responsible for catching Osama bin Laden.

7. Which of the following contributed the LEAST to the fall of the Soviet Union?
   A. the fall of East European Communism
   B. the Soviet economy
   C. Mikhail Gorbachev's policies
   D. the War on Terror

8. Computers and the Internet are just two examples of
   A. new technology that has impacted the United States since 1975.
   B. advanced technology invented during World War II.
   C. circumstances that led to the collapse of the Soviet Union.
   D. technology made better by the Camp David Accords.

Chapter 6 Geographic Understandings

This chapter addresses the following competencies

SS5G1	The student will locate important places in the United States.
SS5G2	The student will explain the reasons for the spatial patterns of economic activities.

6.1 Geographic Features

Physical Features

Physical Features of the United States

Geography is thc study of land, physical features (mountains, waterfalls, gorges, and so on), bodies of water, climate, cultures, natural resources, and so on. **Physical geography** is the study of how specific physical characteristics define a region. Physical features include deserts, bodies of water, mountain ranges, and other land forms. The United States has many important physical features. Some of them are listed on the following page.

Physical Features of the United States

Grand Canyon

The **Grand Canyon** is a gorge located in northwestern Arizona. It is over two hundred and fifty miles long and over a mile deep at its deepest point. The Colorado River's flowing water carved out the canyon over millions of years. The Grand Canyon is one of the earth's greatest natural wonders. It attracts over five million visitors each year.

The Grand Canyon

The Salton Sea

The **Salton Sea** is a salt lake and the largest lake in California. A **salt lake** is a lake that contains salt water rather than fresh water. The Salton Sea is located in the southeastern corner of the California and spans over three hundred and fifty square miles.

Great Salt Lake

The **Great Salt Lake** is the largest salt lake in the Western Hemisphere. It is located in the northern part of Utah. The lake changes in size, depending on the amount of annual rainfall.

The Great Salt Lake

Mojave Desert

A **desert** is a land area that receives fewer than ten inches of rain a year. The **Mojave Desert** covers over twenty-two thousand square miles and is one of the country's major deserts. Most of the Mojave lies in southern California, but portions of it run through Arizona, Nevada, and Utah.

MAN-MADE FEATURES

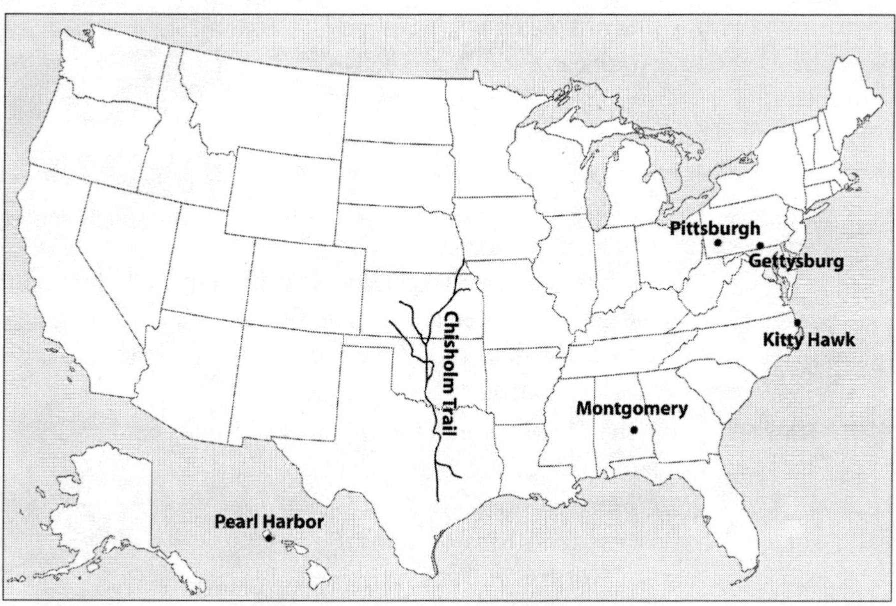

Cities with Man-Made Features

Geography includes the study of **man-made places** (places or features constructed by humans). Examples of man-made features include farms, cities, canals, and roads. For centuries, the geography of the United States has been impacted by humans. Some of these geographical places are listed below and on the following page.

Man-Made Places in the United States

Chisholm Trail The **Chisholm Trail** was a route used in the late nineteenth century to move cattle from Texas to Kansas. The journey could take up to two months. It was often very dangerous. Cattle drives often encountered harsh weather, wild animals, hostile Native Americans, and outlaws.

Pittsburgh, PA **Pittsburgh** is the second-largest city in Pennsylvania after Philadelphia. It is located where the Allegheny and Monongahela Rivers come together to form the Ohio River. Due to these massive rivers, Pittsburgh relies on a number of bridges to deal with traffic and transportation. Pittsburgh has so many bridges that it is often called the "Bridge Capital of the United States." The city's location has made it a key industrial center. The Allegheny, Monongahela, and Ohio Rivers provide key water routes for transporting industrial resources and goods. During the early 1900s, Pittsburgh manufactured almost half of the nation's steel. Today, Pittsburgh is still known as the "Steel City."

Pittsburgh

Gettysburg, PA **Gettysburg, Pennsylvania**, is most famous for the Battle of Gettysburg, one of the key battles of the American Civil War. The Union's victory at Gettysburg ended the Confederates' hopes of invading the North and marked a key turning point in the war. Before Gettysburg, President Abraham Lincoln felt a lot of pressure to make peace with the South. After the battle, however, the Union decided to continue fighting—a decision that kept the Union together. Today, the population of Gettysburg is around eight thousand citizens.

Modern Gettysburg

Kitty Hawk, NC **Kitty Hawk, North Carolina**, is a town on the Outer Banks of North Carolina. The Outer Banks is a series of small islands that line North Carolina's coast. Kitty Hawk became famous as the site of the Wright brothers' first powered airplane flight in 1903.

Wright Brothers Flight

Pearl Harbor, HI **Pearl Harbor, Hawaii**, is located west of Honolulu on the island of Oahu, Hawaii. Its harbor serves as a U.S. naval base. On December 7, 1941, Japanese forces bombed Pearl Harbor in a surprise attack. Japan chose to attack Pearl Harbor because it wanted to expand its empire. Japan's leaders felt that Pearl Harbor was too close to Japan. It feared the U.S. Pacific Fleet would sail for Japan and try to stop Japan's expansion. The attack badly damaged the U.S. fleet, but failed to destroy it. The United States declared war on Japan and entered World War II in response to the Pearl Harbor attack.

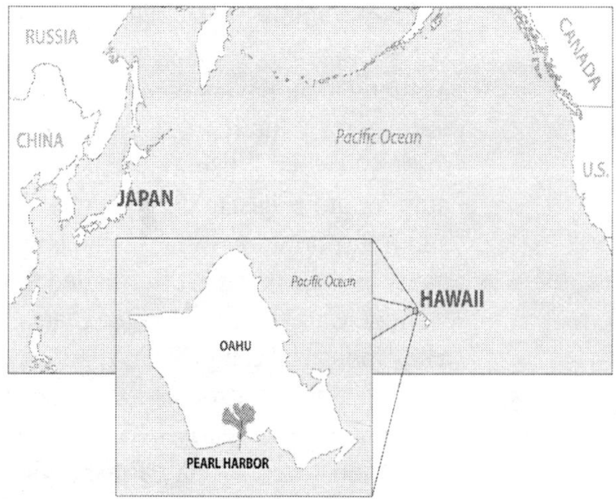

The Island of Oahu

Montgomery, AL **Montgomery, Alabama**, is the capital of Alabama. It is located in the southeast region of the state and has a rich history. Montgomery served as the first capital of the Confederacy after Southern states seceded from the Union in 1860. The city also became well known during the civil rights movement of the 1950s and '60s. The Montgomery bus boycott led to a U.S. Supreme Court decision ending segregation on public buses. It also made Martin Luther King Jr. a national figure and the recognized leader of the civil rights movement.

Montgomery, Alabama, During the Civil Rights Movement

Practice 6.1: Geographic Features

Look at the map below, and answer questions 1 – 3.

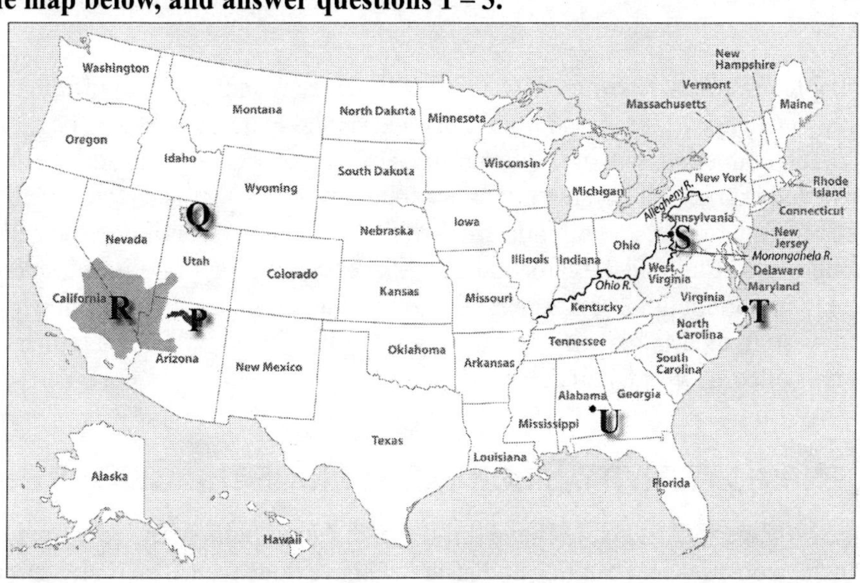

1. Which area depicted on the map is BEST known for its industrial production?

   A. P B. T C. Q D. S

2. Which area depicted on the map was created by the flow of a major river?

   A. Q B. P C. R D. U

3. Which of the areas depicted on the map is closest to Gettysburg?

   A. Q B. R C. S D. T

4. What geographic features helped Pittsburgh grow and become an important U.S. city?

5. How did geography contribute to what happened at Pearl Harbor on December 7, 1941?

6.2 Economic Development of the United States

Industrial Development after the Civil War

Industrialization in the Late 1800s

After the Civil War, the United States became more industrialized. **Industrialization** means that more factories and large businesses developed. Many factors affected industrialization. One was available resources. New York, Philadelphia, Baltimore, Boston, Chicago, New Orleans, San Francisco, and Detroit had large populations. Large populations meant plenty of labor, allowing factories and industries to grow. Accessibility to transportation also increased industrialization. Many cities along large rivers, lakes, and coastlines became industrial centers because they had access to shipping. Later, as railroads expanded, transportation to more areas became easier and industry expanded.

Available resources determined what industries became important in different regions. In the South, where agriculture was important, tobacco and cotton industries (textiles) thrived. Fertilizer production, saw mills, naval stores (products used to build and repair wooden sailing ships), and iron ore all became important southern industries. The North featured important steel, railroad, textile, and oil industries. In the West, new technologies helped industrialize mining, agriculture, and the cattle industry. Places like Northern California and Oregon became home to important timber industries. Oil became an important industry in parts of the Southwest. In the Midwest, agriculture became more industrialized as farmers produced large amounts of corn, wheat, and other products.

Economic Activity Since the Turn of the Century

Since 1900, various industries have thrived in different parts of the country. In the Northeast, financial industries like banking and insurance have done well. The region has also been home to manufacturing and factory production industries. The South has featured textiles and agricultural industries. In recent years, banking has become important as well. Today, Charlotte, North Carolina, is home to Bank of America and Wachovia. It ranks second only to New York as the nation's banking center. Atlanta continues to grow as an industrial center. It is the home of world-famous Coca-Cola, The Home Depot, and Chick-fil-A. Atlanta is also home to a thriving media and entertainment industry. Turner Broadcasting, Cable News Network (CNN), and profitable recording industries are all based in Atlanta.

Coca-Cola Headquarters

New York City Banking

Coal Mining in West Virginia

Agricultural industries continue to do well in the South, Midwest, and parts of the West. Automobile manufacturing became a big part of the northern Midwest's economy during the twentieth century. Other industries, like brewing, became important in Milwaukee. In the Appalachian Mountains, coal mining became important, due to the large amounts of coal available. Fishing industries play an important role in regions along the nation's coastlines. The defense industry (industry that builds weapons for the nation's military) is important in several western states. In the last few decades, Silicon Valley in Northern California and Research Triangle Park in eastern North Carolina have become important centers for the computer and technology industries. As technology changes, industries like communications, finance, computers, real estate, and many service industries continue to grow (except during occasional slumps in the economy). Traditional factory industries, however, have suffered in recent years.

THE UNITED STATES AS A WORLD POWER

AFTER WORLD WAR I

Before **World War I**, the United States was not considered a world power. After the war, however, things changed. European economies were devastated. Property, industries, and infrastructure had been badly damaged. Meanwhile, the war boosted the U.S. economy. Although U.S. troops eventually fought in the war, none of the battle took place in the United States. U.S. businesses were not damaged or destroyed by attacks. Industries grew as the nation produced more goods to support the war effort. Once the war ended, the United States found itself an economic world power. It was producing more goods than ever before, while many other industrialized nations were trying to recover.

World War I

After World War II

Post World War II Industry

The United States became even more of a world power after **World War II**. Once again, the U.S. economy did well, while economies overseas suffered from the destruction caused by war. The United States provided loans and financial aid to rebuild parts of Europe and Southeast Asia. In addition to being an economic power, the United States became one of the world's leading military powers. It developed the world's first nuclear weapons and placed military bases in foreign countries. This led to a rise in defense industries, boosting the U.S. economy even more.

Practice 6.2: Economic Development of the United States

1. Explain how available labor and natural resources affect industrialization.
2. Why were many of the earliest industrial centers located in large cities, and along rivers, lakes, or coastlines?
3. How did the development of railroads impact industrialization?
4. What factors led to the United States becoming a world power after World War I?

Chapter 6 Review

Key Terms, People, and Concepts

physical geography
Grand Canyon
Salton Sea
salt lake
Great Salt Lake
desert
Mojave Desert
man-made places
Chisholm Trail
Pittsburgh
Gettysburg, Pennsylvania
Kitty Hawk, North Carolina
Pearl Harbor, Hawaii
Montgomery, Alabama
industrialization
U.S. economic development after World War I
U.S. economic development after World War II

Multiple Choice Questions

Look at the map below, and answer questions 1 – 3.

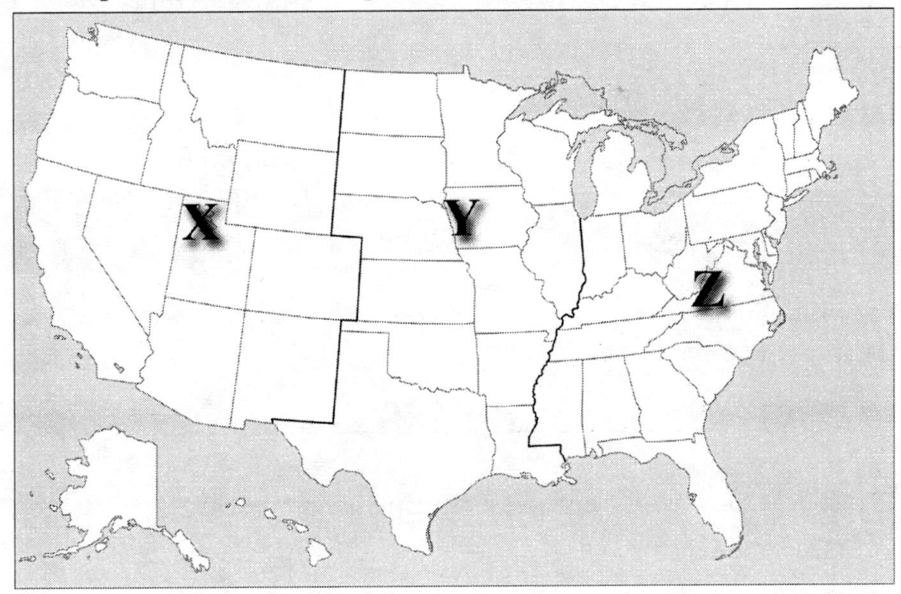

1. In which area would one find the Grand Canyon and the Great Salt Lake?

   A. X B. Y C. Z D. X and Y

2. In which area or areas would one find the sites of both a key Civil War battle and the nation's first powered airplane flight?

   A. X B. Y C. Z D. X and Z

3. In which area would one find the Chisholm Trail?

   A. X

   B. Y

   C. Z

   D. None of these areas include the Chisholm Trail.

Look at the map below, and answer questions 4 and 5.

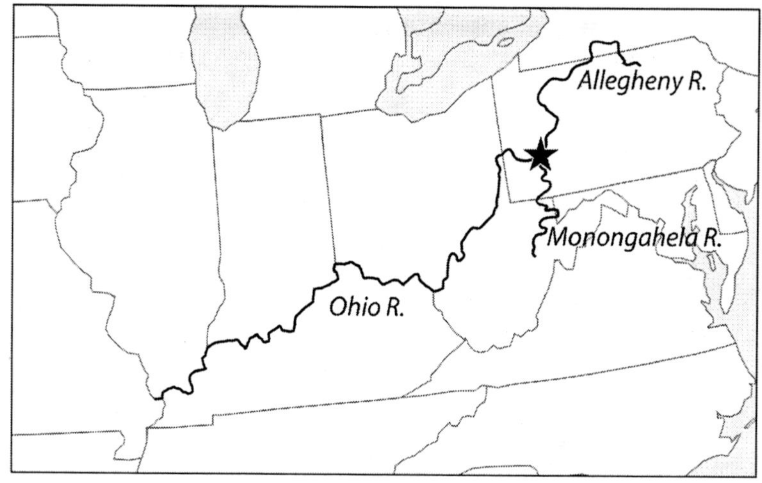

4. What does the star on the map MOST LIKELY represent?
   A. the Grand Canyon
   B. Gettysburg
   C. Kitty Hawk
   D. Pittsburgh

5. What is the area represented by the star MOST famous for?
   A. textiles
   B. a famous Civil War battle
   C. steel production
   D. first airplane flight

6. Which of the following is a geographic factor that led to Japan's decision to bomb Pearl Harbor?
   A. Pearl Harbor is home to a naval base.
   B. Commanders at Pearl Harbor were not expecting to be attacked.
   C. Hawaii is located in the Pacific Ocean.
   D. Japan wanted to expand.

7. A coal miner would MOST LIKELY live and work in
   A. the Mojave Desert.
   B. the Appalachian Mountains.
   C. Pittsburgh, PA.
   D. Utah.

- no fighting took place on U.S. soil
- European industries were destroyed or badly damaged
- U.S. production increased and U.S. industries thrived

8. The BEST heading for the list above would be
   A. World War II After Pearl Harbor
   B. Reasons the United States Won Two World Wars
   C. Reasons the U.S. Became an Economic Power after World War I
   D. Effects of the United States Becoming an Economic Power

Chapter 7
Government and Civics

This chapter addresses the following competencies

SS5CG1	The student will explain how a citizen's rights are protected under the U.S. Constitution.
SS5CG2	The student will explain the process by which amendments to the U.S. Constitution are made.
SS5CG3	The student will explain how amendments to the U.S. Constitution have maintained a representative democracy.

7.1 Civic Responsibility and the Bill of Rights

Responsibilities of U.S. Citizenship

The **United States Constitution** establishes the U.S. government. It also protects the rights of U.S. citizens. These rights are often called **civil rights**. They are meant to protect citizens' freedoms.

Constitutional Convention, 1787

America's leaders wrote the Constitution in 1787. The states ratified (accepted) it the following year. It is the national body of laws that governs the United States of America. In order for the U.S. system to work citizens must be willing to fulfill **civic responsibilities**. The following table lists a few examples of civic responsibilities.

EXAMPLES OF CIVIC RESPONSIBILITIES	
Obeying Laws	**Laws** are rules set by the government that citizens must obey. In order to maintain order and protect the rights of everyone, citizens must be willing to obey local, state, and federal laws. There have been times in history when responsible citizens saw it as their duty to disobey *unjust* laws. One example of such a time was during the civil rights movement of the 1950s and '60s, when many people disobeyed unjust laws that denied equal rights to African Americans.
Paying Taxes	Local, state, and the federal governments each need money to operate. **Taxes** (money citizens and businesses must pay the government) are the number one way governments raise the money that they need. Responsible citizens pay the taxes that they owe so that governments can fulfill their role.
Participation in the Political Process	The United States is a **democracy**. A democracy is a system of government in which citizens elect their leaders and often vote on issues. Democracies give citizens a voice in their government. However, for democracy to work, citizens must participate in the political process. **Voting** is one form of participation. When citizens vote in elections they participate in choosing local, state, and national leaders. Sometimes citizens also vote on referendums, which allow them to help decide what laws their community will live by. **Campaign volunteering** is another way citizens participate. They volunteer to help political candidates win elections. Volunteers may go door-to-door, make phone calls, pass out flyers, or help in many other ways. **Protests** allow citizens to participate by voicing their disagreement with the government. Protests often take the form of marches or rallies (large gatherings centered around a political issue). Serving in **public office** is also an essential means of participation. It would not do any good to have a democracy if citizens were not willing to run for and serve in positions of leadership.
Jury Duty	The Constitution guarantees everyone accused of a crime the right to a fair trial. One of the ways it protects this right is through the use of **juries**. Juries are groups of private citizens who decide whether or not an accused person is guilty. They make sure that people are judged by citizens like themselves rather than government officials. In order for the jury system to work, citizens must be willing to accept **jury duty**. They must be willing to sacrifice the time necessary to sit on juries, hear evidence presented at trials, and make decisions about people's guilt or innocence.
Volunteering	Citizens **volunteer** (agree to accept certain duties without pay) in many ways. Many volunteer to help in their communities, assist with campaigns, help the underprivileged, and so on.
Military Service	In order to protect and defend the rights and freedoms guaranteed by the Constitution, the US government must make sure it has a strong military. The military protects the United States against foreign threats. There have been times when the US military drafted citizens (required them to serve in the military). Today, however, the United States armed forces relies on citizens who choose to enlist (decide on their own to join the military).

U.S. Citizens

Jury Duty

Volunteering

Military Service

The Bill of Rights

At first, a number of states would not accept the Constitution. Their leaders felt it did not do enough to protect civil rights. They feared that the national government would trample on peoples' freedoms. In order to convince these leaders to ratify the Constitution, the framers (leaders who drafted the Constitution) agreed to consider several **amendments** (changes to the Constitution). Following ratification, Congress presented twelve amendments to the states. The states ratified ten of them. These first ten amendments to the Constitution are known as the **Bill of Rights**.

First Amendment

The **First Amendment** guarantees several freedoms:

- Freedom of speech – People can say what they believe so long as it does not cause undue harm or danger.
- Freedom of the press – The media has the right to report news freely and accurately.
- Freedom to petition the government – Citizens may insist that the government take certain actions.
- Freedom to assemble – Citizens may come together for rallies, protests, and other peaceful gatherings.
- Freedom of religion – Citizens may practice whatever religion they wish, so long as they don't interfere with the rights of others.

Freedom of Speech

Freedom of Religion

Second Amendment

The **Second Amendment** protects citizens' right to bear arms (guns). Today, many citizens and political leaders argue whether or not it is a good idea for private citizens to own guns. At the time that the Constitution was ratified, however, many U.S. communities relied on militias for protection. (Militias are local militaries made up of volunteer citizens). The Second Amendment protected the existence of militias by guaranteeing local citizens' rights to own guns.

A Citizen's Right to Bear Arms

Third Amendment

Under the **Third Amendment**, U.S. citizens cannot be forced to house U.S. soldiers in times of peace, and only "in a manner prescribed by law" during times of war.

Fourth Amendment

The Fourth Amendment protects citizens from unlawful searches and seizures. No government agency can enter a citizen's home or search their property without proper authority. Today, the Fourth Amendment means that law enforcement must first have a warrant (document signed by a judge) or probable cause (evidence that a person has committed a crime) before they may search a citizen or a citizen's property.

Law Enforcement Conducting a Search

Fifth Amendment

Due Process

The Fifth Amendment states that the government must obey certain rules when charging someone with a crime. In the case of very serious crimes, citizens must first be indicted by a grand jury (a group of citizens that decides there is enough evidence against a person to have a trial). The Fifth Amendment also protects people from *double jeopardy* and *self-incrimination.* The government may not put a citizen on trial for the same crime more than once. Nor can it force accused people to testify against themselves in court. The Fifth Amendment also addresses *eminent domain.* The government may not take a citizen's property without paying that person for it. For example, if the government needs someone's house because they want the land to finish a highway, then it must pay that person what the land and the house are worth. They cannot simply take the property.

The Fifth Amendment states that no person may be, "deprived of life, liberty, or property without due process of law." **Due process** means that the government must follow the Constitution and respect an accused person's civil rights when arresting or putting that person on trial. It cannot punish someone for a crime or deny them any of their civil rights (taking away their freedom or property) without following the rules set by law.

Sixth Amendment

The Sixth Amendment guarantees an accused citizen the right to a defense lawyer (a lawyer who defends accused people in court). It also promises them the right to a speedy jury trial. A jury is a group of citizens that hears all the evidence and decides a person's guilt or innocence. The Sixth Amendment also states that an accused person may confront witnesses. No one can testify against the accused secretly. The accused must be given a chance to question them. The accused may also call witnesses during a criminal trial.

A Jail Cell

Seventh Amendment

Civil cases are different from criminal cases. In a criminal case, a citizen is accused by the government of committing a criminal act like murder, robbery, burglary, kidnapping, or so on. In a civil case, one private citizen or business accuses another private citizen or business of doing something wrong. Examples of a civil case include a patient suing a doctor for prescribing the wrong medicine, a landlord suing a renter for failing to pay rent, or a client suing a business for failing to stick to a signed contract. The party that sues is called the *plaintiff*. The party being sued is called the *civil defendant*. The Seventh Amendment states that civil defendants have the same right to a jury trial that criminal defendants have.

Eighth Amendment

The Eighth Amendment protects citizens arrested or found guilty of a crime. It says that the government may not charge "excessive bail." Bail is money that accused people must pay to get out of jail until their trial. It is meant to make sure accused people show up for trial. The Eighth Amendment also forbids "excessive fines." When someone is found guilty of a crime, a fine is money they have to pay as part of their punishment. Finally, the Eighth Amendment states that the government cannot use "cruel and unusual punishment." The government must punish guilty people in a way that fits with the crime. For instance, the U.S. Supreme Court has ruled that it is okay to execute (put to death) people found guilty of first-degree murder. However, it is not okay to execute someone found guilty of picking someone's pocket. The punishment would be far too severe for the crime.

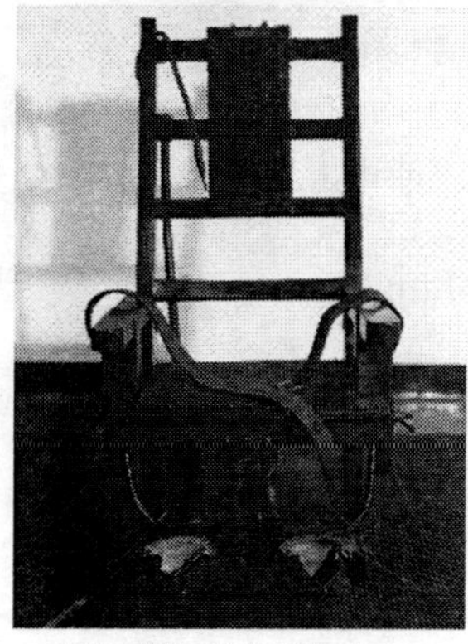
The Electric Chair

Death-Penalty Protest

NINTH AND TENTH AMENDMENTS

The Ninth Amendment states that the rights listed in the Bill of Rights are not the only ones enjoyed by U.S. citizens. The Tenth Amendment says that all powers not given to the federal government or restricted by the Constitution belong to the states. It grants a certain amount of authority to state governments.

Practice 7.1: Civic Responsibility and the Bill of Rights

1. Which amendment to the Constitution protects citizens' freedom of speech?
   A. First Amendment
   B. Second Amendment
   C. Fifth Amendment
   D. Eighth Amendment

2. Which amendment guarantees due process?
   A. First Amendment
   B. Fourth Amendment
   C. Fifth Amendment
   D. Tenth Amendment

3. What is due process? What are some of the ways the Bill of Rights protects it?

7.2 DEMOCRACY AND ONE NATION

THE AMENDMENT PROCESS

President Barack Obama

Vice President Joe Biden

There are two ways that amendments may be added to the Constitution. The first is if two-thirds of both houses of Congress and three-fourths of the states ratify (approve) the amendment. The second is if two-thirds of the states call for a constitutional convention. A constitutional convention involves representatives from each state meeting to consider changes to the constitution. If an amendment is approved by the convention, it then goes to the states. If three-fourths of the states ratify the amendment, it becomes part of the Constitution. Constitutional conventions allow citizens the opportunity to change the constitution without having to wait for Congress to act.

AMENDMENTS SUPPORTING DEMOCRACY

A democracy is a form of government in which citizens participate. They elect their government leaders and often vote on laws and public policy decisions. There have been several amendments added to the constitution that protect and strengthen U.S. democracy.

TWELFTH AMENDMENT (RATIFIED 1804)

The Constitution states that the president and vice president of the United States are to be elected by a body of delegates known as the **Electoral College**. Each state is represented by a number of electors (delegates to the Electoral College) equal to the number of senators and representatives it has in Congress. The **Twelfth Amendment** states that the delegates to the Electoral College shall vote separately for the offices of president and vice president. Before this amendment became law, whoever got the second-highest number of electoral votes for president became the vice president. The weakness in this system became clear during the election of 1800, when Thomas Jefferson and Aaron Burr tied for president. Everyone knew that most of the delegates wanted Jefferson to be president and Burr to be vice president. However, because they had tied, the election had to be decided by the House of Representatives. The states passed the Twelfth Amendment to avoid such confusion in the future.

FIFTEENTH AMENDMENT (RATIFIED 1870)

Following the Civil War, Congress wanted to make sure that freed slaves had the right to vote. The Fifteenth Amendment guaranteed the right to vote to all male citizens, no matter what their race.

African American Men Voting

SEVENTEENTH AMENDMENT (RATIFIED 1913)

Georgia Senator Saxby Chambliss

During the late nineteenth century and early twentieth, U.S. citizens began calling on their leaders to give the public more direct say over their government. In 1913, the states ratified the Seventeenth Amendment. It says that U.S. senators shall be elected directly by the citizens of each state. Before 1913, senators were appointed by state legislators.

Georgia Senator Johnny Isakson

Nineteenth Amendment (Ratified 1920)

The Nineteenth Amendment granted women suffrage (the right to vote). Before the states ratified this amendment, women could only vote in a few states. The Nineteenth Amendment gave them the right to vote nationwide.

Women's Suffrage March in the Early 1900s

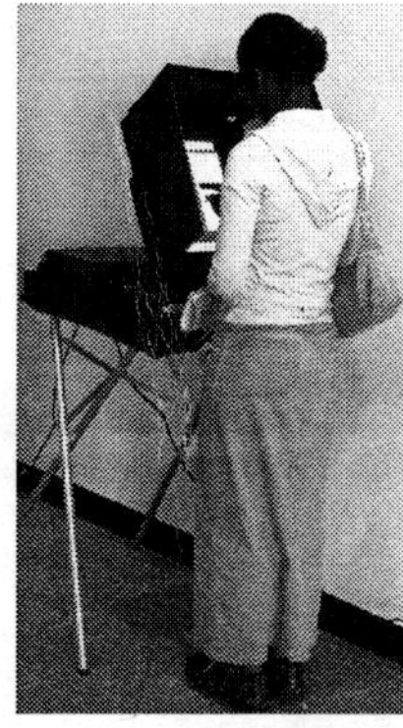

Woman Exercising the Right to Vote

Twenty-third Amendment (Ratified 1961)

Under the Twenty-third Amendment, the District of Columbia is entitled to have electors represent it in the Electoral College. The District of Columbia (Washington, D.C.) is not a state. Therefore, prior to 1961, it was not entitled to have electors participate in the election for president. The Twenty-third Amendment changed this and gives citizens of D.C. a voice in the Electoral College.

The District of Columbia

Twenty-fourth Amendment (Ratified 1964)

After Reconstruction, many southern states used poll taxes to keep African American citizens from voting. The poll tax required voters to pay a fee to vote. Since many African Americans were poor, the law kept many of them from participating in elections. The Twenty-fourth Amendment makes the poll tax illegal. Its effect has been a huge increase in the number of African Americans who vote in elections and serve in public office.

Twenty-sixth Amendment (Ratified 1971)

The Twenty-sixth Amendment states that all U.S. citizens who are at least eighteen years old have the right to vote in elections.

E Pluribus Unum

E pluribus unum is a Latin phrase that means "out of many, one." It serves as a motto of the United States. A motto is a phrase meant to describe a nation, group, or organization. The phrase first arose as a national motto in 1782. It was meant to suggest that out of the many states there is formed one nation. Over time, however, people came to identify the statement as meaning that from many different races, cultures, and backgrounds come one American people. The phrase is found on U.S. currency, national symbols, and the country's official seal.

The United States National Seal

Practice 7.2: Democracy and One Nation

1. Pete and Olivia head a group that supports a proposed amendment to the Constitution. Which of the following will have to happen for their amendment to become national law?

   A. Pete or Olivia will have to win election to Congress because only a member of Congress can recommend amendments.

   B. Pete and Olivia's group will have to convince a member of Congress to introduce the amendment because only Congress can recommend amendments.

   C. Two-thirds of the states must approve a constitutional convention for their amendment to have any chance of becoming law.

   D. Three-fourths of the states will have to ratify the amendment.

2. What does the phrase *E pluribus unum* mean? What did it originally suggest? What do people tend to view it as suggesting today?

3. Pick three amendments discussed in section 7.2 and explain how they impact U.S. democracy.

CHAPTER 7 REVIEW

Key Terms, People, and Concepts

United States Constitution
civil rights
civic responsibilities
laws
taxes
democracy
voting
campaign volunteering
protests
public office
juries
jury duty
volunteer
military service
amendments
Bill of Rights
First Amendment
Second Amendment
Third Amendment
Fourth Amendment
Fifth Amendment
due process
Sixth Amendment
Seventh Amendment
Eight Amendment
Ninth Amendment
Tenth Amendment
constitutional convention
Electoral College
Twelfth Amendment
Fifteenth Amendment
Seventeenth Amendment
Nineteenth Amendment
Twenty-third Amendment
Twenty-fourth Amendment
Twenty-sixth Amendment
E pluribus unum
motto

Multiple Choice Questions

1. Brian is not happy that he owes more than five hundred dollars in taxes to the state. However, he pays them anyway. Brian is

   A. having his civil rights violated.

   B. fulfilling a civic responsibility.

   C. providing an example of *E pluribus unum.*

   D. obeying the Seventeenth Amendment.

2. The national body of laws that governs the United States of America is called the

   A. Bill of Rights.

   B. body of amendments.

   C. U.S. Constitution.

   D. national motto.

3. Mindy stands on a corner downtown and preaches against the war in Iraq while holding a sign that says, "Bring Our Troops Home." Mindy is practicing her

   A. First-Amendment rights.

   B. Second-Amendment rights.

   C. Nineteenth-Amendment rights.

   D. Twelfth-Amendment rights.

4. In 1924, Margaret became the first woman in her family to ever vote in a presidential election. What happened to give Margaret this right that her mother and grandmother did not have?

   A. The U.S. Constitution was ratified.

   B. The Bill of Rights was added to the Constitution.

   C. The states ratified the Nineteenth Amendment.

   D. The states ratified the Twenty-sixth Amendment.

5. Which of the following has had the MOST effect on the roles African Americans play in U.S. democracy?

   A. Seventeenth Amendment

   B. Nineteenth Amendment

   C. Twelfth Amendment

   D. Twenty-fourth Amendment

6. Bobby is arrested and sentenced to prison for a serious crime. However, after reviewing his case, the court rules that the state did not follow the rules set by the Constitution when they investigated, arrested, and tried Bobby. The court has ruled that the state
   A. violated the Twenty-sixth Amendment.
   B. violated Bobby's right to due process.
   C. violated the principle of *E pluribus unum.*
   D. failed to fulfill its civic responsibility.

7. Which of the following BEST represents the modern idea of *E pluribus unum*?
   A. White students sit in a different section of the school cafeteria than African American students.
   B. African American leaders argue that Hispanic immigrants are taking black jobs.
   C. Whites, African Americans, Hispanics, and Asians live together as fellow citizens and friends.
   D. The U.S. government limits immigration to maintain order in society.

Chapter 8
Economic Understanding

This chapter addresses the following competencies

SS5E1	The student will use the basic economic concepts of trade, opportunity cost, specialization, voluntary exchange, productivity, and price incentives to illustrate historical events.
SS5E2	The student will describe the functions of the four major sectors in the United States economy.
SS5E3	The student will describe how consumers and businesses interact in the United States economy.
SS5E4	The student will identify the elements of a personal budget and explain why personal spending and saving decisions are important.

8.1 Economic Principles and Their Impact on U.S. History

Basic Economic Concepts

Economics is the study of how governments, businesses, and people use their money. Since money is limited, most people cannot buy everything they want. They have to make economic choices (decide what to buy with the money they have).

Consumers Shopping

A **market** is where economic exchanges take place. People buy groceries, cars, computers, clothes, houses, and other items in a market. Goods and services are everything bought and sold in a market. Things that can be touched, such as clothing and food, are **goods**. A **service** is work that does not produce something you can touch. Medical checkups and housekeeping are both examples of services. **Price** is the amount of money that **producers** (those who produce a good or service) are willing to sell a good or service for. In order for producers to produce a good or service, they must be able to sell it at a price that is higher than the amount it cost them to produce it. The amount of money the producer makes from the sale of a good or service is called **profit**. Producers want to make as much profit as possible. However, they have to be careful not to charge too high a price. If the price is too high, then **consumers** (those who buy a good or service) will not buy it. **Demand** refers to the goods and services people want and are willing to buy. **Supply** refers to the goods and services that are available that producers have produced.

Opportunity Costs

Whenever someone decides to spend their money on one good or service, they give up something else. The benefit of the good or service they give up is the **opportunity cost**. Mary is hungry and thirsty. She looks in her purse and sees that she only has enough money for a bag of pretzels or a drink. She cannot buy both. If Mary buys the drink, then satisfying her hunger with the pretzels is her opportunity cost. If, on the other hand, she chooses the pretzels, then quenching her thirst with the soda is her opportunity cost.

Economics and U.S. History

Economics affects history. Often, economic and political interests are related. When European powers began establishing colonies in the Western Hemisphere, they wanted to claim territory and expand their empires (political interests). They also wanted the rich resources these areas offered (economic interests). When the American colonies declared independence from Great Britain, they claimed that they had the right to govern themselves (political interests). They also resented British taxes, wanted to trade freely, and hoped to settle land west of the Appalachian Mountains without Britain trying to tell them what to do (economic interests). Following the Spanish-American War, the United States claimed new territories in the Pacific and Caribbean. Part of the reason the United States wanted new territory was to be a world power (political interests). However, the U.S. also wanted the resources and markets in these areas (economic interests). These are just a few examples of how political and economic interests often go hand in hand.

Early Colonization

Signing the Declaration of Independence

World War II Fighting

Historical decisions also have opportunity costs. Whenever the U.S. government decides to do one thing, it must pay the opportunity cost of not doing something else. Take, for example, the **opportunity costs of World War II**. When the war began, the United States decided to stay out of the fighting. The United States reasoned that war was not worth the opportunity costs of peace and economic trade. After the attack on Pearl Harbor, there were more opportunity costs. War production boosted the U.S. economy. However, the government passed laws and encouraged people to give up buying things, so that more could go to support the war effort. The satisfaction citizens would have gotten from buying things for themselves was the opportunity cost.

SPECIALIZATION AND PRICE INCENTIVES

SPECIALIZATION

Southern Cotton Crop

Specialization is when one region, business, or person focuses on producing one thing. Specialization has had a lot of impact on U.S. history. For centuries, the South specialized in cash crops like tobacco and cotton. Cotton led to a great dependence on slavery. Slavery eventually led to the Civil War. Even after the war, the South came to rely on textiles as a major industry due to its abundant cotton. In the North, large industries grew as businesses specialized in steel, oil, automobiles, and other forms of production.

Factory Worker

Specialization also refers to individual workers. As industrialization occurred, more and more factories began to operate. In factories, workers specialized in one task. Each worker became faster and more efficient because they were responsible for just one part of the production process. Specialization tends to improve the quality of products and increase production. More goods are made in a shorter amount of time. This allows companies to sell more, make more money, provide more jobs, and pay employees higher wages. Specialization helps improve peoples' standards of living because it usually results in workers receiving higher pay and the market offering better products. As the United States entered the twentieth century, many people left farms and moved to cities where they could earn more money and improve their standard of living working in specialized industrial jobs. The same thing happened during World War I, the Great Depression, and World War II.

PRICE INCENTIVES

A **price incentive** is when price encourages consumers to buy or producers to produce. Low prices are an incentive to buy. High prices are an incentive to produce and sell.

THE GREAT DEPRESSION

At times, the government has tried to use incentives to get people to spend money. During the **Great Depression**, many businesses failed. People were out of work. Most citizens did not have extra money to spend. This hurt businesses even more and made the depression worse. President Roosevelt's New Deal used government spending to provide incentives for people to spend money. The New Deal cut taxes. By cutting taxes, the New Deal intended to leave businesses with more money to spend on production and citizens with more money to spend in the market. The New Deal also spent borrowed money on government programs to give citizens' jobs. By providing citizens with government jobs, the New Deal hoped to put more money back in peoples' pockets. The government hoped consumers would spend more money and help the economy move in the right direction. Roosevelt also introduced the Social Security system. It provided money to retired people and people out of work. Although the New Deal did not end the Great Depression, it helped provide relief until the economy boomed during World War II.

The Great Depression

VOLUNTARY EXCHANGE AND TRADE

When producers freely choose to sell and consumers freely choose to buy, it is called **voluntary exchange**. Voluntary exchange tends to help both buyers and sellers. Since consumers are free to buy what they want, producers learn what they should produce if they want to make a profit. It also helps consumers by making sure producers are only producing things consumers want or need.

International Trade

Trade is when countries exchange goods with one another. **Imports** are goods countries buy from other nations. **Exports** are goods countries sell to other nations. **Free trade** occurs when nations trade with one another without any restrictions. The only things determining what goods are traded are supply and demand. Sometimes, trade is restricted. Nations will sometimes use **tariffs** (taxes on imports) to raise the price of imported goods and encourage citizens to buy products made in their own country. Other times, nations may use sanctions or embargoes. **Sanctions** limit trade with certain countries. They are meant to punish a nation for some action or policy. **Embargoes** are also meant to punish nations economically by refusing to trade with them at all.

G8 COUNTRIES AND NAFTA

The **G8** is an unofficial organization of industrialized nations. It includes the United States and seven other countries. The G8 nations work together to maintain trade, peace, a clean environment, and address human rights questions. Voluntary exchange between G8 countries helps maintain the economies of these nations. It also enables them to offer financial aid to less-developed countries. When Japan sells products in the United States, it helps Japan's economy. It also helps the United States. By allowing Japan to sell goods in the United States, the United States encourages Japan to allow U.S. producers to sell goods in Japanese markets as well. It also benefits consumers in both nations by providing more competition. The more producers there are in a market, the more choices consumers have. The more choices consumers have, the lower prices tend to be and the better the quality of the goods and services in the market. The less money consumers have to pay for one good, the more they have to spend on others. This keeps people spending money and helps the economy.

G8 Leaders

NAFTA Signing

NAFTA stands for North American Free Trade Agreement. It allows the United States, Canada, and Mexico to trade freely with one another. NAFTA is designed to promote economic activity in all three nations. It allows producers to sell their products more easily in foreign markets, while allowing consumers to benefit from foreign competition. Many support NAFTA as a great way to promote U.S. economic growth. Others have criticized it because they feel it encourages U.S. producers to move jobs to Mexico, where they can hire cheaper labor. Some people also criticize free trade because they believe that richer, more- developed nations, exploit (take advantage of) poorer, less-developed nations by taking their resources and paying very little for labor.

TECHNOLOGY AND PRODUCTION IN U.S. HISTORY

Assembly Line

New technology has always played an important role economic development. **Technology** makes production easier. Eli Whitney's cotton gin made cotton processing much faster and cheaper. It led to the South becoming a "cotton kingdom." New machines and factory assembly lines, like the one designed by Henry Ford for

Technology in Business

automobiles, greatly increased production and led to the United States becoming an industrialized society. Edison's light bulb made the work day much longer and increased production by allowing factories to stay open after dark. The Bessemer process was a new process that made manufacturing steel cheaper and allowed railroads and cities to expand at a faster rate. Today, computers, the Internet, cell phones, and other forms of communications technology make production faster and more efficient. Medical technology enables people to live longer, more comfortable lives. Energy technology helps improve the environment and leads to cheaper sources of energy. These are just a few examples of how technology has affected, and continues to impact, the United States.

Practice 8.1: Economic Principles and Their Impact on U.S. History

1. A market is the

   A. number of producers making a certain good.

   B. amount of a good available.

   C. place where economic exchanges take place.

   D. benefit one gives up when they buy something else.

2. Shortly before the attack on Pearl Harbor, the United States imposed an embargo against Japan. Which of the following was an opportunity cost of this decision?

   A. the attack on Pearl Harbor

   B. war with Japan

   C. benefits of trading with Japan

   D. sanctions against Japan

3. What is a *price incentive*? What kind of incentives did the New Deal offer during the Great Depression?

4. Describe how countries can benefit from voluntary exchange and free trade. Why do some in the United States and other countries criticize agreements like NAFTA?

5. Give some examples of how technology has contributed to the United States' economic development.

8.2 U.S. Economics

Households

A **household** is any group of people that lives together and functions as a "family" unit. Members of a household are often related. But they do not have to be related. For example, roommates qualify as a household.

Households are key factors in the economy. They provide labor for businesses and the government. They also pay taxes and act as consumers. Households buy the products that businesses or the government produce.

Most households rely on jobs for income (money the household takes in). When income is high, households consume more. This helps businesses and governments because profits and tax revenues increase. When income is low, businesses and governments suffer. People do not have as much to spend in the economy and they often pay less in taxes.

PRIVATE BUSINESS

Private businesses drive the U.S. economy. They produce the goods and services that consumers buy. Private businesses range in size. Many are small businesses owned by one person or a partnership of only a few people. Others are very large and may have interests all over the nation. Some are even international. Larger businesses are often owned by numerous stockholders (people who buy a share of ownership in the business). Private businesses produce goods that they think they can sell for a profit. They provide what consumers need or want at a price consumers are willing to pay. Businesses also provide jobs that people depend on for income. People use their income to buy things. When businesses do well, the economy tends to grow. When businesses fail, people lose jobs, have less money to spend, buy less, and the economy can enter a down time.

Small Business Owner

BANKS

Banks are private businesses that specialize in loaning money. Banks are important to the economy because they allow people to buy things they normally could not afford. For instance, most people don't have enough money to buy a house. However, they may have enough to pay for part of the house. They rely on banks or other lending institutions to borrow the rest. They then pay **interest** (additional money a borrower pays a lender for the use of money) on the loan. Loans allow consumers to buy more expensive items or invest in things (such as starting their own business) that they normally could not afford. They also allow banks to make money off of interest. When banks make money, they loan to more people, boosting economic activity. When banks do poorly, they have less money. Less money means fewer loans and less economic activity.

Bank of America Building

GOVERNMENT

Governments also impact the economy (review section 8.1 regarding the Great Depression). The U.S. government affects the economy in different ways. One is through fiscal policy. **Fiscal policy** concerns how much the government taxes and spends. When the government raises taxes, it tends to decrease the amount of money in the economy. Businesses and citizens have to give more of their money to the government. Businesses have less to spend on production and employing workers, while citizens have less to spend in the market. On the other hand, when the government cuts taxes, it often boosts economic activity. Businesses and citizens have more money to spend.

Diverse Citizens

A **tax** is money citizens or businesses must pay the government. Taxes are the number-one way governments raise the money they need to operate. Governments use taxes to provide certain services. Park maintenance, law enforcement, fire protection, national defense, and public education are a few examples of services provided by the government. Sometimes taxes are used to help farmers or failing businesses that the government thinks are very important to the U.S. economy. The government also uses tax money to provide social programs meant to help the poor, elderly, and those with special needs. It sometimes provides relief to foreign nations as well.

Monetary policy concerns the nation's money supply. If the government does not believe there is enough economic activity, the **Federal Reserve** will often take action to increase the money supply. The Federal Reserve loans money to banks and determines how much money banks must keep on hand rather than loaning. By lowering or raising interest rates, the Federal Reserve affects how much money banks loan. The more they loan, the more is in the economy. The more is in the economy, the more economic activity there is.

Chairman of the Federal Reserve
Ben Bernanke

How Consumers and Businesses Interact

Effects of Competition

Competitors Coke and Pepsi

Competition is an important part of the U.S. economy. Competition occurs when businesses compete with one another for consumers. Since consumers are free to buy from whatever producer they want, producers have to compete to convince consumers to buy from them. Price and quality are the two main areas where producers compete. **Price** is how much the good or service costs. **Quality** is how well the product is made or the service is performed. Consumers tend to buy goods and services that have low prices and high quality. Sometimes, consumers are willing to give up a certain amount of quality in order to get a lower price. For instance, they might give up the extra comfort and features of a luxury car in order to buy a cheaper car that is less comfortable. On the other hand, sometimes people are willing to pay a higher price to get better quality. A man who is about to propose to his girlfriend might pass on a cheaper ring in order to buy a more expensive, high-quality ring. In order to compete, businesses must price their goods and services at a level that consumers are willing to pay. If they don't, the consumers will buy from someone else. Businesses that can't compete must improve their quality, lower their prices, or go out of business. Competition is good for consumers because it usually keeps prices low and quality high.

INCOME

Labor is the work that people do. People sell their labor to businesses for **income**. Income is the money businesses are willing to pay for labor. Income usually increases based on the amount of skill needed to perform a job. It also increases depending on how important the position is to the profitability of the company. Businesses pay workers income for their labor. Workers then spend part of their income in the market as consumers. The more they spend, the better businesses do. The better businesses do, the more they produce and the more workers they hire. People and businesses depend on each other in order to keep the economy going.

White-Collar Workers

Blue-Collar Workers

ENTREPRENEURS

Entrepreneurs are people who start businesses. Entrepreneurs take financial risks. They spend their own money (or money they have borrowed) to start new businesses that they believe will eventually earn profits. Without entrepreneurs, the U.S. economy could not stay strong. Entrepreneurs introduce new ideas and innovations, provide competition, and employ workers. Some entrepreneurs' businesses remain relatively small. Others grow their businesses into huge corporations.

Large Corporation

Practice 8.2: U.S. Economics

1. After years of working as a contract writer, Phil decides to open his own publishing house. Which of the following is true?

   A. Phil is a publishing consumer.

   B. Phil is an entrepreneur.

   C. Phil has no competition in publishing.

   D. Phil will sell his labor to a publishing house.

2. Private businesses help the economy by providing

   A. labor for consumers.

   B. entrepreneurs for government.

   C. income for workers.

   D. loans to banks.

3. Describe how competition affects the economy and people's behavior.

4. Describe how the government can affect the economy.

8.3 Personal Economics

Having a Budget

Making a Household Budget

Every citizen needs to learn how to manage their own money. Having a budget is an important part of any money-management plan. A **budget** is a record of how you plan to spend your money. It helps keep you from spending too much. People who spend too much end up falling into debt. **Debt** is the amount of money that you owe. People get in debt when they spend more money than they have and are forced to borrow to pay for things.

INCOME AND EXPENSES

The first step to making a budget is to know your **income**. Income is how much money you make. For most people, their income is the amount of money they are paid by their employer. If they are self-employed, then income would be the money they make through their own business. A regular allowance from your parents is also income. Since most people are paid every two weeks or once a month, most people operate on a weekly or monthly budget. It is important to know your income first, so that you know how much money you are able to spend.

BigCorp Inc.
1280 Main St.
Building 550
Atlanta, GA 30010

John Jones
1117 Meryll Street
Lithonia, GA 30038

Work ID: 972825
Department: 00012

Earnings Statement
Period Ending: 08/01/2008
Pay Date: 08/08/2008

Earnings	rate	hours
Regular	18.00	80.00
Overtime		
Other		
Gross Pay		$1440.00

Deductions	
Federal	$240.80
State	67.10
Social Security	105.00
Medicare	89.30
Medical	29.00
Dental	15.00
Net Pay	$894.10

BigCorp Inc. 0255
DATE 08/08/2008
PAY TO THE ORDER OF John Jones $ 894.10
eight hundred ninety-four dollars 10/100
⑆0012245575⑆ 0012245577⑈ 255

Employee Paycheck

Once you know your income, the second step is to write down all of your **expenses**. Expenses are the things you spend money on. When you know your income and expenses, you can then decide how much income to spend on each expense. The key is to make sure that expenses are less than income. Once you have a budget that works, you then need to stick to it. Spend only what your budget allows because you know you can afford it. When people don't stick to a budget, they run the risk of getting into financial trouble.

STAYING OUT OF DEBT

It is important to stay out of debt as much as possible. **Debt** occurs when people have to borrow to pay for things. Sometimes, debt is not bad. Most people could not afford expensive items, such as cars or houses, if they could not borrow money to pay for them. Many people, however, get into trouble when they borrow more money than they can pay back. It is important to remember that when someone borrows money, they have to pay **interest**. Interest is extra money the borrower pays in addition to the amount they borrowed. Interest is how lenders, such as banks or credit card companies, make money. They let you use their money to buy something in exchange for you paying them even more money later. A lot of people get in trouble because they use credit to buy things they really can't afford. Later, when the time comes to pay the money back with interest, they find that they are unable to pay. People can lose their homes, cars, other possessions, and their ability to borrow money in the future if they fail to pay back the money they borrowed.

Credit Cards

Saving Money

Spending is when you give money in return for a good or service. You spend money to buy a video game, go to Six Flags, or buy a soda at the convenience store. **Saving** is when you take money you *could spend* and, instead, put it aside for a later time. People save money in different ways. Many put money in savings accounts. These are accounts people have with banks or other financial institutions. Savings accounts allow a person's money to gain interest.

The Stock Market

Investing is one of the most popular ways people save money. Investing is when you allow businesses to use part of your money in return for interest or a share of their profits. It could be your own business that you invest in. Often, however, it is other peoples' businesses. People invest in a variety of ways. Many buy stocks, which make them part owner of a company. Others buy bonds, which does not give them ownership but rather allows them to lend money to a business or institution. Many participate in mutual funds, which are made up of many companies. Mutual funds are safer because if one company in the fund does poorly, others are usually doing well. Others might invest in CDs (certificates of deposit) which keep their money in a special account for a set period of time. When the time expires, the depositor withdraws the money with interest.

Reasons to Save

Buying a New Home

Retirees

There are lots of **reasons why people save**. Sometimes, they save because they want to buy something they can't afford to buy right away. Young couples often save to buy their first home. Teenagers often save to buy a car. Parents usually save to pay for their kids' college education. Families might save to take a nice vacation. One of the most important things citizens save for is retirement. When a person retires, it means that they no longer work. People may retire because they are sick or because they simply don't want to work anymore. The most common reason people retire is age. However, even retired people still need money to live on. If they are not working and earning a salary (money paid by an employer), then this money must come from somewhere else. For many, it comes from retirement savings. Many people participate in retirement savings plans at work. Others set up IRAs (individual retirement accounts). IRAs allow people to save money over time for when they are older. The earlier people set up or participate in such accounts, the longer their money grows and the more they have for retirement. Many people count on Social Security to provide their retirement income. Social Security is a federal government program that gives money to retired citizens.

But Social Security does not provide enough money for most people to live on. Therefore, citizens need to save on their own as well. By investing wisely and starting early, citizens can do a good job of saving for retirement.

College Students

Why Saving is Important

Saving money is important for many reasons. People don't know what will happen in the future. They could lose their job, get hurt and be unable to work, have a huge expense that they did not plan on, or face other financial challenges. People who save money have an easier time dealing with such problems. They have money in savings that they can use to pay their bills. Those that don't save often find themselves in trouble because they lack money. Saving money takes discipline. It is usually more fun to spend. But wise and responsible citizens will save some of their income rather than spending all of it.

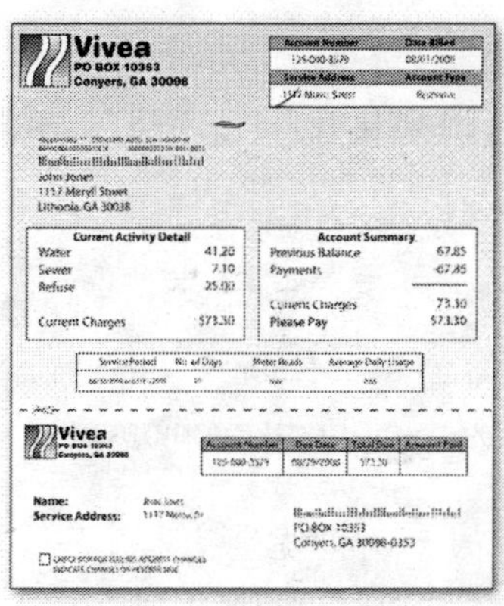

Monthly Bill

Practice 8.3: Personal Economics

1. Bill makes $2500 a month working at Danbar, Inc. He pays $900 a month in rent and usually spends at least $1200 a month on other things. The remaining $400 a month goes in the bank. Which of the following statements is true?
   A. Bill saves most of his income.
   B. Bill's expenses equal $2500 a month.
   C. Bill spends more than he makes.
   D. Bill's expenses equal $2100 a month.

2. If Amy wants to make sure that she spends less money than she makes, then she should
   A. make a budget.
   B. go into debt.
   C. forget about saving.
   D. borrow money.

3. Why should people be careful not to go into debt?

4. Why is it important to save money?

CHAPTER 8 REVIEW

Key Terms, People, and Concepts

economics
market
goods
services
price
producers
profit
consumers
demand
supply
opportunity cost
opportunity costs of Word War II
specialization
price incentive
depression
Great Depression
voluntary exchange
trade
imports
exports
free trade
tariffs
sanctions
embargoes
G8
NAFTA
technology
private businesses
banks
interest
government's impact on the economy
fiscal policy
tax
monetary policy
Federal Reserve
competition
quality
labor
income
entrepreneurs
budget
debt
expenses
spending
saving
investing
reasons people save
why saving is important

Multiple Choice Questions

1. Goods and services are bought and sold in a/an
   A. budget.
   B. opportunity cost.
   C. market.
   D. monetary policy.

2. In order to have a good budget, one must make sure that
   A. they never have debt.
   B. their income is less than their expenses.
   C. their spending is greater than their savings.
   D. they spend less money than they make.

3. When businesses lower the cost of a good to encourage people to buy it, they are offering consumers a
   A. fiscal policy.
   B. price incentive.
   C. savings plan.
   D. form of specialization.

4. When the United States entered World War II, citizens and the government had to make economic sacrifices. These sacrifices were
   A. debts.
   B. imports.
   C. tariffs.
   D. opportunity costs.

5. Lydia owns a company in Rome, Georgia. Last week, she made large profits selling her goods in Canada and Mexico because her prices are lower than much of her competition. It sounds like Lydia is benefiting from
   A. NAFTA.
   B. the United States being part of the G8.
   C. restricted trade.
   D. tariffs.

6. Emails, faster airline travel, and video conferencing are all examples of
   A. technology that has impacted the economy.
   B. the effects of NAFTA on the U.S. economy.
   C. reasons the G8 was formed.
   D. ways banks have helped private businesses.

7. In which of the following ways do entrepreneurs LEAST affect the U.S. economy?
   A. providing jobs
   B. introducing innovations
   C. preventing debt
   D. increasing competition

8. Banks help the U.S. economy by
   A. loaning money to consumers and businesses.
   B. keeping people out of debt.
   C. letting people and businesses borrow money without having to pay interest.
   D. preventing economic opportunity costs.

Mastering the Georgia 5th Grade CRCT in SS
Practice Test 1

The purpose of this practice test is to measure your progress in social studies. This test is based on the GPS-based Georgia CRCT in Social Studies and adheres to the sample question format provided by the Georgia Department of Education.

General Directions:

1. Read all directions carefully.

2. Read each question or sample. Then choose the best answer.

3. Choose only one answer for each question. If you change an answer, be sure to erase your original answer completely.

1. Which of the following people would have been MOST affected by the Fifteenth Amendment? SS5CG3
   A. a poor black male farmer
   B. a rich white male landowner
   C. a black female servant
   D. a white male serving in the army

2. In 1932, an Oklahoma farmer and his family would have been MOST affected by SS5H5
   A. the Dust Bowl.
   B. the Civilian Conservation Corps.
   C. the Social Security Act.
   D. the Tennessee Valley Authority.

3. What is the MAIN purpose of the United Nations? SS5H6
   A. to ensure that the United States and Great Britain maintained control of all international policies and laws
   B. to divide Germany in two
   C. to maintain peace, protect human rights, and make sure nations obeyed international law
   D. to assist the United States during the arms race

4. After the Civil War, cities like New York, Chicago, Boston, and San Francisco became industrialized. Which factors MOST LIKELY contributed to this economic growth? SS5G2
   A. natural resources such as cotton and tobacco
   B. large labor populations and accessibility to water for easy shipping
   C. plenty of land for cattle grazing and lumber industries
   D. availability of saw mills and fertilizer production

5. What is the PRIMARY function of private businesses in the United States? SS5E2
   A. to produce the goods and services that consumers buy
   B. to encourage free trade within the nation
   C. to decide how much people should pay in taxes
   D. to loan people money

6. Michelle voted in the 1924 presidential election. This was the first time it was legal for her to participate in an election. What MOST LIKELY made this possible? SS5CG3
   A. Due process was established by the federal government.
   B. The states ratified the Twenty-sixth Amendment.
   C. Michelle was a participant in double jeopardy.
   D. The states ratified the Nineteenth Amendment.

Use the image below to answer question number 7.

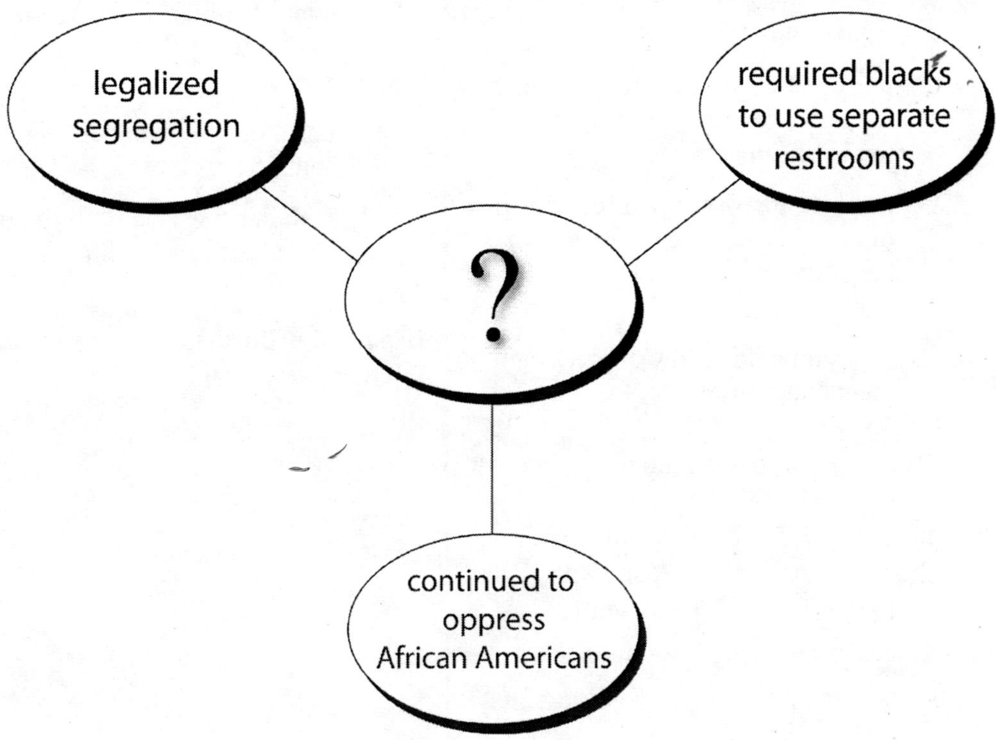

7. Which of the following BEST completes the web? SS5H2

   A. Reconstruction

   B. Jim Crow Laws

   C. black codes

   D. Freedman's Bureau

8. What was the MAIN purpose of the North Atlantic Treaty Organization? SS5H7

   A. to give money to European nations

   B. to remove Communism from all European nations

   C. to remove nuclear missiles from European nations

   D. to provide a military force to fight any Communist attack in Europe

9. How did the Allegheny, Monongahela, and Ohio Rivers help Pittsburgh become an important U.S. city? SS5G1

   A. by providing key routes for transporting goods

   B. by protecting the city from foreign invasion and attacks

   C. by providing running water to the suburbs of Pittsburgh

   D. by providing irrigation water for the crops

10. If an amendment is approved by the constitutional convention, it SS5CG2

A. immediately becomes part of the Constitution.

B. must be ratified by three-fourths of the states before becoming part of the U.S. Constitution.

C. must be approved by three-fourths of both houses of Congress before becoming part of the U.S. Constitution.

D. is put on hold until Congress can meet and ratify it.

11. Rita is an African American living in Montgomery, Alabama in 1955. She wants to support the cause inspired by Rosa Parks. Rita will MOST LIKELY refuse to SS5H8

A. eat in segregated restaurants.

B. ride the public bus.

C. be seen in public parks.

D. speak to any white people.

12. Why did the United States initially declare the war on terror? SS5H9

A. because of the September 11th attacks

B. in response to the Camp David Accords

C. because of a false report about al Qaeda planning an attack

D. to prevent a nuclear war in the United States

13. The U.S. Bill of Rights SS5CG1

A. was the first part of the U.S. Constitution written.

B. consists of ten amendments to the Constitution that protect citizens' rights.

C. upset people who believed in personal freedoms.

D. includes the Twelfth through the Nineteenth Amendments.

Use the timeline below to answer the following question.

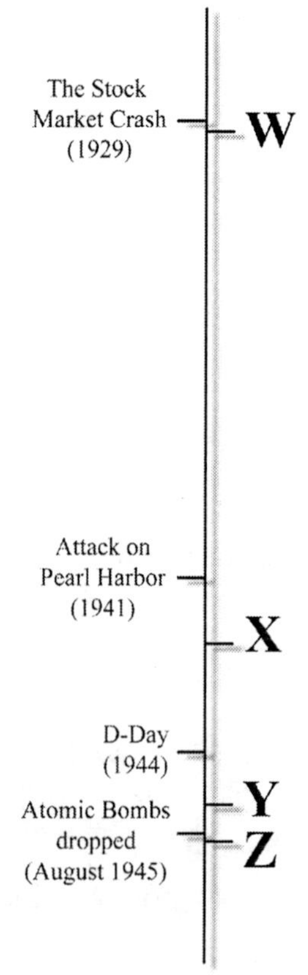

14. On the timeline above, where should V-J Day be listed? SS5H6

A. letter W

B. letter X

C. letter Y

D. letter Z

15. These were important battles in the Civil War. What is the correct order in which they took place? SS5H1
    1. Gettysburg
    2. march to the sea
    3. Fort Sumter

    A. 1, 3, 2
    B. 2, 3, 1
    C. 3, 1, 2
    D. 1, 2, 3

16. After World War I, many European economies were devastated. How did this influence the United States? SS5G2
    A. It led to the decline of the U.S. political system.
    B. It contributed to the U.S. becoming a world power.
    C. It did not influence the U.S. economy at all.
    D. It led to the failure of many U.S. businesses.

17. What was MOST important about the *Lusitania*? SS5H4
    A. It was a German submarine that spied on U.S. ships during World War I.
    B. It was a ship that Germany sank, leading to U.S. involvement in World War I.
    C. It secretly carried Spanish missiles to Cuba during the Spanish American War.
    D. It was the plane that dropped the first atomic bomb.

18. When businesses lower the cost of a good to encourage people to buy it, they are offering consumers SS5E1
    A. a savings plan.
    B. an opportunity cost.
    C. a price incentive.
    D. specialization.

19. The Seventeenth Amendment states that SS5CG3
    A. delegates of the Electoral College must vote separately for president and vice president.
    B. U.S. senators shall be elected directly by the citizens of each state.
    C. all U.S. citizens who are at least eighteen years old have the right to vote.
    D. the poll tax is illegal.

20. In order to prevent African Americans from voting, Southern lawmakers SS5H2
    A. enforced poll taxes and literacy tests.
    B. refused to ratify the Fifteenth Amendment.
    C. ended Jim Crow laws.
    D. passed Radical Reconstruction.

21. Which amendment to the Constitution protects citizens' freedom of speech? SS5CG1
    A. First Amendment
    B. Second Amendment
    C. Third Amendment
    D. Fourth Amendment

Use the map below to answer the following three questions.

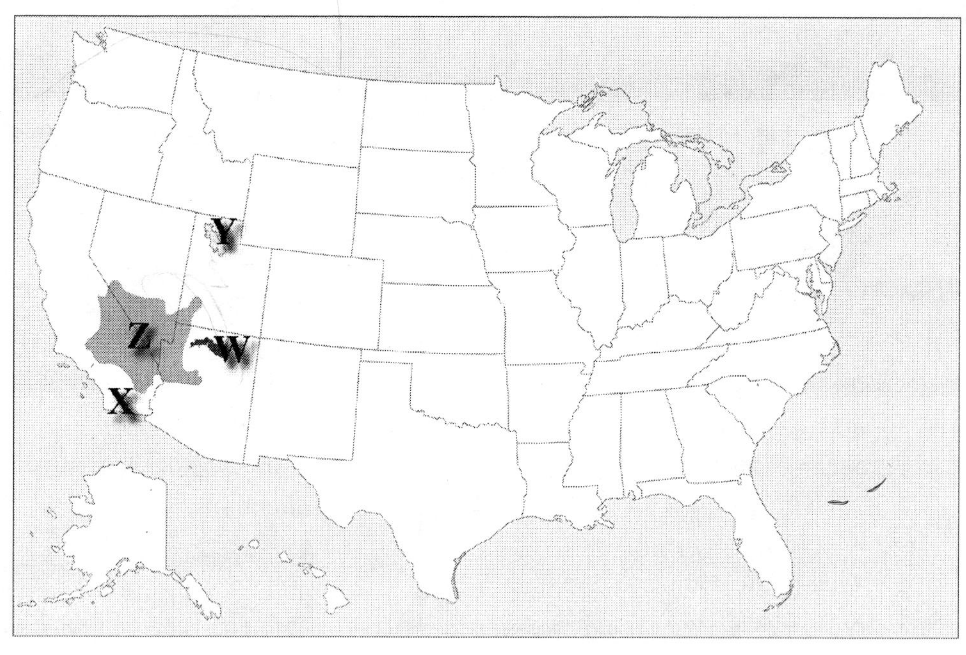

22. Which letter represents the largest salt lake in the Western Hemisphere? SS5G1

    A. W B. X C. Y D. Z

23. Which letter represents one of the country's major deserts? SS5G1

    A. W B. X C. Y D. Z

24. What letter represents a natural wonder that is over a mile deep at its deepest point? SS5G1

    A. W B. X C. Y D. Z

25. After ten years of working as a riding instructor, Victoria decides to open her own horse stable. Which of the following is MOST accurate? SS5E3
    A. Victoria will have no competition.
    B. Victoria is an entrepreneur.
    C. Victoria will provide loans to clients.
    D. Victoria's actions are an example of fiscal policy.

Use the passage below to answer the following question.

> It originated from Theodore Roosevelt's ideas of expansion. It was finally completed in 1914. It allowed ships to travel between the Atlantic and Pacific Oceans without having to go around South America.

26. What is the passage MOST LIKELY referring to? SS5H3
    A. Suez Canal
    B. Panama Canal
    C. Great Lakes Waterway
    D. industrial canal

27. People often go into debt because SS5E4
    A. they save all their money instead of paying bills.
    B. they cannot pay back the money that they borrowed.
    C. their income is greater than the amount they owe.
    D. they make a careful budget plan and stick to it.

28. How did Louis Armstrong influence the early 1920s? SS5H4
    A. He was one of the most famous jazz musicians in history.
    B. He wrote poems and stories about black life in America.
    C. He invented the first automobile.
    D. He created beautiful works of art.

29. Over a period of months in the late 1940s, U.S. airplanes dropped food and supplies into democratic West Berlin. What was this event called? SS5H7
    A. the Berlin Wall
    B. charity food drop
    C. the Berlin airlift
    D. British air league

30. Which of the following BEST describes President Franklin Roosevelt's New Deal? SS5H5
    A. an agreement between the U.S. and Canada about land boundaries
    B. a company that provided the Midwest with electricity
    C. government programs intended to help the U.S. economy
    D. a strategy to improve foreign relations with the Soviet Union

31. Rosa Parks is MOST associated with SS5H8
    A. the march on Washington.
    B. the Nation of Islam.
    C. the Montgomery bus boycott.
    D. the women's movement.

32. The Fifteenth Amendment guarantees SS5CG3
    A. male citizens the right to vote regardless of their race.
    B. women the right to vote.
    C. a certain amount of authority to state governments.
    D. civil defendants the right to a jury trial.

33. Which of the following is the BEST heading for the list below? SS5E2
    - money for the government
    - services like law enforcement and national defense
    - relief to foreign nations
    - special programs for the poor and elderly

    A. Reasons Citizens Pay Taxes
    B. Causes of Market Competition
    C. Economic Factors that Influence Trade
    D. Primary Purposes of Banks in the United States

34. What conflict occurred between U.S. troops and Iraqis in the small nation of Kuwait? SS5H9
    A. War on Terror
    B. Lebanon
    C. al Qaeda
    D. Persian Gulf War

Read the list below, and answer the following question.

- Cuba
- Guam
- The Philippines
- Puerto Rico

35. What is the BEST heading for the list above? SS5H3
    A. Democratic Nations During World War I
    B. Enemies of the United States in 1898
    C. Territories Involved in the Spanish-American War
    D. Nations That Sent Millions of Immigrants to the United States in the Early 1900s

36. Mary would like to get a job. The only job available requires her to work during the hours of cheerleading practice. She cannot do both. If she takes the job, what is the opportunity cost? SS5E1
    A. getting paid to be a cheerleader
    B. There would be no opportunity cost.
    C. cheerleading
    D. She would not make enough money.

37. Which amendment made slavery illegal in the United States? SS5H2
    A. the Twelfth Amendment
    B. the Thirteenth Amendment
    C. the Fourteenth Amendment
    D. the Fifteenth Amendment

Use the image below to answer question number 38.

38. What American hero of the 1920s does the image above portray? SS5H4

    A. Hank Aaron
    B. Babe Ruth
    C. Charles Lindbergh
    D. Henry Ford

39. How did geography contribute to the attack on Pearl Harbor? SS5G2

    A. Japan's leaders felt that Hawaii was too close to Japan.
    B. Geography did not contribute to the attack.
    C. Pearl Harbor is located in the Atlantic Ocean.
    D. The mountains of the region provided little protection from the Japanese fighter planes.

40. What was the effect of the Civil War on the South? SS5H1

    A. Its economy suffered.
    B. Its economy prospered.
    C. Industries and manufacturing grew.
    D. Nothing changed in the South.

41. Which of the following is an example of how the U.S. Constitution protects individual rights? SS5CG1
   A. The minimum wage amendment guarantees the right to a living wage.
   B. The Fourth Amendment prevents searches and seizures without a warrant.
   C. The press is not allowed to report news that offends people.
   D. People are not allowed to carry guns so that citizens feel safe.

42. Brian works for a publishing company. Brian receives what for his labor? SS5E3
   A. bartering
   B. income
   C. inflation
   D. free trade

43. Which of the following has had the MOST effect on the role of African Americans in the voting process? SS5CG3
   A. Twenty-third Amendment
   B. Twenty-fourth Amendment
   C. Seventeenth Amendment
   D. Nineteenth Amendment

44. Which city is known for its steel production? SS5G1
   A. Gettysburg
   B. Kitty Hawk
   C. Pittsburgh
   D. Charlotte

Read the passage below, and answer the following question.

> It was established in 1935. It was part of the Second New Deal, and it provided jobs for unskilled workers. It hired people to build government buildings, roads, and other public projects.

45. What is the passage above MOST LIKELY referring to? SS5H5
   A. Tennessee Valley Authority
   B. Works Progress Administration
   C. Social Security
   D. Civilian Conservation Corps

46. When someone borrows money, they often have to pay SS5E4
   A. a profit.
   B. expenses.
   C. interest.
   D. savings.

47. During World War II, Rosie the Riveter symbolized SS5H6
   A. the suffering of the Jewish people during Hitler's reign.
   B. the strength of the United Nations.
   C. women who fought in the armed forces during the war.
   D. women who joined the work force during the war.

Read the passage below, and answer the following question.

> It provided food, education, clothes, and medical attention to African Americans coming out of slavery. It was established in 1865. It was an attempt to help African Americans adjust to life after slavery.

48. What is the above passage referring to? SS5H2
    A. African Amends Bureau
    B. Radical Reconstruction
    C. the Freedman's Bureau
    D. the New Deal

49. For centuries, the South focused on crops like tobacco and cotton. What is this called? SS5E1
    A. specialization
    B. opportunity cost
    C. embargoes
    D. free trade

50. The Cuban Missile Crisis is evidence of SS5H8
    A. the potential for a nuclear war.
    B. the Soviets' power over the United States.
    C. the impact of poverty on Cuba.
    D. the international belief that Communism is wrong.

51. Which amendment protects citizens' right to bear arms? SS5CG1
    A. First Amendment
    B. Second Amendment
    C. Third Amendment
    D. Seventh Amendment

52. What senator accused high-ranking U.S. military officers of being Communists? SS5H7
    A. Dwight Eisenhower
    B. Thurgood Marshall
    C. John F. Kennedy
    D. Joseph McCarthy

53. The first airplane was flown in 1903. Who is responsible for this great American invention? SS5H3
    A. the Wright brothers
    B. Theodore Roosevelt
    C. Thomas Edison
    D. John Brown

54. Why did Franklin Roosevelt call December 7, 1941, "a date that will live in infamy"? SS5G2
    A. The first powered airplane flight occurred.
    B. The Japanese bombed Pearl Harbor.
    C. The Battle of Gettysburg was fought.
    D. Pittsburgh was attacked by the Chinese.

55. Which of the following was the bloodiest battle of the Civil War, ending Lee's attempts to invade the North? SS5H1
    A. Fort Sumter
    B. Gettysburg
    C. Harpers Ferry
    D. march to the sea

56. The Montgomery bus boycott helped start

A. the Civil War.

B. the Civil Rights Movement.

C. World War I.

D. during the attack on Pearl Harbor.

57. Who is the list below MOST LIKELY referring to? SS5H5

- an African American
- won four gold medals at the 1936 Olympics
- famous track and field athlete

A. Joe Louis

B. Sinclair Lewis

C. Jesse Owens

D. Hank Aaron

58. The Twelfth Amendment states that SS5CG3

A. delegates of the Electoral College vote separately for president and vice president.

B. the U.S. government limits immigration in order to maintain order in our society.

C. all U.S. citizens who are at least eighteen years old have the right to vote.

D. the poll tax is illegal.

59. Which of the following BEST promotes economic activity between nations? SS5E1

A. embargoes

B. tariffs

C. NAFTA

D. personal investing

60. How did Henry Ford change the automobile industry? SS5H4

A. He had nothing to do with the automobile industry.

B. He discovered a way to sell cars overseas.

C. He copyrighted the automobile so even fewer people could buy cars.

D. He used an assembly line to mass-produce cars.

61. U.S. citizens cannot be forced to house soldiers during times of peace. Which amendment guarantees this protection? SS5CG1

A. Second Amendment

B. Third Amendment

C. Seventh Amendment

D. Eighth Amendment

62. Which of the following made African Americans U.S. citizens? SS5H2

A. the Thirteenth Amendment

B. black codes

C. the Fifteenth Amendment

D. the Fourteenth Amendment

63. Computers, the Internet, and cell phones are all examples of SS5E1

A. things that prevent economic growth.

B. the effects of NAFTA on International trade.

C. technology that has impacted the economy.

D. reasons for the formation of the G8.

Use the map below to answer the following question.

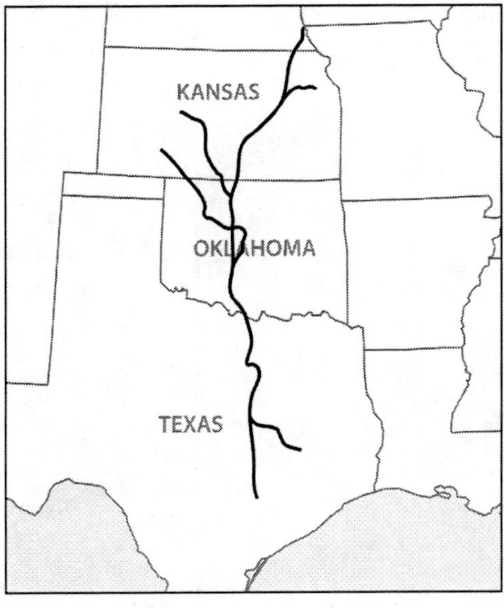

64. What does the map above MOST LIKELY represent? SS5H3
    - A. iron curtain
    - B. Chisholm Trail
    - C. D-day
    - D. march on Washington

65. The establishment of the Voting Rights Act of 1965 SS5H8
    - A. made it easier for African Americans to vote.
    - B. made it easier for poor white men to vote.
    - C. made it impossible for African Americans to vote.
    - D. stated that all male U.S. citizens over the age of thirty could vote.

66. Citizens and businesses must give the government money. What is this process called? SS5CG1
    - A. paying taxes
    - B. volunteering
    - C. jury duty
    - D. protesting

67. Who was the only president of the Confederate States of America? SS5H1
    - A. Abraham Lincoln
    - B. Thomas "Stonewall" Jackson
    - C. Jefferson Davis
    - D. Robert E. Lee

Read the list below, and answer the following question.

- preached a hatred for Jews
- controlled Germany by 1933
- called his empire the Third Reich

68. Who is the list referring to? SS5H6

A. Joseph Stalin

B. Adolf Hitler

C. Emperor Hirohito

D. Benito Mussolini

69. Jack turned eighteen in 1972. Which amendment guarantees him the right to vote? SS5CG3

A. the Seventeenth Amendment

B. the Nineteenth Amendment

C. the Twenty-sixth Amendment

D. the Twenty-third Amendment

Read the passage below, and answer the following question.

> The country should never forget these African American fighter pilots. They contributed greatly to the war effort, successfully protecting every U.S. bomber they escorted.

70. Which of the following is the passage referring to? SS5H6

A. the Tuskegee Airmen

B. code talkers

C. African American riveters

D. members of the WAC

Mastering the Georgia 5th Grade CRCT in SS
Practice Test 2

The purpose of this practice test is to measure your progress in social studies. This test is based on the GPS-based Georgia CRCT in Social Studies and adheres to the sample question format provided by the Georgia Department of Education.

General Directions:

1. Read all directions carefully.

2. Read each question or sample. Then choose the best answer.

3. Choose only one answer for each question. If you change an answer, be sure to erase your original answer completely.

1. Which of the following were MOST affected by the Seventeenth Amendment? SS5CG3

   A. U.S. congressmen

   B. the president of the United States

   C. state governors

   D. U.S. Senators

2. Who is the following statement referring to? SS5H1

   > On October 16, 1859, he seized the United States arsenal at Harpers Ferry. He wanted to give weapons to slaves so they could fight for their freedom, but he was caught by Union soldiers. The government hanged him a few days later.

   A. Thomas Jackson

   B. Uncle Tom

   C. Jefferson Davis

   D. John Brown

3. Which of the following is MOST accurate about President Franklin Roosevelt? SS5H5

   A. He was very positive and offered hope to America.

   B. He was a ruthless president who made the Depression worse.

   C. He was the only president to be impeached.

   D. He only served one term as president.

4. Communist Eastern Europe and democratic Western Europe were separated by an imaginary line. This was known as the SS5H7

   A. Great Divide.

   B. Communist shield.

   C. iron curtain.

   D. Berlin Wall.

5. After World War II, the United States and its allies established a group to help maintain international peace. What was this organization called? SS5H6

   A. the League of Nations

   B. the United Nations

   C. the Potsdam Declaration

   D. the Allies bargain

6. Private businesses help the economy by providing SS5E2

   A. labor for consumers.

   B. income for workers.

   C. loans for U.S. citizens.

   D. lower taxes for goods.

7. Which amendment to the U.S. Constitution gave women the right to vote? SS5CG3

   A. Eighteenth

   B. Twenty-fourth

   C. Nineteenth

   D. Twenty-sixth

8. The image above depicts a type of German ship used in World War I. What was it called? SS5H4

   A. a U-boat

   B. a diver

   C. a bomber

   D. an underwater marine

9. Which of the following involves state representatives meeting to consider changes to the constitution? SS5CG2

   A. campaign volunteering

   B. constitutional convention

   C. *E pluribus unum*

   D. due process

10. Which of the following is an example of a price incentive? SS5E1

    A. a customer purchasing items with a credit card

    B. a hardware store increasing the cost of lumber

    C. an increase in supply and demand

    D. a department store putting clothes on sale

11. What do Rosa Parks and Martin Luther King, Jr. have MOST in common? SS5H8

    A. They both contributed to the Montgomery bus boycotts.

    B. They were both members of the Nation of Islam.

    C. They both were assassinated for their civil rights efforts.

    D. They were both key figures in the *Brown v. Board of Education* case.

12. When did the United States first become a world power? SS5G2

    A. after the Civil War ended

    B. after World War I ended

    C. after Japan attacked Pearl Harbor

    D. after the Battle of Gettysburg

13. The first ten amendments to the Constitution are known as SS5CG1

A. due process.

B. the Bill of Rights.

C. Civil Rights.

D. E pluribus unum.

Use the timeline below to answer the following question.

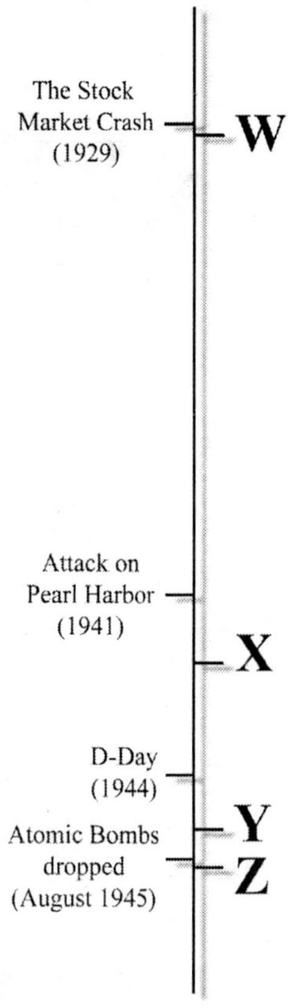

14. On the timeline above, where should the Great Depression be listed? SS5H6

A. at the letter W

B. at the letter X

C. at the letter Y

D. at the letter Z

15. What significant event happened at Appomattox Court House? SS5H1

A. Sherman started his march to the sea.

B. General Lee surrendered to Grant, ending the Civil War.

C. Lincoln gave his famous Gettysburg Address.

D. The first battle of the Civil War.

16. Which of the following was the first federal relief agency in U.S. history? SS5H2

A. the New Deal

B. Radical Reconstruction

C. Social Security

D. the Freedman's Bureau

17. What do Hiroshima and Nagasaki have in common? SS5H6

A. The United States dropped atomic bombs on both cities in 1945.

B. They were both emperors of Japan in the 1900s.

C. They were fighter planes used in WWII.

D. They were destroyed in the Korean War.

18. What event contributed MOST to the U.S. becoming involved in World War I? SS5H4

A. the sinking of the *USS Maine*

B. the sinking of the *Lusitania*

C. its alliance with Central Powers

D. its hatred of Mexico

Read the passage below, and answer the following question.

> It was passed by the Senate in 1911 and by the House in 1912. It states that Senators shall be elected directly by people of a state rather than state legislators. The first direct election of U.S. senators occurred in 1914.

19. Which amendment is this passage referring to? SS5CG3
    A. the Fifteenth Amendment
    B. the Twelfth Amendment
    C. the Seventeenth Amendment
    D. the Nineteenth Amendment

20. Why is competition good for consumers? SS5E3
    A. It makes prices much higher.
    B. It creates interest-free purchases
    C. It usually keeps prices low and quality high.
    D. It causes quality of goods to decrease.

21. Louis Armstrong was BEST known for being a SS5H4
    A. great jazz musician.
    B. famous baseball player.
    C. poet and novelist.
    D. fighter pilot.

22. If Mark wants to make sure that he spends less money than he makes, he should SS5E4
    A. apply for a loan.
    B. forget about saving.
    C. work two jobs.
    D. make a budget.

23. Which of the following is LEAST associated with a constitutional convention? SS5CG2
    A. a meeting between representatives from each state
    B. one way that amendments may be added to the Constitution
    C. possible changes to U.S. law
    D. a meeting between both houses of Congress

24. A group of nations was formed to protect each other if attacked by the Soviet Union. What was this organization called? SS5H7
    A. NAACP
    B. NATO
    C. militant movements
    D. the Allied Forces

25. What role did Hoovervilles play during the Great Depression? SS5H5
    A. They provided money, food, and employment to poor people.
    B. They were communities of poor, homeless people.
    C. They had no role during the Great Depression.
    D. They enlisted men to build homes for those in need.

26. What is it called when one region, business, or person focuses on producing one thing? SS5E1
    A. specialization
    B. voluntary exchange
    C. an embargo
    D. free trade

Use the map below to answer question numbers 26, 27, and 28.

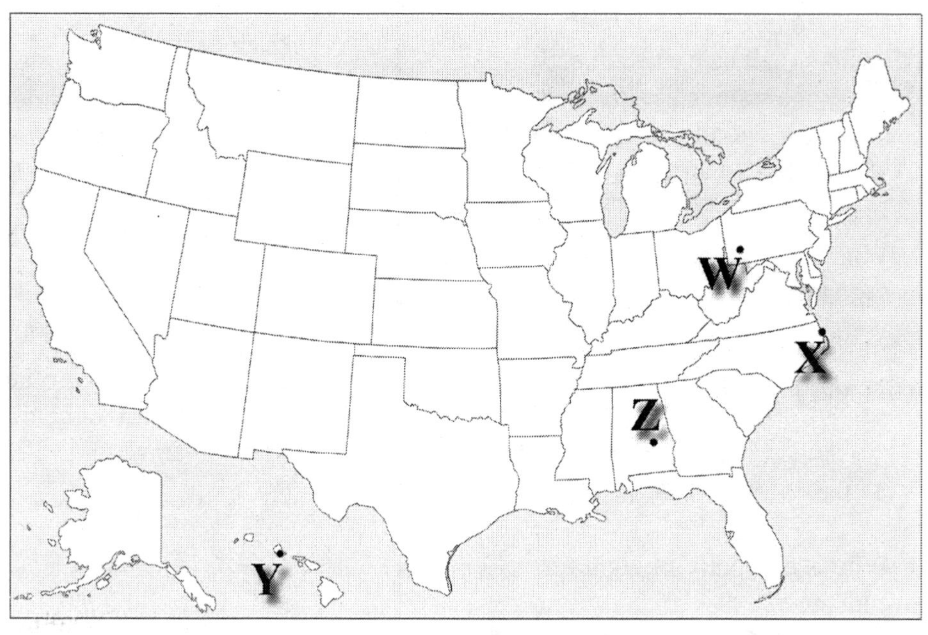

27. Which area depicted on the map is known for steel production? SS5G1

    A. W B. X C. Y D. Z

28. Which area depicted on the map was home to the FIRST powered airplane flight? SS5G1

    A. W B. X C. Y D. Z

29. Which region on the map became well known for its role in the civil rights movement? SS5G1

    A. W B. X C. Y D. Z

30. How did the assassination of Robert Kennedy impact the United States? SS5H8
    A. It signaled the end of the Vietnam War.
    B. It saddened many people who had hoped he would end the war in Vietnam.
    C. It did not impact the nation at all.
    D. It contributed to the nation's involvement in the Cuban Missile Crisis.

31. The Patriot Act and the Department of Homeland Security are SS5H9
    A. intended to protect the United States from terrorist attacks.
    B. things that led to the collapse of the Soviet Union.
    C. responsible for the September 11th attacks.
    D. intended to build weapons of mass destruction.

32. All male citizens are guaranteed the right to vote under the SS5CG3
    A. Twenty-third Amendment.
    B. Seventeenth Amendment.
    C. Fifteenth Amendment.
    D. Nineteenth Amendment.

33. How do banks help the U.S. economy? SS5E2
    A. by encouraging people to spend money
    B. by providing interest-free loans
    C. by loaning people money
    D. by keeping people out of debt

34. How did Alexander Graham Bell's invention impact the world? SS5H3
    A. It helped mail reach people much quicker.
    B. It allowed people to talk to one another over great distances.
    C. It led to the creation of the motion-picture industry.
    D. It made long-distance travel easier.

Read the list below, and answer the following question.

- freedom of the press
- freedom of religion
- freedom of speech

35. What is the BEST heading for the list above? SS5CG1
    A. Rights Guaranteed by the First Amendment
    B. Rights Guaranteed by the Third Amendment
    C. Examples of Civic Responsibilities
    D. Participation in the Political Process

36. If someone has a choice between two options, the loss of the option that he or she does not select is SS5E1
    A. economic incentive.
    B. opportunity cost.
    C. demand rate.
    D. free trade.

Read the passage below, and answer the following question.

> The army burned buildings, destroyed rail lines, set fire to factories, and demolished bridges. They hoped to end the South's ability to make and ship supplies, forcing them to surrender.

37. What is the passage above MOST LIKELY referring to? SS5H1

A. D-Day

B. Sherman's march to the sea

C. Battle of Gettysburg

D. attack on Fort Sumter

38. How did the Twenty-fourth Amendment contribute to increased voter participation by African Americans? SS5CG3

A. by making the poll tax illegal

B. by making it legal for eighteen-year-old males to vote

C. by allowing African American women to vote

D. by forbidding white males under age twenty-one to vote

39. Places constructed by humans are called SS5G1

A. physical features.

B. man-made features.

C. industrialization.

D. natural resources.

Read the list below, and answer the following question.

- A New Deal program
- Provided cheap electricity to the South
- Created many jobs
- Helped poor regions in the South prosper

40. What is the BEST heading for the list above? SS5H5

A. Social Security Act

B. Tennessee Valley Authority

C. Public Works Administration

D. Radical Reconstruction

41. The United States entered World War II after SS5H6

A. Japan attacked Pearl Harbor.

B. Hitler was planning an invasion of the United States.

C. Germany and Great Britain signed an alliance.

D. Hitler's troops invaded Poland.

42. Which of the following is MOST accurate in regard to the Sixth Amendment? SS5CG1

A. The government may charge excessive bail to guilty criminals.

B. Convicted criminals are able to choose their own punishment.

C. All powers given to the federal government belong to the citizens.

D. Citizens are guaranteed the right to a defense lawyer and a trial by jury.

Since 1900, various industries have thrived in different parts of the United States. For the following three questions, use the map below to locate primary industries.

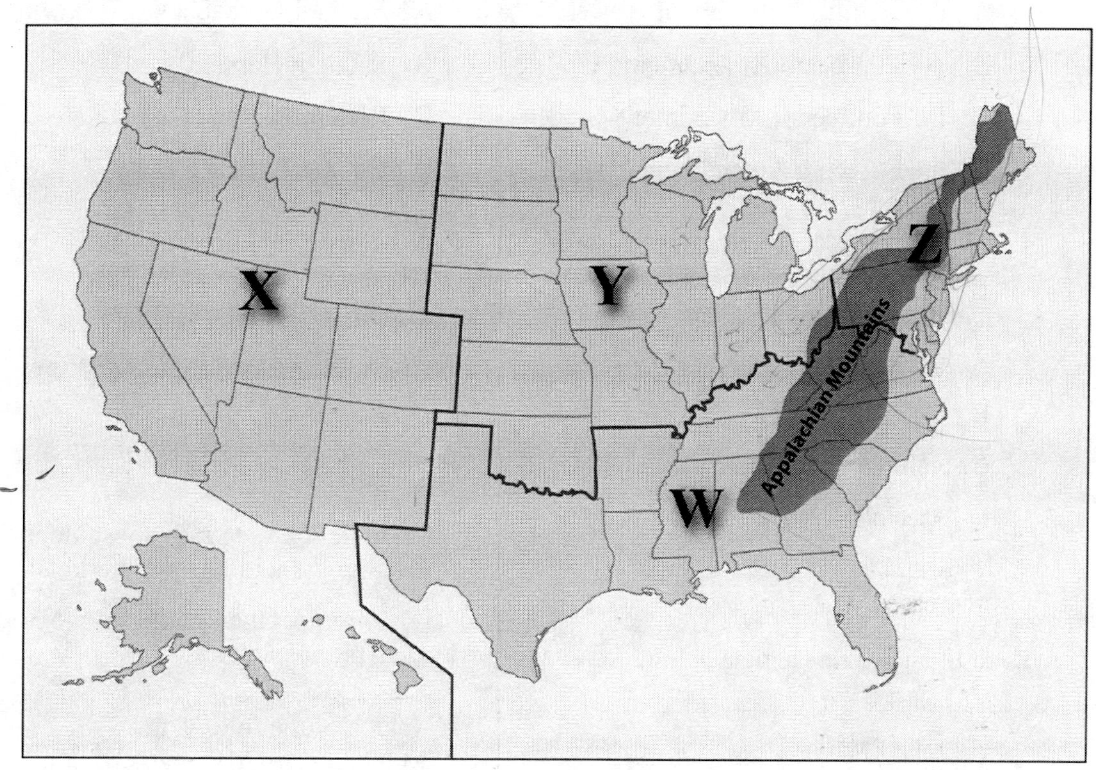

43. Which region has featured both textiles and agriculture? SS5G2

A. W B. X C. W and Y D. X and Z

44. Where have MOST banking, insurance, and manufacturing industries thrived? SS5G2

A. the Appalachian Mountains
B. X
C. Y
D. Z

45. In which area did coal mining become highly successful? SS5G2

A. X
B. Y
C. the Appalachian Mountains
D. Z

46. Which of the following was meant to protect African Americans' right to vote? SS5H2
   A. the Twelfth Amendment
   B. the Thirteenth Amendment
   C. the Fourteenth Amendment
   D. the Fifteenth Amendment

47. When producers freely choose to sell and consumers freely choose to buy, it is called SS5E1
   A. competition.
   B. a closed market.
   C. voluntary exchange.
   D. specialization.

Read the magazine article below.

It was the closest the world ever came to nuclear war. The United States armed forces were at their highest state of readiness ever, and Soviet field commanders were prepared to use battlefield nuclear weapons to defend the island.

48. Which of the following is the magazine article referring to? SS5H8
   A. the Korean War
   B. the Vietcong
   C. the Cuban Missile Crisis
   D. nuclear arms race

49. Whose policies contributed MOST to the collapse of the Soviet Union? SS5H9
   A. Mikhail Gorbachev
   B. Saddam Hussein
   C. Richard Nixon
   D. George Bush

50. What was the purpose of the Chisholm and Great Western Cattle Trails? SS5H3
   A. to sell cows to people in small towns
   B. to move cows west for better grazing lands
   C. to get cows to railway stations to ship them to Eastern markets
   D. to protect their cattle from Native American attacks

51. Which of the following MOST LIKELY supported states' rights in 1860? SS5H1
   A. a southern leader
   B. a Radical Republican
   C. an abolitionist
   D. Abraham Lincoln

52. The national body of laws that form the framework of the United States government is called SS5CG1
   A. the Bill of Rights.
   B. the U.S. Constitution.
   C. *E pluribus unum.*
   D. the Electoral College.

Use the map below to answer the following question.

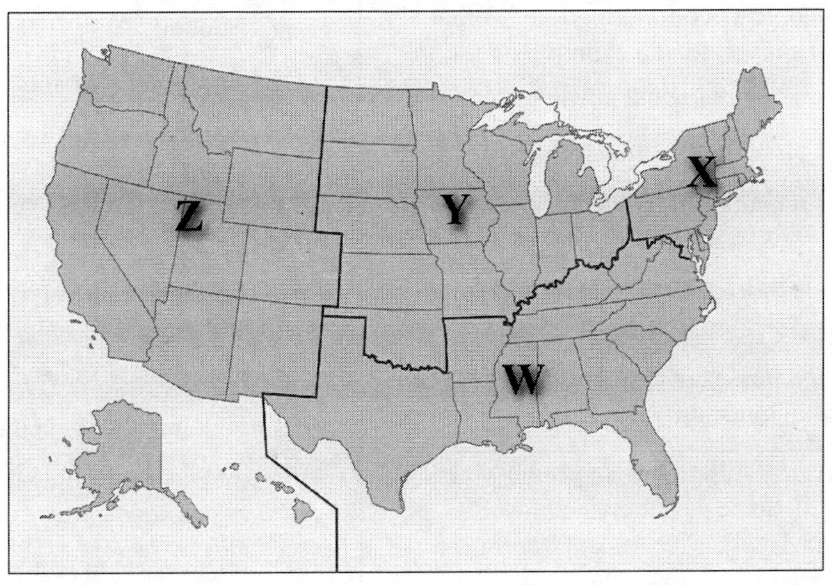

53. In which area did tobacco, cotton, and sawmills flourish? SS5G2

A. W B. X C. Y D. Z

54. Which of the following served as FIRST secretary of the USSR's Communist Party during the 1950s and '60s? SS5H7

A. Benito Mussolini

B. Joseph McCarthy

C. Nikita Khrushchev

D. Joseph Stalin

55. Who was the FIRST person to fly a solo flight nonstop across the Atlantic Ocean? SS5H4

A. Charles Lindbergh

B. Zora Neale Hurston

C. Langston Hughes

D. Woodrow Wilson

56. The Twelfth Amendment was ratified in 1804. What was the MAIN purpose of this amendment? SS5CG3

A. to ensure that all males over the age of eighteen could vote

B. to limit immigration into the United States

C. to avoid confusion concerning the offices of president and vice president

D. to ensure U.S. senators were elected directly by citizens

57. Eli Whitney's cotton gin made cotton processing much faster and cheaper. It led the South to become a "cotton kingdom." What is Eli's invention an example of? SS5E1

A. a technological advancement

B. an item to be traded freely

C. an opportunity cost of World War II

D. a tariff

Read the passage below, and answer the following question.

> Over six million Jewish people were killed. Some were executed immediately, while others were shipped to camps. In the camps, they were forced to work, and they were often brutally tortured. This was part of Hitler's plan to exterminate the Jewish race.

58. What is the passage above referring to? SS5H6

A. Hiroshima

B. the Holocaust

C. World War I

D. D-Day

59. On Election Day, Jack goes to his county office to cast his vote. Jack is SS5CG1

A. obeying the Ninth Amendment.

B. fulfilling a civic responsibility.

C. having his civil rights violated.

D. paying his taxes.

60. Who was the attorney who won the *Brown v. Board of Education* case? SS5H8

A. Malcolm X

B. Thurgood Marshall

C. Douglas McCarthy

D. Robert Nixon

61. What was the primary purpose of the Thirteenth Amendment? SS5H2

A. give money to newly freed slaves

B. guarantee women the right to vote

C. make slavery illegal in the United States

D. make African Americans citizens

62. Which amendment states that all U.S. citizens who are at least eighteen years old have the right to vote? SS5CG3

A. the Seventeenth Amendment

B. the Nineteenth Amendment

C. the Twenty-third Amendment

D. the Twenty-sixth Amendment

63. Which of the following attacks started the Civil War? SS5H1

A. Gettysburg

B. Fort Sumter

C. Appomattox

D. Bull Run

64. Duke Ellington became famous for his contributions in SS5H5

A. writing.

B. sports.

C. jazz.

D. acting.

65. What is the BEST heading for the list below? SS5G2

- large working population
- availability of natural resources
- access to rivers, lakes, or coastlines

A. Negative Factors That Caused a Decline in Industrialization

B. Reasons the Midwest Became the First Industrialized Region

C. Positive Factors That Influenced Industrial Locations

D. Led to the Development of Agriculture in Boston and New York

66. Which amendment states that the government must obey certain rules when charging someone with a crime? SS5H1

A. the Second Amendment

B. the Third Amendment

C. the Fourth Amendment

D. the Fifth Amendment

67. How did sharecropping MOST LIKELY affect African Americans? SS5H2

A. made them feel equal to white southerners

B. made them wealthy landowners

C. continued to oppress them as they provided labor to white landowners

D. led them to protest violently against white landowners

68. What is the following quote describing? SS5H1

> It was a fictional story that was published in 1852. It showed the cruelty of slavery. Many people became very angry and even more determined to end slavery. This fueled the abolitionist movement.

A. The Freedmen's Bureau

B. Harpers Ferry

C. *Uncle Tom's Cabin*

D. march to the sea

69. What was a major contribution of George Washington Carver? SS5H3

A. sharecropping

B. invention of the electrical plow

C. crop rotation

D. designed the first tractor

70. During the early twentieth century, who greatly contributed to the mass production of the automobile? SS5H4

A. Langston Hughes

B. Henry Ford

C. Harry Truman

D. Zora Neale Hurston

Numerics

A

B

C

D

E

F

Mastering the Georgia 5th Grade CRCT in Social Studies

Answer Key

August 2008

American Book Company
PO Box 2638
Woodstock, GA 30188-1383
Toll Free: 1 (888) 264-5877 Phone: (770) 928-2834
Fax: (770) 928-7483 Toll Free Fax: 1 (866) 827-3240
www.americanbookcompany.com

Georgia 5 CRCT Social Studies Standards Chart

Georgia 5 CRCT Social Studies

Chart of Standards

The following chart correlates each question on the Diagnostic Test, Practice Test 1, and Practice Test 2 to the Georgia 5 CRCT competency goals ***standards and benchmarks published by the Georgia Department of Education***. These test questions are also correlated with chapters in *Georgia 5 CRCT Social Studies*.

Chapter Number	Diagnostic Test Questions	Practice Test 1 Questions	Practice Test 2 Questions
Historical Understandings			
SS5H1 The student will explain the causes, major events, and consequences of the Civil War. a. Identify Uncle Tom's Cabin and John Brown's raid on Harper's Ferry and explain how each of these events was related to the Civil War. b. Discuss how the issues of states' rights and slavery increased tensions between the North and South. c. Identify major battles and campaigns: Fort Sumter, Gettysburg, the Atlanta Campaign, Sherman's March to the Sea, and Appomattox Court House. d. Describe the roles of Abraham Lincoln, Robert E. Lee, Ulysses S. Grant, Jefferson Davis, and Thomas "Stonewall" Jackson. e. Describe the effects of war on the North and South.			
1	2, 20, 37, 43, 52, 70	15, 40, 55, 67	2, 15, 37, 51, 63, 66, 68
SS5H2 The student will analyze the effects of Reconstruction on American life. a. Describe the purpose of the 13th, 14th, and 15th Amendments. b. Explain the work of the Freedmen's Bureau. c. Explain how slavery was replaced by sharecropping and how African Americans were prevented from exercising their newly won rights; include a discussion of Jim Crow laws and customs.			
1	13, 25, 53, 55	7, 20, 37, 48, 62	16, 46, 61, 67

Standards Chart

<table>
<tr><td colspan="4">SS5H3 The student will describe how life changed in America at the turn of the century.
a. Describe the role of the cattle trails in the late 19th century; include the Black Cowboys of Texas, the Great Western Cattle Trail, and the Chisholm Trail.
b. Describe the impact on American life of the Wright brothers (flight), George Washington Carver (science), Alexander Graham Bell (communication), and Thomas Edison (electricity).
c. Explain how William McKinley and Theodore Roosevelt expanded America's role in the world; include the Spanish-American War and the building of the Panama Canal.
d. Describe the reasons people emigrated to the United States, from where they emigrated, and where they settled.</td></tr>
<tr><td>2</td><td>19, 26, 49, 57</td><td>26, 35, 53, 64</td><td>34, 50, 69</td></tr>
<tr><td colspan="4">SS5H4 The student will describe U.S. involvement in World War I and post-World War I America.
a. Explain how German attacks on U.S. shipping during the war in Europe (1914 – 1917) ultimately led the U.S. to join the fight against Germany; include the sinking of the Lusitania and concerns over safety of U.S. ships.
b. Describe the cultural developments and individual contributions in the 1920s of the Jazz Age (Louis Armstrong), the Harlem Renaissance (Langston Hughes), baseball (Babe Ruth), the automobile (Henry Ford), and the airplane (Charles Lindbergh).</td></tr>
<tr><td>2</td><td>14, 29, 46, 58</td><td>17, 28, 38, 60</td><td>8, 18, 21, 55, 70</td></tr>
<tr><td colspan="4">SS5H5 The student will explain how the Great Depression and New Deal affected the lives of millions of Americans.
a. Discuss the Stock Market Crash of 1929, Herbert Hoover, Franklin Roosevelt, the Dust Bowl, and soup kitchens.
b. Analyze the main features of the New Deal; include the significance of the Civilian Conservation Corps, Works Progress Administration, and the Tennessee Valley Authority.
c. Discuss important cultural elements of the 1930s; include Duke Ellington, Margaret Mitchell, and Jesse Owens.</td></tr>
<tr><td>3</td><td>3, 30, 59, 66</td><td>2, 30, 45, 57</td><td>3, 25, 40, 64</td></tr>
<tr><td colspan="4">SS5H6 The student will explain the reasons for America's involvement in World War II.
a. Describe Germany's aggression in Europe and Japan's aggression in Asia.
b. Describe major events in the war in both Europe and the Pacific; include Pearl Harbor, Iwo Jima, D-Day, VE and VJ Days, and the Holocaust.
c. Discuss President Truman's decision to drop the atomic bombs on Hiroshima and Nagasaki.
d. Identify Roosevelt, Stalin, Churchill, Hirohito, Truman, Mussolini, and Hitler.
e. Describe the effects of rationing and the changing role of women and African Americans; include "Rosie the Riveter" and the Tuskegee Airmen.
f. Explain the U.S. role in the formation of the United Nations.</td></tr>
<tr><td>3</td><td>10, 36, 45</td><td>3, 14, 47, 68, 70</td><td>5, 14, 17, 41, 58</td></tr>
</table>

Georgia 5 CRCT Social Studies

<table>
<tr><td colspan="4">SS5H7 The student will discuss the origins and consequences of the Cold War.
a. Explain the origin and meaning of the term “Iron Curtain.”
b. Explain how the United States sought to stop the spread of communism through the Berlin airlift, the Korean War, and the North Atlantic Treaty Organization.
c. Identify Joseph McCarthy and Nikita Khrushchev.</td></tr>
<tr><td>4</td><td>4, 22, 40, 51</td><td>8, 29, 52</td><td>4, 24, 54</td></tr>
<tr><td colspan="4">SS5H8 The student will describe the importance of key people, events, and developments between 1950 – 1975.
a. Discuss the importance of the Cuban Missile Crisis and the Vietnam War.
b. Explain the key events and people of the Civil Rights movement; include Brown v. Board of Education (1954), Montgomery Bus Boycott, the March on Washington, Civil Rights Act, Voting Rights Act, and civil rights activities of Thurgood Marshall, Rosa Parks, and Martin Luther King, Jr.
c. Describe the impact on American society of the assassinations of President John F. Kennedy, Robert F. Kennedy, and Martin Luther King, Jr.
d. Discuss the significance of the technologies of television and space exploration.</td></tr>
<tr><td>4</td><td>17, 27, 50, 62</td><td>11, 31, 50, 65</td><td>11, 30, 48, 60</td></tr>
<tr><td colspan="4">SS5H9 The student will trace important developments in America since 1975.
a. Describe U.S. involvement in world events; include efforts to bring peace to the Middle East, the collapse of the Soviet Union, Persian Gulf War, and the War on Terrorism in response to September 11, 2001.
b. Explain the impact the development of the personal computer and Internet has had on American life.</td></tr>
<tr><td>5</td><td>8, 32, 54</td><td>12, 34</td><td>31, 49</td></tr>
<tr><td colspan="4">Geographic Understandings</td></tr>
<tr><td colspan="4">SS5G1 The student will locate important places in the United States.
a. Locate important physical features; include the Grand Canyon, Salton Sea, Great Salt Lake, and the Mojave Desert.
b. Locate important man-made places; include the Chisholm Trail; Pittsburgh, PA; Gettysburg, PA; Kitty Hawk, NC; Pearl Harbor, HI; and Montgomery, AL.</td></tr>
<tr><td>6</td><td>15, 24, 42, 60, 63, 67, 69</td><td>9, 22, 23, 24, 44, 56</td><td>27, 28, 29, 39</td></tr>
<tr><td colspan="4">SS5G2 The student will explain the reasons for the spatial patterns of economic activities.
a. Identify and explain the factors influencing industrial location in the United States after the Civil War.
b. Define, map, and explain the dispersion of the primary economic activities within the United States since the turn of the century.
c. Map and explain how the dispersion of global economic activities contributed to the United States emerging from World War I as a world power.</td></tr>
<tr><td>6</td><td>7, 28, 44</td><td>4, 16, 39, 54</td><td>12, 43, 44, 45, 53, 65</td></tr>
</table>

Standards Chart

<table>
<tr><th colspan="4">Government/Civic Understandings</th></tr>
<tr><td colspan="4">SS5CG1 The student will explain how a citizen's rights are protected under the U.S. Constitution.
a. Explain the responsibilities of a citizen.
b. Explain the freedoms granted by the Bill of Rights.
c. Explain the concept of due process of law.
d. Describe how the Constitution protects a citizen's rights by due process.</td></tr>
<tr><td>7</td><td>6, 21, 38, 61, 64</td><td>13, 21, 41, 51, 61, 66</td><td>13, 35, 42, 52, 59</td></tr>
<tr><td colspan="4">SS5CG2 The student will explain the process by which amendments to the U.S. Constitution are made.
a. Explain the amendment process outlined in the Constitution.
b. Describe the purpose for the amendment process.</td></tr>
<tr><td>7</td><td>18, 35</td><td>10</td><td>9, 23</td></tr>
<tr><td colspan="4">SS5CG3 The student will explain how amendments to the U.S. constitution have maintained a representative democracy.
a. Explain the purpose of the 12th and 17th amendments.
b. Explain how voting rights were protected by the 15th, 19th, 23rd, 24th, and 26th amendments.</td></tr>
<tr><td>7</td><td>1, 12, 33, 41, 48, 65</td><td>1, 6, 19, 32, 43, 58, 69</td><td>1, 7, 19, 32, 38, 56, 62</td></tr>
<tr><th colspan="4">Economic Understandings</th></tr>
<tr><td colspan="4">SS5E1 The student will use the basic economic concepts of trade, opportunity cost, specialization, voluntary exchange, productivity, and price incentives to illustrate historical events.
a. Describe opportunity costs and their relationship to decision-making across time (such as decisions to remain unengaged at the beginning of World War II in Europe).
b. Explain how price incentives affect people's behavior and choices (such as monetary policy during the Great Depression).
c. Describe how specialization improves standards of living, (such as how specific economies in the north and south developed at the beginning of the 20th century).
d. Explain how voluntary exchange helps both buyers and sellers (such as among the G8 countries).
e. Describe how trade promotes economic activity (such as trade activities today under NAFTA).
f. Give examples of technological advancements and their impact on business productivity during the development of the United States.</td></tr>
<tr><td>8</td><td>9, 23, 47, 56, 68</td><td>18, 36, 49, 59, 63</td><td>10, 26, 36, 47, 57</td></tr>
</table>

Georgia 5 CRCT Social Studies

<table>
<tr><td colspan="4">SS5E2 The student will describe the functions of the three major institutions in the U.S. economy in each era of United States history.
a. Describe the private business function in producing goods and services.
b. Describe the bank function in providing checking accounts, savings accounts, and loans.
c. Describe the government function in taxation and providing certain goods and services.</td></tr>
<tr><td>8</td><td>11, 39</td><td>5, 33</td><td>6, 33</td></tr>
<tr><td colspan="4">SS5E3 The student will describe how consumers and businesses interact in the United States economy across time.
a. Describe how competition, markets, and prices influence people's behavior.
b. Describe how people earn income by selling their labor to businesses.
c. Describe how entrepreneurs take risks to develop new goods and services to start a business.</td></tr>
<tr><td>8</td><td>16, 31</td><td>25, 42</td><td>20</td></tr>
<tr><td colspan="4">SS5E4 The student will identify the elements of a personal budget and explain why personal spending and saving decisions are important.</td></tr>
<tr><td>8</td><td>5, 34</td><td>27, 46</td><td>22</td></tr>
</table>

Standards Chart

Diagnostic Test

Pages

1. B	11. B	21. A	31. B	41. A	51. B	61. A
2. A	12. D	22. B	32. D	42. B	52. B	62. C
3. D	13. A	23. A	33. A	43. B	53. C	63. A
4. C	14. C	24. C	34. A	44. A	54. C	64. A
5. B	15. B	25. A	35. C	45. B	55. A	65. B
6. D	16. C	26. B	36. C	46. B	56. D	66. A
7. C	17. B	27. C	37. D	47. B	57. A	67. B
8. B	18. B	28. C	38. B	48. B	58. C	68. C
9. A	19. A	29. C	39. B	49. D	59. B	69. D
10. A	20. A	30. A	40. B	50. A	60. B	70. B

CHAPTER 1: HISTORICAL UNDERSTANDINGS: THE CIVIL WAR AND RECONSTRUCTION

Practice 1.1: Causes of the Civil War

Page 22

1. B 2. A

3. John Brown was a white abolitionist. He thought the only way to end slavery was through force. That night, he led a group of his friends to take over a United States arsenal at Harpers Ferry, Virginia. Brown wanted to give weapons to slaves who could then use them to fight for their freedom. The plan failed when Union troops surrounded the arsenal. The soldiers killed some of Brown's men and captured Brown. The government hanged Brown just a few days later. Many northerners called Brown a hero. Southerners thought he was an example of how radical abolitionists had become. More and more slaveholders began to believe that it would take bloodshed to protect the South's way of life.
4. In 1852, Stowe published a book called *Uncle Tom's Cabin*. It was a fictional story that showed how cruel slavery truly was. The story made many people angry. Northerners became even more determined to abolish slavery. Southerners, on the other hand, were angry and said that not all slave owners treated their slaves cruelly.
5. The power of the states should be greater than the power of the federal government.

Practice 1.2: The Civil War

Page 28

1. C 2. B

3. The war affected the northern and southern economies differently in that the North prospered. Its manufacturing and industries grew and more people were employed as the Union worked to support its war effort. The southern economy, on the other hand, suffered. The South had depended on cash crops. The end of slavery meant that it no longer had its main source of labor. Since most of the fighting took place in the South, many of the region's farms and industries had been destroyed. At the end of the war, the North had grown stronger. The South faced an uncertain future.

Practice 1.3: Reconstruction

Page 31

1. A 2. B 3. B

4. They put in place black codes and systems like sharecropping to keep African Americans living like slaves on white-owned land. They often used violence. They used Jim Crow laws and creative laws to disenfranchise blacks: poll taxes, literacy tests.
5. It was the first federal relief agency in US history. The Freedmen's Bureau provided clothes, medical attention, food, education, and even land to African Americans coming out of slavery.

Chapter 1 Review

Key Terms, People, and Concepts

Pages 32 – 34

slavery – the capturing, selling, and ownership of black Africans. American colonists began buying slaves in 1619. Slaves lived very hard lives and were often treated badly. Until 1776, all American colonies had slaves. The North and South became divided over the issue of slavery. The Civil War ended legal slavery in 1865.

cash crops – crops grown in large amounts so that they could be sold and traded both at home and overseas. Tobacco, rice, indigo, and sugar were important southern cash crops.

cotton gin - a machine that made processing cotton much faster. It was invented in the 1790s by Eli Whitney.

cotton – the South's most important cash crop. Cotton made many southern landowners wealthy. Slavery was important to the southern cotton industry.

plantations – the huge farms on which large southern landowners raised their cash crops. Plantations required a lot of labor. Plantation owners relied on slaves to work the fields and harvest crops. They also used slaves for many other tasks, such as cooking, cleaning, and helping to run the plantation.

abolished - doing away with slavery. By the middle of the nineteenth century, many northern states had abolished slavery.

slave states – During the fight over slavery, most southern states became slave states.

free states – During the debate over slavery, most northern states became free states.

Missouri Compromise – was established to settle the issue of slavery in the North. The Missouri Compromise allowed Missouri to enter the Union as a slave state while Maine entered as a free state. It also stated that all future states admitted north of Missouri's southern border would be free states. All those admitted south of the same border would be slave states. The Missouri Compromise helped keep peace between those who opposed slavery and those who supported it.

Compromise of 1850 – allowed California to enter the Union as a free state. It also let people in the Utah and New Mexico territories decide the issue by popular sovereignty.

popular sovereignty – After the Compromise of 1850, people in Utah and New Mexico were allowed to vote on whether or not to allow slavery. This was called popular sovereignty.

Fugitive Slave Law – stated that northerners must return runaway slaves to their southern masters. Many northerners did not like the law and did not obey it.

abolitionist movement – existed in the North by the 1850s. Abolitionists wanted to end slavery. Both whites and blacks took part.

Harriet Beecher Stowe – one of the most famous abolitionists of all time. In 1852, Stowe published a book called *Uncle Tom's Cabin.*

Uncle Tom's Cabin – a fictional story that showed the cruelty of slavery. The story made many people angry. Abolitionists became even more determined to end slavery. They believed that all slaves were treated as badly as those in *Uncle Tom's Cabin.* Slaveowners believed that *Uncle Tom's Cabin* did not present the truth. They were angry and argued that not all slaves were treated cruelly.

Kansas-Nebraska Act – a law that was passed in 1854. The law said that people in the Kansas and Nebraska territories could decide by popular sovereignty whether or not to have slaves. This upset a lot of people because, under the Missouri Compromise, these territories were supposed to be free. The Kansas-Nebraska Act only increased the tension between the North and South.

Bleeding Kansas – Soon after the Kansas-Nebraska Act was passed, Kansans who supported slavery and those who were against it began fighting. The violence was so bad that the territory became known as Bleeding Kansas.

Dred Scott decision – After his master died, a slave named Dred Scott sued for his freedom. The United States Supreme Court ruled that Scott was not a citizen and had no right to sue. The Court also stated that a slave master could keep his or her slaves even if they entered a free state. Abolitionists were furious, but many southerners were very pleased with this decision.

John Brown's Raid – took place in 1859. John Brown was a white abolitionist. He thought the only way to end slavery was through force, and he raided the United States arsenal at Harpers Ferry, Virginia. Brown wanted to give the weapons to slaves who could use them to fight for freedom. The plan failed when Union troops surrounded the arsenal. The soldiers killed some of the raiders and captured Brown. The government hanged John Brown just a few days later. Many northerners called Brown a hero. Southern slave owners thought he was an example of how radical abolitionists had become.

states' rights – Southern leaders defended slavery by arguing for states' rights. Those who preached states' rights believed that the federal government could not tell states what to do. They believed that the Founding Fathers wanted the states to have most of the governing power, not the central government. Supporters of states' rights saw federal attempts to limit slavery as unlawful acts.

presidential election of 1860 – Slavery was the main issue of the election of 1860. The Democratic Party split. Northern Democrats supported Stephen Douglas, who favored popular sovereignty. Southern Democrats wanted a pro-slavery candidate. Republicans hoped to stop the spread of slavery into new territories. Some of them were even abolitionists.

Abraham Lincoln – Southerners did not want Lincoln as president because they feared he would seek to end slavery. Shortly after Lincoln won the election, South Carolina left the Union. Other states soon followed.

Confederate States of America – the southern states that left the Union after Lincoln won the election of 1860. The states were South Carolina, Mississippi, Alabama, Georgia, Florida, Louisiana, and Texas. They declared themselves a new nation, the Confederate States of America.

Fort Sumter – In 1861, the Union had troops at Fort Sumter, South Carolina. The Confederates opened fire on the fort, forcing the Union troops to surrender and leave. By attacking Fort Sumter, the Confederacy made many Northerners angry. They now viewed the Union as under attack. This gave Lincoln the support that he needed for war.

Civil War – The Civil War began after the attack on Fort Sumter. Lincoln called for 75,000 volunteers to fight for the Union. The Confederacy called for volunteers as well. Slave states that had not yet seceded had to decide which side to support. Kentucky, Maryland, Missouri, and the western portions of Virginia voted to stay with the Union. North Carolina, Arkansas, Tennessee, and most of Virginia joined the Confederacy. The Union won the war in 1865. The Civil War ended legal slavery.

First Battle of Bull Run – the first major battle of the Civil War. It occurred near Bull Run Creek in 1861. It was also called the First Battle of Manassas. It was a surprising loss for the Union. The Confederacy defeated the Union Army and could have invaded Washington if its troops had been better trained. First Bull Run showed both sides that the war would not be so short after all.

Robert E. Lee – a Confederate General. In 1862, he tried to invade the North. He did a good job of keeping his invasion a secret, until Union soldiers found a copy of his plans in an abandoned camp. The Union stopped Lee's invasion at the Battle of Antietam.

Battle of Antietam – the bloodiest single day of the war. The battle occurred in Maryland. The Union stopped Lee's invasion, forcing the Confederates to retreat into Virginia. The victory gave Lincoln the support he needed to issue the Emancipation Proclamation.

Emancipation Proclamation – an executive order that declared the slaves in the Confederate states free. It did not grant freedom to slaves in states loyal to the Union. That was because Lincoln still needed the support of these states to win the war. Once the Emancipation Proclamation became known, many African Americans volunteered to fight in the Union military.

Battle of Gettysburg – the bloodiest battle of the entire war. It occurred in early June 1863. Lee's Confederate Army met the army of Union General George Meade. Roughly 50,000 men died or were wounded. The Union won the battle, ending Lee's last attempt to invade the North. Four months after the battle, President Lincoln stood on the battlefield and gave a speech known as the Gettysburg Address.

Gettysburg Address – a famous speech made by President Lincoln. He gave the speech at the battlefield of Gettysburg. He honored the men who had died there and expressed his hope that the war would soon end and the nation be healed.

Ulysses S. Grant – appointed overall commander of the entire Union army in 1864 by Lincoln. **William T. Sherman** – in charge of Grant's western Union forces. In May, Sherman began an invasion of Georgia. Sherman captured Atlanta in September of 1864.

Atlanta Campaign – After taking Atlanta, Sherman ordered much of the city burned. Sherman's capture of Atlanta placed the city under Union control. It also increased support for President Lincoln in the North. After Sherman's success, northerners believed the war could be won and re-elected Lincoln.

March to the Sea – Sherman's march from Atlanta to Savannah. Sherman's army burned buildings, destroyed rail lines, set fire to factories, and demolished bridges. Sherman hoped to end the South's ability to make and ship supplies. Without supplies, the South would have to surrender. People in Savannah were so scared by news of the destruction that they surrendered to Sherman without a fight.

Appomattox Courthouse - On April 9, 1865 Robert E. Lee surrendered to Ulysses S. Grant at Appomattox Courthouse in Virginia. Although some fighting continued afterwards, this effectively ended the war.

major effects of the Civil War – Thousands of young men from the North and the South died or were wounded during the war. Both sides experienced great human suffering.

Economically, the North prospered. Manufacturing and industries grew and more people were employed as the Union worked to support its war effort. The southern economy suffered. The South had depended on cash crops. The end of slavery meant that it no longer had its main source of labor. Since most of the fighting took place in the South, many of the region's farms, railroads, and industries had been destroyed.

Andrew Johnson – After Lincoln was assassinated, Andrew Johnson became president.

Radical Republicans – a group of congressmen who wanted to force the South to accept strict conditions before rejoining the Union. They also wanted to protect the rights of newly freed African Americans in the southern states.

Reconstruction – the process of rebuilding the South after the Civil War.

Thirteenth Amendment – In 1865, Congress and the states ratified the Thirteenth Amendment. It made slavery illegal throughout the United States. Eventually, the Radical Republicans won control of reconstruction and passed two other key amendments.

Fourteenth Amendment – made African Americans citizens.

Fifteenth Amendment – guaranteed all men the right to vote, no matter what their race.

Freedmen's Bureau – the first federal relief agency in US history. The Freedmen's Bureau provided clothes, medical attention, food, education, and even land to African Americans coming out of slavery. It helped many freed African Americans throughout the South, but lacking support, it ended in 1869.

black codes – laws that made it illegal for African Americans to live or work in certain areas. They also allowed African Americans who were not working to be arrested and forced to work for white landowners. Black codes kept blacks living like slaves by keeping them on the plantations. These codes were later outlawed under Radical Reconstruction.

sharecropping – African American sharecroppers farmed land owned by white landowners. In exchange, they were given a place to live and a portion of the crop. Sharecroppers often fell victim to dishonest landlords who cheated them and treated them like slaves. Unable to pay their debts, sharecroppers often remained chained to the land and forced to provide labor for white landowners.

Ku Klux Klan – The Klan was a secretive organization that dressed in hooded white robes. It used threats, violence, and murder to intimidate blacks and those who helped them. The Klan often practiced lynchings.

Compromise of 1877 – The presidential election of 1876 was settled the following year by a political compromise known as the Compromise of 1877. Democrats agreed to allow the Republican, Rutherford Hayes, to become president. In exchange, the Republican-led federal government agreed to end reconstruction. The compromise allowed southern states to have more authority over their own affairs.

Jim Crow laws – laws passed by southern states soon after the Compromise of 1877. These laws legalized segregation by requiring whites and blacks to use separate facilities.

segregation – separation of races.

disenfranchise – to keep from voting. Southern whites wanted to keep blacks from voting. blacks. They found creative ways to keep them from voting such as poll taxes, literacy tests, and grandfather clauses.

poll taxes – required people to pay to vote. Since most African Americans were poor, many of them could not afford to pay the tax. This kept blacks from voting.

literacy tests – Voters had to prove they could read and write. African Americans were often uneducated and had a hard time passing these tests. This kept blacks from voting.

grandfather clauses – stated that men whose ancestors had voted before or whose ancestors had served in the Confederate military could vote without having to pass a literacy test or pay a poll tax. Since it was usually only whites who met these conditions, grandfather clauses allowed poor, illiterate whites to vote while still keeping most blacks from voting.

Multiple Choice

1. C 2. B 3. A 4. D 5. C 6. C 7. B 8. B 9. C 10. D

CHAPTER 2: HISTORICAL UNDERSTANDINGS: THE TURN OF THE CENTURY, WORLD WAR I, AND THE 1920S

Practice 2.1: The Turn of the Century

Page 40

1. C 2. B 3. C

4. George Washington Carver was one of the first African Americans to make great contributions in science. He is greatly remembered for his crop rotation system and finding new uses for the peanut.

Practice 2.2: America's Expanding Role in the World

Page 46

1. B 2. A

3. Immigrants are people who move to the US from other countries. Nativists did not like immigrants because they feared they'd take their jobs and they did not trust their foreign ways.

Practice 2.3: World War I and the 1920s

Page 51

1. D 2. B

3. Henry Ford invented a new kind of engine. It was powered by fuel rather than steam. His cars didn't cost as much to make. Ford also introduced the idea of mass producing cars. To accomplish his goal, Ford introduced a new kind of assembly line. Unlike earlier assembly lines that required workers to walk from station to station, Ford's brought the parts to the workers. His employees could stand in one spot while the parts came to them. This made the work much faster and increased production. Ford also paid his employees $5 a day (a good salary back then) so that they could also afford to buy his cars. Henry Ford's first mass-produced car was known as the Model T. It revolutionized the auto industry. Meanwhile, Ford's ideas about mass production and his assembly line helped make other businesses better as well.

Chapter 2 Review

Key Terms, People, and Concepts

Pages 52 – 54

turn of the century – The end of the nineteenth century and the beginning of the twentieth was a time of great change in the United States. Many people moved west to claim land and seek opportunities. Many settlers became farmers. They took advantage of new inventions like the steel plow, mechanical reaper, and windmill to farm the Great Plains and other parts of the Midwest. Others became miners. Following the discovery of gold in California and other parts of the West, many settlers moved to these regions hoping to strike it rich.

reservations – The US government forced Native Americans to move to special areas so that whites could have their land. Each time settlers discovered gold or white citizens demanded more land, these same Native Americans were often forced to move again. The government constantly broke promises to Native American tribes as it forced them to give up more and more territory. This caused several wars between the US Army and Native Americans.

Battle of Little Bighorn – a battle that occurred in 1876 between Native Americans and the United States Army. A US commander named George Armstrong Custer thought he could surprise and defeat a band of Sioux warriors. Custer had only a few hundred men. He did not know that the Sioux had thousands. He and the men under his command rushed recklessly into battle. They were quickly surrounded and killed by the Sioux.

Custer's last stand – the name given to the Native American Victory at the Battle of Little Bighorn. It was the last major victory for Native Americans over US forces.

Cowboys – became legendary figures in US history during the late 1800s. Cowboys drove large herds of cattle from ranches to towns and markets where they could be shipped and sold.

cattle drives – journeys taken to drive cattle herds to markets. They could often take days or weeks.

black cowboys – common in places like Texas. Often, these black cowboys were freed slaves who made their way west following the Civil War.

cattle trails – developed during the late 1800s. Cattle trails were known routes used by cowboys to drive cattle great distances.

Chisholm Trail – a cattle trail that ran from Texas, north through Oklahoma and into Kansas. Texas cowboys used it to drive herds to Kansas towns where the cattle could then be loaded onto trains and shipped east to market.

Great Western Cattle Trail – another famous path used by cowboys. It ran from Texas to Kansas, ending in Dodge City. Cowboys relied on the Great Western Cattle Trail to get their herds to railway stations so that the cattle could be transported by train.

Wilbur and Orville Wright – Two brothers who built the world's first successful airplane. Orville piloted their first flight. It was short (only twelve seconds), but it marked the beginning of air travel. Planes eventually made travel much easier and faster for everyday citizens.

Alexander Graham Bell – During the 1870s, he invented the telephone. His telephone greatly improved communication by allowing people to talk to one another despite being separated by great distances.

Thomas Edison – an inventor who was interested in sound. While trying to improve the telegraph machine, he discovered how to record spoken words. Edison named his new invention the phonograph. Later, he invented the motion picture camera as well. He is most famous for inventing the electric light bulb.

electric light bulb – Thomas Edison invented the electric light bulb. The light bulb changed business and how people lived. Before Edison's light bulb, people could only work in the daytime or by the dim light of oil lamps. After the invention of the light bulb, factories could stay open later. More goods were produced. People could enjoy more nighttime entertainment and stay up later.

George Washington Carver – one of the first African Americans to make great contributions in science. He developed the crop rotation method.

crop rotation method – George Washington Carver invented the crop rotation method. Carver taught growers to plant crops that enriched the soil every other year. In between cotton crops, farmers planted peanuts, peas, soybeans, sweet potatoes, and pecans. To make sure that the farmers could sell their products, Carver discovered new uses for the crops they grew.

William McKinley – became the president of the United States in 1897. He entered office at a time when many US citizens wanted the nation to expand.

Cuba – Cuba was ruled by Spain in the late 1890s. The Cuban people wanted their independence and many of them revolted. The Spanish responded with military force. Large numbers of Cubans were removed from their homes and put in prison camps. In the United States, many newspapers and political leaders called for war.

USS Maine – mysteriously exploded in a Cuban harbor. This event caused the US to blame Spain and declare war. This was the beginning of the Spanish-American War.

Spanish-American War – began in 1898. The war quickly spread to other parts of the world. US naval commander Commodore George Dewey, learned Congress had declared war, he set sail for another Spanish colony, the Philippines. He easily defeated the Spanish navy and took control of the islands. Meanwhile, in Cuba, the US forces defeated Spain is just a few months. Most people in the United States saw it as an easy victory.

The Philippines – US commander George Dewey took control of the Philippines during the Spanish-American War.

Platt Amendment – gave the US a say in how Cubans ran their country, allowed the US to take action in Cuba if it thought it was necessary, and gave the US permanent control of two Cuban naval bases. The Platt Amendment stayed in effect until the 1930s.

Imperialists – people who favored expansion. They wanted to keep the Philippines because of its natural resources and location in Southeast Asia. They felt it would give US businesses access to East Asian markets and provide a good base for the US Navy.

Isolationists – people who were against expansion. They believed the US should give up the Philippines and let it be an independent nation. Isolationists feared trying to control the Philippines would only lead to more wars. Many of them also believed it was morally wrong: the United States was supposed to stand for democracy and freedom.

Theodore Roosevelt – Roosevelt was the Assistant Secretary of the Navy. He believed strongly in expansion. He also thought that a war with Spain would be good for the country. When the fighting started, he resigned from his position in Washington, DC, and became the commander of a unit fighting in Cuba known as the Rough Riders.

Rough Riders – a US unit that was led by Roosevelt. The Rough Riders' charge up San Juan Hill became famous and helped make Roosevelt a hero. In 1901, he became vice president of the United States. A few months later, he became the president after an assassin shot and killed President William McKinley.

Panama Canal – a man-made waterway that officially opened in 1914. It allowed ships to travel back and forth between the Atlantic and Pacific Oceans without having to sail round South America.

Roosevelt Corollary – a policy that stated the United States had the right to keep European nations from trying to occupy territories in Latin America. Its purpose was to protect the United States' economic interest and keep it the dominant country in the Western Hemisphere.

immigrants – people who moved to the US from a foreign land. Between 1870 and 1900, more than twelve million immigrants moved to the United States. They brought with them new languages, unfamiliar religions, and different customs. Most immigrants settled in large cities like New York. They provided labor for the new factories and industries that were developing. Immigrants helped the US urban population grow greatly around the turn of the century.

Tenements – cheap, dirty, overcrowded apartments that often housed more than one family. Immigrants commonly lived in tenements.

Ghettoes – neighborhoods where immigrants from the same country lived because of the similarities they shared. Because most immigrants were poor and ghettoes were over crowded, people in these neighborhoods lived in poverty. The ghettoes featured poor sanitation, unclean air, and disease.

Nativists – people born in the United States who disliked immigrants. Nativists feared that people from other countries would take their jobs. They also did not trust the foreign customs that immigrants had and were prejudiced against those that looked different, talked differently, and practiced different religions. Nativists succeeded in convincing the government to limit the number of immigrants who could come from certain countries during the late 1800s and early twentieth century.

alliances – In an alliance, countries agree to help each other if one of them is attacked. Germany and Austria-Hungary formed an alliance called the Central Powers. Russia, Great Britain, and France became the leaders of an alliance known as the Triple Entente.

World War I – a war that took place primarily in Europe between 1914 and 1918. The war started when Archduke Franz Ferdinand was assassinated by Serbian nationalists. Ferdinand was heir to the Austria-Hungary throne. The two major alliances of the war were the Central Powers and the Triple Entente. Eventually, the US joined the war as well. The war ended in 1918 when Germany signed an armistice with the alliances.

Woodrow Wilson – President Woodrow Wilson won re-election in 1916. He wanted to keep the US out of World War I, but eventually the US was involved in the war.

U-boats – submarines that could stay hidden beneath the surface of the water as they fired torpedoes that sank ships. German U-boats fired not only on enemy ships but also on ships from other countries.

Lusitania – In May of 1915, German submarines sank the US passenger ship *Lusitania.* Over a hundred of the passengers killed were Americans. People in the United States were furious.

Zimmerman Telegram – Germany's foreign minister, Arthur Zimmerman, sent a telegram to Mexico City asking Mexico to attack the United States if the US ever went to war with Germany. In return, Germany promised to help Mexico win back parts of North America it had lost to the US during the 1800s. Mexico did not agree to the deal, but when people in the US learned of the offer, they were alarmed. The Zimmerman Telegram led more and more citizens to support the idea of going to war.

armistice – an agreement to stop fighting. In November of 1918, Germany signed an armistice with the Allies (Great Britain, France, Italy, and the United States) in November 1918. This ended World War I.

Treaty of Versailles – a treaty that was drafted at the end of World War I. It forced Germany to take total blame for the war. It also made Germany pay for the war and greatly decrease the size of its military. Many of the German people grew very bitter because of the treaty. Many in the US feared that the treaty would lead the US into alliances with foreign countries. The Senate refused to ratify it, claiming it feared the Treaty of Versailles could lead to future wars.

Jazz Age – the first years of the 1920s were called the Jazz Age. Jazz was a new form of music that made its way from New Orleans to northern cities early in the decade. African American musicians created it. It is a style of music in which performers use brass, woodwind, and percussion instruments to improvise rather than rely on sheet music. The fast and spirited beat of jazz made it popular with both blacks and whites. Jazz led to the creation of several new dances during the 1920s.

Louis Armstrong – one of the most famous jazz musicians in history during the 1920s.

Harlem Renaissance – an important movement among the African American community. It involved black writers and artists. It was named for Harlem, New York, the mostly black community where it began.

Langston Hughes – became famous for his poems and stories about black life in America.

Zora Neal Hurston – a well-known writer during the Harlem Renaissance.

Henry Ford – invented a new kind of automobile engine. It was powered by fuel rather than steam. His cars didn't cost as much to make. Henry Ford revolutionized the automobile industry, making it affordable for most people to own.

mass producing – Henry Ford began to mass produce cars. He wanted to make so many cars that he could afford to sell them much cheaper than other manufacturers and still make a profit. Ford's ideas about mass production and his assembly line helped make other businesses better as well.

assembly line – An assembly line allows workers to focus on one task rather than trying to assemble the whole product. Each of Ford's workers was responsible for assembling one part of each car. Unlike earlier assembly lines that required workers to walk from station to station, Ford's brought the parts to the workers. His employees could stand in one spot while the parts came to them. This made the work much faster and increased production.

Babe Ruth – a popular baseball player. Ruth played most of his career with the New York Yankees. He became famous for his powerful hitting during the 1920s and, before he left the game, became the all-time home run leader. His 714 homeruns stood as a record until 1974, when an Atlanta Brave named Hank Aaron finally broke it. Babe Ruth still ranks third on the all-time homerun leaders list.

Charles Lindbergh – the first person in history to fly a solo flight non-stop across the Atlantic Ocean. He flew from the United States to Paris, France, in 1927 aboard a plane called the *Spirit of St. Louis*. Today, Lindbergh's plane hangs from the ceiling of the National Air and Space Museum in Washington, DC.

Multiple Choice

1. C 2. C 3. D 4. A 5. B 6. D 7. A 8. C 9. B 10. B

CHAPTER 3: HISTORICAL UNDERSTANDINGS: THE GREAT DEPRESSION AND WORLD WAR II

Practice 3.1: The Great Depression and the New Deal

Page 58

1. B 2. B

3. The Stock Market Crash of 1929 marked the start of the Great Depression. It was the worse economic crisis in US history, and it affected countries all over the world. At one point roughly one-fourth of the nation was unemployed. Many had to rely on soup kitchens to survive. Soup kitchens were locations that gave out free food to the poor. Hoovervilles appeared in cities. Hoovervilles were communities made of shacks where poor, homeless people lived.

4. The New Deal was a set of government programs introduced by Franklin Roosevelt. It relied on deficit spending. The government went into debt, spending borrowed money. Roosevelt hoped it would get people back to work and the economy headed in the right direction.

Practice 3.2: Important Cultural Elements of the 1930s

Page 60

1. D

2. She authored the popular book *Gone with the Wind.* It ended up becoming a movie that won more Academy Awards than any other movie up to that time.

3. He won four gold medals at the Olympics. The fact that he was African American and won them in Germany was extra significant because Germany's Nazi Party was racist and believed that white athletes were superior to black athletes.

Practice 3.3: World War II

Page 69

1. C 2. D 3. C

4. The government used rationing to limit how much citizens could buy of certain goods. Rationing was intended to force people to conserve goods needed for the war effort.
5. Japan wanted to destroy the US Pacific Fleet so that it could not threaten their plans to expand.
6. Japan would not surrender unconditionally. Truman believed it was necessary to force Japan's unconditional surrender and end the war.
7. The UN is an international organization founded in 1945. Its purpose was to monitor relations between countries. Today, the UN continues to seek peaceful solutions to international problems while providing relief to human suffering around the world.

Chapter 3 Review

Key Terms, People, and Concepts

Pages 70 – 72

Stock Market Crash of 1929 – In 1929, the Stock Market crashed. Many people had invested in stocks in the 1920s. When stock prices fell, many of these investors lost everything! The crash caused others to panic and sell off the stock they had. Soon banks were recalling loans and many even closed. Many citizens who had put their money in banks lost their life savings. The Stock Market Crash was the start of the Great Depression.

The Great Depression – the worst economic crisis in US history. Many people were unemployed, homeless, and very poor. The Stock Market Crash of 1929 marked the start of the Great Depression.

soup kitchens– places that gave out free food to the poor. Many people relied on soup kitchens during the Great Depression.

Hoovervilles – communities made of shacks where poor, homeless people lived. They popped up in cities during the Great Depression. They were named after Herbert Hoover.

Herbert Hoover – Hoover was president when the Great Depression struck. Most citizens viewed his economic policies as a failure and blamed him for the Great Depression.

Dust Bowl – a series of windstorms that carried the soil high into the air. These storms created massive dark clouds of dust. Some of these storms were so big that they buried entire homes and blanketed cities. The Dust Bowl forced many Midwest farmers to leave their farms and move to other parts of the country in hopes of starting over.

Franklin D. Roosevelt - Known to many as FDR, Roosevelt was very positive and offered hope to hurting Americans. He became president in 1932. He was also prepared to try new things to deal with the Depression. He introduced the New Deal and deficit spending.

New Deal – a set of government programs that was introduced by Franklin Roosevelt. He was trying new things in order to deal with the depression. The New Deal relied on deficit spending.

deficit spending – Part of Roosevelt's New Deal, the government went into debt, hoping that its programs would get people back to work and the economy headed in the right direction.

Civilian Conservation Corps – a New Deal program. The CCC provided employment for young, unmarried men. These young men worked in the national parks installing electric lines, building fire towers, and planting new trees. The government provided many of their basic needs so that much of their pay could be sent home to their families.

Tennessee Valley Authority – The TVA built hydroelectric dams. It created jobs and supplied cheap electricity to parts of the South that had never had electric power before. The southern Appalachians were one of the poorest areas in the nation. With the help of the TVA, this region prospered as never before.

Works Progress Administration – was part of a second group of New Deal programs, sometimes called the Second New Deal. It provided jobs for unskilled workers. The WPA hired people to build government buildings, roads, and other public projects. It also provided money for the arts.

Social Security – a New Deal program that promised government money to the unemployed and those over sixty-five years of age. Social Security is the only New Deal program that still exists today.

Margaret Mitchell's – an important author of the 1930s. She wrote *Gone with the Wind*, a best-selling novel.

Gone with the Wind – a best-selling novel written by Margaret Mitchell. It depicted life on a southern plantation during the Civil War. Published in 1936, it became a movie in 1939 and won more Academy Awards than any other film up to that time.

Duke Ellington – a talented musician who increased the popularity of jazz and big band music. Ellington assembled one of the most talented jazz orchestras in history, recorded many jazz classics, and appeared in movies.

Sinclair Lewis – a novelist who became the first American in history to win the Nobel Prize in Literature.

Pearl Buck – the first US woman to win the Nobel Prize in Literature.

Joe Louis – One of the most famous athletes of the 1930s. He was heavyweight boxing champion. He was nicknamed "The Brown Bomber." Louis became known for his powerful punches. In 1938, Louis won a famous fight against German boxer Max Schmeling.

Jesse Owens – an African American athlete. He won four gold medals in track and field at the 1936 Olympic Games. His victories were even more significant because the games took place in Berlin, Germany. Owens defeated a host of white athletes as Nazi leader Adolf Hitler looked on.

Germany – After World War I, Germany's economy suffered because they were forced to pay for the war. The worldwide depression hit Germany hard. Many angry Germans blamed other European nations and German Jews for their hardships.

Adolf Hitler – Many Germans wanted new leadership after World War I. Hitler took advantage of the unhappiness to lead his Nazi Party to power. Hitler preached hatred of the Jews and promised to return Germany to greatness. By 1933, he was firmly in power.

Third Reich – Hitler called his empire the Third Reich. He wanted to expand his empire even further. He invaded the Rhineland, Austria, and parts of Czechoslovakia. Since other European nations did not want another war, they did little to stop him.

appeasement – the belief that it is best to let an aggressive nation have what it wants. The hope is that this will satisfy its leaders and stop the aggression. Many nations used appeasement with Hitler, but he had no intention of stopping. He soon signed an alliance with two other aggressive nations: Italy and Japan.

World War II – World War II started in Europe when Germany invaded Poland in 1939. By the end of 1940, Hitler's forces had conquered other European nations, including France. They had also attacked Great Britain and were preparing to invade the Soviet Union. The United States entered the war after the attack by the Japanese on Pearl Harbor.

Japan – Beginning in the 1920s, Japan decided to expand its territory in Southeast Asia. As a tiny island nation, Japan lacked natural resources. Many in the military saw the invasion of other territories as the best way to solve this problem. By the late 1930s, Japan controlled most of the Chinese coast and was determined to conquer other territories as well.

Emperor Hirohito – Emperor of Japan in the 1930s. Hirohito did not desire war, but he did not possess most of the power in Japan. The government fell under the control of the military.

Pearl Harbor – On December 7, 1941 Japanese planes launched a surprise attack on Pearl Harbor that was intended to destroy the fleet and keep it from interfering with Japan's plans. The attack destroyed US ships and planes. It also killed or wounded nearly three thousand people. The next day, President Roosevelt asked Congress to declare war. Congress agreed. Because Germany and Japan were allies, the United States soon found itself at war with Germany as well. The United States had entered World War II.

victory gardens – During World War II, US citizens began to conserve goods so that more could go to the soldiers. They planted victory gardens, raising their own vegetables.

rationing – During World War II, the government introduced rationing, limiting how much citizens could buy. Rationing forced people to conserve certain goods because they could not simply go buy more whenever they wanted.

WAC (Women's Army Corps) – the largest military division of women during World War II. Military women served in nearly every role of service except combat.

Rosie the Riveter – During World War II, thousands of women went to work in the nation's factories and industries because many of the men were at war. Rosie the Riveter became the symbol of such women. It was the title of a song about a woman who went to work as a riveter while her husband went off to war.

Tuskegee Airmen – African American fighter pilots during World War II. As a squadron they successfully protected every US bomber they escorted during the war.

code talkers – a group of Native American Marines. The Marine Corps developed a coded radio language based on the Navajo language. Code talkers played an important role in secret communications. The code proved very effective. The Japanese never figured it out.

442nd - an important army infantry regiment. It was made up totally of Japanese American soldiers. The 442nd fought in Europe and became the most decorated unit in US history.

civil rights movement – Race relations changed due to the war. Although they served honorably, African American soldiers remained segregated from white soldiers. Many African Americans resented that the government expected them to fight for a country that did not give them equal rights. African American soldiers returned home no longer willing to accept inequality. Many of them helped lead a new civil rights movement that challenged American's view of race.

internment of Japanese Americans – one of the most tragic events of World War II. After Pearl Harbor, many in the US government feared that Japanese Americans would help Japan. In an effort to avoid spying and sabotage, President Roosevelt signed an executive order. The executive order called for the government to relocate thousands of Japanese Americans to interment camps. Many Japanese Americans had to leave their homes. Some lost their jobs or their own businesses. Although some German and Italian Americans were interned as well, these groups did not face nearly as much racism or suspicion as Japanese Americans.

Allies – During World War II, the United States, Great Britain, the USSR and a number of other nations stood together as the Allies.

Axis Powers – During World War II, Germany, Italy, and Japan formed the Axis Powers.

Joseph Stalin – leader of the Soviet Union during World War II.

Winston Churchill – Great Britain's Prime Minister during World War II.

Benito Mussolini – leader of Italy during World War II. He escaped to the north where he became the leader of a puppet government under Adolf Hitler.

Dwight D. Eisenhower – the US general who planned and commanded the Allies' invasion of Western Europe. On June 6, 1944, Allied troops from various nations launched a surprise invasion of Northern France.

D-Day – On June 6, 1944 Allied troops from various nations launched a surprise invasion of Northern France. It became known as D-Day, and it was a huge success. As the Soviets marched towards Berlin from the east, the western Allies liberated France and other countries as they advanced from the west.

VE Day – Victory in Europe Day. The Allies celebrated VE Day when Germany surrendered in May of 1945.

Harry Truman – became the new president in 1945 after Roosevelt died.

concentration camps – areas that housed thousands of starving and tortured prisoners during World War II. Most of these prisoners were Jewish. They were tortured and murdered in these camps. It was part of Hitler's plan to exterminate the Jewish people.

Holocaust – Hitler tired to exterminate the Jewish race. Over six million Jewish people perished during this time period. It became known as the Holocaust.

Battle of Midway – Midway was a tiny island in the Pacific Ocean. The US considered it important militarily because it helped protect Hawaii and the west coast of the United States. Japan's leading admiral hoped he could force the US to fight Japan at Midway. He planned to attack while the US fleet was still weak. Japan succeeded in forcing a fight, but its naval commanders failed to win the battle. The US defeated Japan and turned the tide of the war in the Pacific.

island hopping – a strategy used by the US military during World War II. It involved US forces conquering one set of islands after another in the Pacific as they fought their way towards Japan

Iwo Jima – one of the fiercest battles occurred on this island. It took more than 100,000 US soldiers nearly a month to defeat a Japanese force of 25,000.

Potsdam Declaration – President Truman, Churchill, and Stalin signed the Potsdam Declaration after Germany surrendered from World War II. It restated the Allies' policy of unconditional surrender.

unconditional surrender – meant that the Allies would set all the rules for Japan's surrender; Japan would have no say. In truth, Japan was ready to surrender. The Japanese had suffered greatly from the war. They knew that they could not keep the Allies from reaching Japan. Japan's leaders would not accept unconditional surrender. They wanted a guarantee that Japan would still have an emperor after the war. The Allies refused to listen to Japan's request.

atomic bomb – Developed by the United States, it was the world's first nuclear weapon. It was far more powerful than any weapon ever invented. When Japan refused to surrender unconditionally, Truman ordered the bomb dropped on the Japanese city of Hiroshima.

Hiroshima – On August 6, 1945, a US plane called the *Enola Gay* dropped the bomb on Hiroshima, Japan. It destroyed Hiroshima. Thousands of Japanese people were killed. Thousands more died later as a result of the radiation caused by the explosion.

Nagasaki – When Japan didn't immediately surrender after Hiroshima, a second atomic bomb was dropped on Nagasaki. The death and destruction caused by these horrifying weapons forced Japan to surrender.

VJ Day – Victory over Japan Day. After the war, the Allies allowed Japan to keep its emperor. Hirohito remained the emperor of Japan until his death in 1986.

United Nations (UN) – In October of 1945 the United Nations was formed. Its purpose was to maintain peace between countries, make sure nations obeyed international law, and protect human rights. Although nations from around the world sent representatives, most of the decision making power fell to five permanent members of the UN Security Council.

UN Security Council – the United States, Soviet Union, China, Great Britain, and France. Most of the decision making of the United Nations fell to these countries. In order for the UN to take any military action to enforce its decisions all five of the permanent members had to agree. Today, the Soviet Union no longer exists. Its former seat belongs to Russia. The UN continues to seek peaceful solutions to international problems while providing relief to human suffering around the world.

Multiple Choice

1. C 2. D 3. B 4. D 5. C 6. D 7. B 8. A 9. C 10. D

CHAPTER 4: HISTORICAL UNDERSTANDINGS: THE COLD WAR AND US SOCIETY FROM 1950 TO 1975

Practice 4.1: The Cold War

Page 79

1. C 2. A 3. D

4. Just before the end of the Berlin Airlift, the United States signed a treaty with Canada and several European nations. Each nation vowed to help the others if the Soviets attacked. They also formed NATO (the North Atlantic Treaty Organization). NATO would provide a combined military force to fight against any attack from Eastern Europe.

5. Cuban leader, Fidel Castro, struck a deal with the Soviet Union and allowed it to place nuclear missiles in Cuba. When President Kennedy learned of the missiles he called on Khrushchev to remove them and ordered a blockade of the island. (A blockade is when naval ships prevent any other ships from leaving or docking in a country's ports). For thirteen days the world watched and feared that the Cuban

Missile Crisis might lead to nuclear war. Finally, the Soviets agreed to remove the missiles and the US promised never to invade Cuba. The US also made a secret pledge to remove missiles from Turkey.

6. Vietnam was unlike any other war. For one, the Vietcong fought differently. They struck quickly and unexpectedly. After killing or wounding as many US soldiers as they could, they would then retreat back into the thick jungle. Also, It was the first war to occur during the age of television. Vietnam also occurred during a time in which more young citizens were attending colleges and universities than ever before. During the 1960s, many college students began to question traditional values authority figures, including their own government. A huge anti-war movement arose and the nation became divided over Vietnam. Finally, Vietnam was different because the United States lost.

Practice 4.2: The Civil Rights Movement

Page 83

1. B 2. C

3. Dr. King became the recognized leader of the Civil Rights Movement. He believed in non-violence and civil disobedience. King believed that the best way for African Americans to win equal rights was through non-violent protests and through peacefully disobeying unjust laws. King used television to his advantage. As people across the country watched film of peaceful civil rights protestors being beaten by police and racist citizens, support for the movement grew. Soon, whites as well as blacks were traveling to the South to help the movement.

4. The 1964 Civil Rights Act made segregation and discrimination illegal in many public places, such as hotels, restaurants, and theatres. The Twenty-fourth Amendment to the Constitution ended the poll tax and made it easier for African Americans to vote. The Voting Rights Act of 1965 authorized the president to outlaw literacy tests and to send federal officials to make sure blacks got a fair chance to vote in elections.

Practice 4.3: Social Unrest

Page 86

1. Kennedy and Nixon met in the first televised debate. Most of the citizens who heard the debate on the radio thought that Nixon had won. But most of those who watched on television thought the younger, more confident looking Kennedy had. Many historians believe that television helped Kennedy win the election.

2. President Kennedy was loved by many citizens, and the entire nation mourned his death. Historians often debate how history might have been different if Kennedy had lived. Some believe the Vietnam War never would have happened. Robert Kennedy's assassination saddened many who had hoped he would end the war in Vietnam and end many of the country's social problems. A few months later, the Democratic convention became a scene of disorder and chaos when the Democrats nominated Vice President Hubert Humphrey. Humphrey lost the election to Richard Nixon, and the Vietnam War continued on for nearly five more years.

Chapter 4 Review

Key Terms, People, and Concepts

Pages 87 – 88

capitalist democracy – the US is a capitalist democracy. It allows citizens and businesses to own private property, determine economic production, and pursue profits. Its Constitution also guarantees basic human rights and allows citizens to have a role in their government.

communist dictatorship – The Soviet Union was a communist dictatorship. Joseph Stalin was the dictator. Communism meant that the state, not citizens or businesses, owned nearly all the property and determined production.

Cold War – a time when people around the world feared the tension between the US and USSR would eventually lead to war. The Cold War was a result of Stalin's conquest of new territories. He turned them into communist governments, and the US and Great Britain feared that he wanted to spread communism throughout Western Europe.

Berlin – After World War II, the Allies divided Germany. Berlin was the capital of Germany, and the allied powers governed a portion of the city. Even though Berlin was in the Soviet sector of Germany, each of the allied powers governed a portion of the city.

Iron Curtain – Since Stalin would not give up East Germany, it remained a communist nation. Western Europe became a capitalist democracy. Former British Prime Mininster Winston Churchill described Europe as being divided by an "Iron Curtain."

containment policy – Containment meant that the US would not attempt to remove communism from places where it already existed. However, it would do all it could to make sure that communism didn't spread to other parts of the world.

Truman Doctrine – President Truman's vow to help other nations resist communism became known as the Truman Doctrine.

Marshall Plan. This plan involved the US government giving money to European nations. The money helped them rebuild after the war. By helping nations rebuild, the US believed it would help prevent the spread of communism.

Berlin Airlift – When Stalin's army surrounded West Berlin and would not let any supplies in or out, Truman responded with the Berlin Airlift. For several months in 1948 and '49, the US and its allies flew planes delivering supplies across the Soviet lines and into West Berlin. Not wanting a war, Stalin finally gave up. But the Berlin Airlift only made the two sides angrier with one another.

NATO – the North Atlantic Treaty Organization. An alliance between the US, Canada, and several European nations. Each nation vowed to help the others if the Soviets attacked. NATO would provide a combined military force to fight against any attack from Eastern Europe.

nuclear arms race – developed between the US and the USSR after Hiroshima. Both nations created more and more nuclear weapons. Soon both sides had nuclear missiles that could travel thousands of miles in minutes and destroy cities on the other side of the world. People lived in fear that the Cold War might result in a nuclear war that would destroy the entire planet.

38th parallel – served as a dividing line between North and South Korea after World War II. North Korea became a communist state. South Korea became a capitalist democracy.

Korean War – started as a result of the split in North and South Korea after World War II. In 1950, North Korean troops crossed the 38th parallel and quickly conquered much of South Korea. The United Nations elected to send troops to stop the invasion. The US drove back the North Koreans. Before he could fully defeat them, however, Chinese troops crossed the border to help the North Koreans. It continued until 1953, resulting in a cease-fire that left the country divided at almost the same place as before the war began.

Joseph McCarthy – a US senator from the state of Wisconsin. During the 1950s, he became convinced that Communists were trying to gain control of the US government. He vowed to find these Communists and drive them out. He accused high-ranking military officers of being Communists. When McCarthy tried to make his case on television during a series of congressional hearings, most people thought he came off looking cruel, paranoid, and perhaps crazy. The hearing ruined McCarthy's political career.

John F. Kennedy – He became president in 1961. He approved an attempt to overthrow Castro's Cuban government. The plan failed and increased Castro's fear that the US might try to invade Cuba. Castro struck a deal with the Soviet Union and its leader Nikita Khrushchev.

Nikita Khrushchev – the leader of the Soviet Union. Khrushchev had taken over as First Secretary of the USSR's Communist Party after Stalin died in 1953. Although the Soviet government was no longer a dictatorship under Khrushchev, the new leader was still a tough politician who distrusted the US. He also tried to bully the US and its allies into abandoning West Berlin in 1958. He eventually backed down when President Eisenhower strengthened NATO's armed forces there.

Cuban Missile Crisis – Cuba allowed the Soviets to place nuclear missiles in Cuba in 1962. When President Kennedy learned of the missiles he called on Khrushchev to remove them and ordered a blockade of the island. For thirteen days the world watched and feared that the Cuban Missile Crisis might lead to nuclear war. Finally, the Soviets agreed to remove the missiles and the US promised never to invade Cuba.

Vietnam War – In 1954, an international treaty divided the tiny Southeast Asian country of Vietnam. Communists ruled North Vietnam. A pro-US government ruled South Vietnam. Soon the two sides were at war. Because the southern leader was corrupt, many peasants in South Vietnam formed a rebel army called the Vietcong and fought alongside of the North Vietnamese. The Vietnam War escalated in the 1960s and was unlike any war the United States had ever fought. Even though the US military was much stronger, the Vietcong struck quickly and unexpectedly. The Vietcong did not try to win battles as much as they simply tried to make the US tired of fighting. In 1973, the United States signed a peace agreement that pulled US troops out of Vietnam. Soon, however, war erupted again between North and South Vietnam. In 1975, the Communist took the South Vietnamese capital. After a long and bloody war, the Communist finally controlled the entire country.

television's effect on the Vietnam War – Vietnam was the first war in which citizens could actually see much of the death and destruction from their own living rooms. Such scenes led many citizens to have strong opinions about the war. Many questioned the way their government was fighting the war. Others opposed the war completely.

anti-war movement – During the 1960s, a huge anti-war movement arose on many campuses and spread to other parts of society. Unlike World War II, the nation became divided over Vietnam.

Civil Rights Movement – Following World War II, legalized segregation still existed in the South. African Americans usually had to remain separate from whites in public places. After World War II, many African Americans called for an end to segregation and injustice. Their protests helped give birth to the Civil Rights Movement.

NAACP – National Association for the Advancement of Colored People**.** The NAACP argued in court that segregation violated the Constitution. It stated that segregation was unlawful because black schools were not as equally equipped as white schools. It wanted the courts to stop segregation in public education. The NAACP won their case with the help of Thurgood Marshall.

Thurgood Marshall – a talented lawyer who helped the NAACP win the case against school segregation. Thirteen years later, Thurgood Marshall became the first African American ever appointed to the United States Supreme Court.

Brown v. Board of Education – The Supreme Court struck down school segregation in a case known as *Brown v. Board of Education.*

Rosa Parks – In 1955, An African American woman refused to give up her bus seat to a white person. This took place in Montgomery, Alabama. City officials arrested Rosa Parks. This caused anger among the African American community.

Martin Luther King, Jr. – a young Baptist minister who helped organize and lead the Montgomery Bus Boycott. King became the recognized leader of the Civil Rights Movement.

Montgomery Bus Boycott – A boycott led by Martin Luther King, Jr. African Americans refused to ride public buses. They walked or carpooled instead. The boycott cost the city a lot of money because many of the citizens who usually paid to ride the buses were black. The boycott ended after the Supreme Court ruled in 1956 that Montgomery could no longer segregate its buses.

non-violence – Martin Luther King believed in non-violence as a solution. He felt the best way for African Americans to win equal rights was through non-violent protests.

civil disobedience – King believed that the best way for African Americans to win equal rights was through non-violent protests and peacefully disobeying unjust laws. Many African Americans were arrested for sitting in all-white areas or assembling for civil rights protests and rallies. King, himself, was arrested a number of times and wrote one of his most famous letters from the jail in Birmingham, Alabama.

television's effects on the Civil Rights Movement – Martin Luther King used television to his advantage. As people across the country watched news clips of peaceful civil rights protestors being beaten by police and insulted by racists, support for the movement grew. Soon, whites as well as blacks were traveling to the South to help the movement.

March on Washington – One of the most famous events of the Civil Rights Movement. In August of 1963, more than 200,000 civil rights supporters marched in the nation's capital. Dr. King gave perhaps his most famous speech standing in front of the Lincoln Memorial. Many know it as his "I have a dream" speech, because he spoke of his dream that, one day, all US citizens would be judged by the "content of their character" rather than the color of their skin.

Militant movements – African Americans that felt violence was a better way to win equality. Such movements attracted many younger, more radical blacks. The Nation of Islam and the Black Panthers were two of the most famous militant groups.

Malcolm X – The most famous militant leader. Malcolm became part of the Nation of Islam and preached distrust of all whites. He later left the "Nation" and, after going on a Muslim pilgrimage, came to believe that some whites were good. He began preaching cooperation rather than hatred of all whites. Some blacks did not like Malcolm changing his message. On February 21, 1965, three African American men assassinated Malcolm X while he spoke at a rally in New York.

effects of Martin Luther King's assassination –On April 4, 1968, a white gunman assassinated Dr. King as he stood on a hotel balcony in Memphis, Tennessee. African American communities in a number of US cities erupted in violence. Riots broke out across the country. People as far away as South Africa mourned his death. Although King was dead, his dream and his cause lived on. The Civil Rights Movement continued to make gains and win rights for African Americans.

Civil Rights Act - made segregation and discrimination illegal in many public places, such as hotels, restaurants, and theaters. It was established in 1964.

Twenty-fourth Amendment – ended the poll tax and made it easier for African Americans to vote.

Voting Rights Act – In 1965, the Voting Rights Act authorized the president to outlaw literacy tests and to send federal officials to make sure blacks got a fair chance to vote in elections.

John F. Kennedy – In 1960, Kennedy defeated Vice President Richard Nixon in one of the closest presidential races in history. It was the first time television played a major role in the election. Only forty-three years old when he took office, he was the youngest man ever elected president. His skills as a communicator, good looks, and sense of humor only added to his popularity. After the Cuban Missile Crisis, many citizens also viewed him as a good leader.

1960 televised debate – the first televised debate occurred between Kennedy and Nixon. Most of the citizens who heard the debate on the radio thought that Nixon had won. But most of those who watched on television thought the younger, more confident looking Kennedy had. Many historians believe that television helped Kennedy win the election. Kennedy became a very popular president.

space exploration – During the 1950s, the Soviet Union had successfully launched satellites and put a man in space. Kennedy and others feared that falling behind in the space race was dangerous. They were convinced the Soviets would use their space technology to build more powerful nuclear weapons. Kennedy challenged the US space program to put a man on the moon by the end of the '60s. In 1969, US Astronaut Neil Armstrong became the first human being to walk on the moon. Today, thanks to such early efforts, the United States often sends people into outer space.

satellites – machines that orbit the Earth providing communication signals and pictures. Satellites have greatly impacted the way people live. Satellites enable people to watch live events on the other side of the world, hear accurate weather forecasts on their local news network, and get instant traveling directions as they drive in their cars.

effects of John F. Kennedy's assassination – Citizens of the United States were shocked on November 22, 1963, when Lee Harvey Oswald assassinated President Kennedy in Dallas, Texas. The young president was loved by many citizens, and the entire nation mourned his death. Vice President Lyndon Johnson became president in his place. Historians often debate how history might have been different if Kennedy had lived. Some believe the Vietnam War never would have happened.

Robert Kennedy – President Kennedy's younger brother. He served as President Kennedy's attorney general and played a key role in bringing a peaceful end to the Cuban Missile Crisis. He worked hard to battle organized crime and eventually became a strong supporter of civil rights. He became an opponent of the Vietnam War and supported a number of social causes. In 1968, Robert Kennedy decided to run for president. Many thought he would win the Democratic Party's nomination, especially after his victory in the California primary. That same night, however, as Kennedy made his victory speech, an assassin shot him at close range.

effects of Robert Kennedy's assassination – saddened many who had hoped he would end the war in Vietnam and deal with many of the country's social problems.

Multiple Choice

1. C 2. A 3. A 4. D 5. A 6. D 7. D 8. B

CHAPTER 5: THE UNITED STATES SINCE 1975

Practice 5.1: US Involvement in World Events

Page 93

1. B 2. C

3. No one was ever able to prove that Saddam had ties to Al Qaeda. Even more serious, the US could not find any weapons of mass destruction. Many in the US criticized the war and accused Bush of lying. Others defended Bush's decision. Attacks from insurgent groups also made the country very unstable and resulted in the deaths of thousands of US soldiers.

4. President Bush established a new government department: the Department of Homeland Security. Its role is to combat terrorism at home, as well as provide aid to parts of the country hurt by natural disasters. Security measures for airports and other public places became much stricter, causing passengers a great deal of inconvenience and making air travel more difficult. Congress also passed laws like the Patriot Act, which gives law enforcement more power to listen in on citizens' phone calls, read emails, and conduct investigations without warrants. The courts have also granted the government the right to arrest and hold suspected terrorists, without having to hold to traditional rules regarding due process.

Practice 5.2: End of the Cold War and Advent of Modern America

Page 95

1. D 2. C

3. The Soviet Union could not keep spending billions of dollars on nuclear weapons; it needed to spend more on improving production and providing basic needs for its citizens. Under Gorbachev, the USSR made changes that allowed more freedom and allowed some capitalism. It also did not try to control Eastern Europe as much. Once the people in these countries got a taste of freedom, they did not want to remain citizens under communist governments anymore. By the late '80s, communist governments began to fall. Many Eastern European countries replaced their old communist regimes with more democratic forms of government and allowed more capitalism. Germany became a unified country once again. Even the Soviet Union dissolved in the early '90s.

4. Answers will vary.

Chapter 5 Review

Key Terms, People, and Concepts

Pages 96 – 98

Israel – In 1948, the United Nations recognized Israel as an independent Jewish state. Many Arab nations dislike Israel because it took land away from the Palestinians.

Palestinians – The Palestinians had long hoped for independence after living for decades under European authority. They believe to this day that they, not Israelis, are entitled to the land that forms modern Israel.

Israeli-Palestinian Conflict – For over sixty years, the Israeli-Palestinian Conflict has resulted in much violence. The US has traditionally supported Israel. Arab nations support the Palestinians and consider Israel an enemy. The United States and other countries want peace in the Middle East because it is an important region. Many trade routes are found in the area as well as an abundance of oil.

oil – The Middle East is home to one of the world's most abundant supplies of oil. A number of Middle East countries rely on oil exports for most of their revenue. Wars and other conflicts can affect oil supplies, raise oil prices, and have harsh effects on nations' economies.

Camp David Accords – a peace agreement between Israel and Egypt. Jimmy Carter helped negotiate this agreement in 1977. Many applauded the three leaders. Some Arabs were upset with the Egyptian president, Sadat. They felt he had sold out the Palestinian people by not insisting that they be given land in Palestine. The Camp David Accords improved Egyptian-Israeli relations, but it did little to end fighting between Israelis and Palestinians.

Lebanon – President Reagan sent US troops to Lebanon in the early '80s. The troops were part of a United Nations force. Reagan claimed that the troops were there to establish peace after fighting broke out between Israelis and Palestinians who had fled to Lebanon. Some Lebanese citizens welcomed the UN force. Others saw it as a foreign army sent to support Israel. In October 1983, a suicide bomber drove a car full of explosives into a US Marine barracks, killing over two hundred people. When the US forces finally left, Lebanon was still an unstable country.

Saddam Hussein – The president of Iraq. In 2003, several world leaders proclaimed that Iraqi President Saddam Hussein had weapons of mass destruction. The US also claimed Saddam had ties to Al Qaeda. The US overthrew Saddam's government and helped establish a new, democratic Iraqi government. The new government eventually tried Saddam following his capture and hanged him in December 2006. No one was ever able to prove that Saddam had ties to Al Qaeda nor did they find any weapons of mass destruction.

Persian Gulf War – lasted only forty-two days and resulted in Iraq's withdrawal from Kuwait. The Persian Gulf War occurred because Saddam Hussein invaded Kuwait. Thousands of Iraqis died in the war, compared to just a few hundred of the UN forces.

War on Terror – George W. Bush declared the War on Terror after terrorists from the Middle East attacked the United States on September 11, 2001.

September 11, 2001- terrorists from the Middle East hijacked four US commercial airplanes. Two of the planes flew into the World Trade Center towers in New York City. The nation watched in horror as the massive towers crashed to the ground, killing thousands. Meanwhile, a third plane crashed into the Pentagon in Washington, DC. The fourth plane crashed in a field in Pennsylvania after the passengers revolted against the hijackers. In a single day, thousands of Americans died at the hands of terrorists. Citizens were shocked, sad, and angry.

Al Qaeda – the terrorist group that carried out the September 11th attacks.

Osama bin Laden – the leader of Al Qaeda. President Bush was determined to capture bin Laden. Bin Laden and his followers hid and trained in Afghanistan. When Afghanistan's leaders would not hand over the terrorists, President Bush organized an international force that invaded the country and overthrew the government. Bin Laden, however, got away. In 2008, international forces are still searching for him as they try to establish a new, stable government.

weapons of mass destruction - weapons capable of killing massive amounts of people, such as nuclear or chemical weapons. In 2003, world leaders claimed Saddam Hussein had weapons of mass destruction in Iraq. They based this claim on intelligence reports, Saddam's history of using chemical weapons, and Saddam's refusal to allow UN investigators into Iraq to see if such weapons existed. After Saddam was tried and hanged in 2006, the US never found any weapons of mass destruction.

Department of Homeland Security – established by President Bush after the September 11th attacks. Its role is to combat terrorism at home, as well as provide aid to parts of the country hurt by natural disasters. Security measures for airports and other public places became much stricter, causing passengers a great deal of inconvenience and making air travel more difficult.

Patriot Act – gives law enforcement more power to listen in on citizens' phone calls, read emails, and conduct investigations without warrants. At times, the government has also arrested and held suspected terrorists without following traditional rules of due process.

Mikhail Gorbachev - became the leader of the Soviet Union in 1985. Under Gorbachev, the USSR made changes that allowed more freedom and some capitalism. Eventually, this led to the collapse of the Soviet Union in the early '90s.

Personal computers – have greatly changed the world in the last thirty years. Today, nearly every household in the United States has a personal computer. Many people have laptop computers that are portable and can be used from nearly anywhere. Today's computers can compute information in mere seconds and perform countless tasks. Computers allow businesses, governments, and citizens to work much faster and produce much more than in past decades. Televisions, cell phones, cars, and many other devices are often equipped with advanced computers.

Internet – a communication system people access using their computer. It links homes, businesses, libraries, government institutions, universities, and schools all over the world. The Internet has changed the way students do research, study, practice for tests, and go to school. Citizens use the internet to gather news, shop, or exchange information. The Internet has impacted politics by allowing citizens to learn more and gather up to date information about political issues and candidates quickly.

internet's impact on politics – The Internet has impacted politics by allowing citizens to learn more and gather up to date information about political issues and candidates quickly.

new problems presented by the internet – Sometimes, harmful, illegal, and/or dangerous information travels over the Internet. Criminals often use the Internet to access people's personal information in order to steal money and/or their identity. People who go on-line have to be careful about who they interact with. Otherwise, they could become a victim of on-line predators.

Multiple Choice

1. B 2. C 3. A 4. C 5. A 6. C 7. D 8. A

CHAPTER 6: GEOGRAPHIC UNDERSTANDINGS

Practice 6.1: Geographic Features

Page 103

1. D 2. B 3. C

4. The Monongahela, Allegheny, and Ohio Rivers

5. Japan chose to attack Pearl Harbor because it wanted to expand its empire. Japan's leaders felt that Pearl Harbor was too close to Japan. It feared the US Pacific Fleet would sail for Japan and try to stop Japan's expansion. Japan's leaders decided to destroy the fleet so it could not interfere.

Practice 6.2: Economic Development of the United States

Page 106

1. Industries require labor and resources for production. Industrialization tends to increase in areas where there are high populations. What natural resources are easily accessible also tends to determine what industries are important to different regions.
2. Large cities provided labor. Rivers, lakes, and coastlines provided access to water routes for transporting goods.
3. As railroads expanded, transportation to more areas became easier and industry expanded.
4. After the war, European countries had been hurt badly by the war. In addition to the millions of lives lost, European economies were devastated. Property, industries, and infrastructure had been badly damaged. Meanwhile, the war boosted the US economy. Although US troops eventually fought in the war, none of the fighting took place in the United States. US businesses were not damaged or destroyed by attacks. Industries grew as the nation produced more goods to support the war effort. Once the war ended, the United States found itself an economic world power. It was producing more at a time when many of the nations that would have competed economically found themselves trying to recover.

Chapter 6 Review

Key Terms, People, and Concepts

Pages 106 – 108

physical geography – the study of how specific physical characteristics define a region. Physical features include deserts, bodies of water, mountain ranges, and other land forms.

Grand Canyon – a gorge located in northwestern Arizona. It is over two hundred and fifty miles long and over a mile deep at its deepest point. The Colorado River's flowing water carved out the canyon over millions of years. The Grand Canyon is one of the earth's greatest natural wonders and attracts over five million visitors each year.

Salton Sea – a salt lake and the largest lake in California. The Salton Sea is located in the southeastern corner of the California and spans over three hundred and fifty square miles.

salt lake – a lake that contains salt water rather than fresh water.

Great Salt Lake – the largest salt lake in the Western Hemisphere. It is located in the northern part of Utah. The lake changes in size, depending on the amount of annual rainfall. It is home to millions of native birds, shrimp, and waterfowl.

desert – a land area that receives less than ten inches of rain a year.

Mojave Desert – over 22,000 square miles and is one of the country's major deserts. Most of the Mojave lies in southern California, but portions of it run through Arizona, Nevada, and Utah.

man-made places – places or features constructed by humans. Examples of man-made features include farms, cities, canals, and roads.

Chisholm Trail – a route used in the late nineteenth century to move cattle from Texas to Kansas. The journey could take up to two months. It was often very dangerous. Cattle drives often encountered harsh weather, wild animals, hostile Native Americans, and outlaws.

Pittsburgh – The second largest city in Pennsylvania after Philadelphia. It is located where the Allegheny and Monongahela Rivers come together to form the Ohio River. The city's location has made it a key industrial center. The Allegheny, Monongahela, and Ohio Rivers provide key water routes for transporting industrial resources and goods. During the early 1900s, Pittsburgh manufactured almost half of the nation's steel. Today, Pittsburgh is still known as the "Steel City."

Gettysburg, Pennsylvania – most famous for the Battle of Gettysburg, one of the key battles of the American Civil War. The Union's victory at Gettysburg ended the Confederate's hopes of invading the North and marked a key turning point in the war. Before Gettysburg, President Abraham Lincoln felt a lot of pressure to make peace with the South. After the battle, however, the Union decided to continue fighting—a decision that kept the Union together. Today, the population of Gettysburg is around eight thousand citizens.

Kitty Hawk, North Carolina – a town on the Outer Banks of North Carolina. The Outer Banks is a series of small islands that line North Carolina's Atlantic coast. Kitty Hawk became famous as the site of the Wright brothers' first powered airplane flight in 1903.

Pearl Harbor, Hawaii – located west of Honolulu on the island of Oahu, Hawaii. Its harbor serves as a US naval base. On December 7, 1941, Japanese forces bombed Pearl Harbor in a surprise attack. Japan chose to attack Pearl Harbor because it wanted to expand its empire. Japan's leaders felt that Pearl Harbor was too close to Japan. It feared the US Pacific Fleet would sail for Japan and try to stop Japan's expansion. Japan's leaders decided to destroy the fleet so it could not interfere. The attack badly damaged the fleet but failed to destroy it. The United States declared war on Japan and entered World War II in response to the Pearl Harbor attack.

Montgomery, Alabama – the capital of Alabama. It is located in the southeast region of the state and has a rich history. Montgomery served as the first capital of the Confederacy after southern states seceded from the Union in 1860. The city also became well-known during the Civil Rights Movement of the 1950s and '60s. The Montgomery Bus Boycott led to a US Supreme Court decision ending segregation on public buses. It also made Martin Luther King, Jr. a national figure and the recognized leader of the Civil Rights Movement.

Industrialization – Many factors affect industrialization including available resources, large labor populations, and accessibility to transportation. After the Civil War, the US became more industrialized. In the South, where agriculture was important, tobacco and cotton industries thrived. The North featured important steel, railroad, textile, and oil industries. In the West, new technologies helped industrialize mining, agriculture, and the cattle industry. Places like Northern California and Oregon became home to important timber industries. Oil became an important industry in parts of the Southwest. In the Midwest, agriculture became more industrialized as farmers produced large amounts of corn, wheat, and other products to be transported by train and sold to other parts of the country and overseas.

US economic development after World War I – Before World War I, the United States was not considered a world power. Things changed after the war. European countries had been hurt badly by the war. In addition to the millions of lives lost, European economies were devastated. Property, industries, and infrastructure had been badly damaged. Meanwhile, the war boosted the US economy. Although US troops eventually fought in the war, none of the fighting took place in the United States. US businesses were not damaged or destroyed by attacks. Industries grew as the nation produced more goods to support the war effort. Once the war ended, the United States found itself an economic world power. It was producing more at a time when many of the nations that would have competed economically found themselves trying to recover.

US economic development after World War II – After World War II, the US economy did well while economies overseas suffered from the destruction caused by war. The US provided loans and financial aid to rebuild parts of Europe and Southeast Asia. In addition to being an economic power, the US became one of the world's leading military powers. It developed the world's first nuclear weapons and placed military bases in foreign countries. This led to a rise in defense industries, boosting the US economy even more.

Multiple Choice

1. A 2. C 3. B 4. D 5. C 6. C 7. B 8. C

CHAPTER 7: GOVERNMENT AND CIVICS

Practice 7.1: Civic Responsibility and the Bill of Rights

Page 114

1. A 2. C

3. Due process means that the government must follow the Constitution and respect an accused person's civil rights when arresting or putting that person on trial. It cannot punish someone for a crime without following the rules set by law. The Constitution guarantees it by setting rules about searches and seizures, indictments, double jeopardy, self incrimination, eminent domain, and rules about how trials are conducted.

Practice 7.2: Democracy and One Nation

Page 117

1. D

2. *E pluribus unum* is a Latin phrase that means "out of many, one." It was meant to suggest that out of the many states there is formed one nation. Over time, however, people came to identify the statement as meaning that from many different races, cultures, and backgrounds come one American people.

3. Answers will vary.

Chapter 7 Review

Key Terms, People, and Concepts

Pages 118 – 120

United States Constitution – the national body of laws that govern the United States of America. The Constitution forms the framework of US government. It also protects the rights of US citizens. America's leaders wrote the Constitution in 1787. The states ratified it the following year.

civil rights – rights that are meant to protect citizens' freedom. The civil rights are protected under the United States Constitution.

civic responsibilities – In order to protect civil rights and make sure that the US system of government works, citizens must be willing to fulfill civic responsibilities. Some of these are obeying laws, paying taxes, voting, jury duty, and volunteering.

laws – rules set by the government that citizens must obey. In order to maintain order and protect the rights of everyone, citizens must be willing to obey local, state, and federal laws.

taxes – the number one way that local, state, and the federal governments raise the money that they need to operate. Responsible citizens pay the taxes that they owe so that governments can fulfill their role.

democracy – a system of government in which citizens elect their leaders and often vote on issues. Democracies give citizens a voice in their government. The United States is a democracy.

voting – a form of political participation. When citizens vote in elections they participate in choosing local, state, and national leaders. Sometimes citizens also vote on referendums, which allow them to help decide what laws their community will live by.

campaign volunteering – a form of political participation. Citizens volunteer to help political candidates win elections. Volunteers may go door-to-door, make phone calls, pass out flyers, or help in many other ways.

protests – allow citizens to participate by voicing their disagreement with the government. Protests often take the form of marches or rallies.

public office – serving in public office is an essential means of political participation. It would not do any good to have a democracy if citizens were not willing to run for and serve in positions of leadership.

juries – The Constitution guarantees everyone accused of a crime the right to a fair trial. One of the ways it protects this right is through the use of juries. Juries are groups of private citizens who decide whether or not an accused person is guilty. They make sure that people are judged by citizens like themselves rather than government officials.

jury duty – In order for the jury system to work, citizens must be willing to accept jury duty. They must be willing to sacrifice the time necessary to sit on juries, hear evidence presented at trials, and make decisions about people's guilt or innocence.

volunteer – agreeing to accept certain duties without pay in many ways. Many citizens volunteer to help in their communities, assist with campaigns, help the underprivileged, and so on.

military service – The military protects the United States against foreign threats. There have been times when the US military drafted citizens. Today, the United States armed forces relies on citizens who choose to enlist.

amendments – changes to the Constitution. Following ratification, Congress presented twelve amendments to the states. The states ratified ten of them.

Bill of Rights – the first ten amendments to the Constitution.

First Amendment – guarantees freedom of speech, freedom of the press, freedom to petition to government, freedom to assemble, and freedom of religion,

Second Amendment – protects citizens' right to bear arms.

Third Amendment – US citizens cannot be forced to house US soldiers in times of peace, and only "in a manner prescribed by law" during times of war.

Fourth Amendment – protects citizens from unlawful searches and seizures by the government. No government agency can enter a citizen's home or search their property without proper authority.

Fifth Amendment – states that the government must obey certain rules when charging someone with a crime. In the case of very serious crimes, citizens must first be indicted by a grand jury. It also protects people from double jeopardy and self incrimination. The government may not put a citizen on trial for the same crime more than once. Nor can it force accused people to testify against themselves in court. The Fifth Amendment also addresses eminent domain. The government may not take a citizen's property without paying them for it. The Fifth Amendment states that no person may be, "deprived of life, liberty, or property without due process of law."

due process – the government must follow the Constitution and respect an accused person's civil rights when arresting or putting that person on trial. It cannot punish someone for a crime or deny them any of their civil rights without following the rules set by law.

Sixth Amendment – guarantees an accused citizen the right to a defense lawyer. It also promises them the right to a speedy jury trial. The Sixth Amendment also states that an accused person may confront witnesses. No one can testify against the accused secretly. The accused must be given a chance to question them. The accused may also call witnesses during a criminal trial.

Seventh Amendment – states that civil defendants have the same right to a jury trial that criminal defendants have.

Eighth Amendment – protects citizens arrested or found guilty of a crime. It says that the government may not charge "excessive bail." It also forbids "excessive fines." The Eighth Amendment also states that the government cannot use "cruel and unusual punishment." The government must punish guilty people in a way that is consistent with the crime.

Ninth Amendment – states that the rights listed in the Bill of Rights are not the only ones enjoyed by US citizens.

Tenth Amendment – all powers not given to the federal government or restricted by the Constitution belong to the states. It grants a certain amount of authority to state governments.

constitutional convention – one of the ways that an amendment may be added to the Constitution. A constitutional convention involves representatives from each state meeting to consider changes to the constitution. If an amendment is approved by the convention, it then goes to the states. If three-fourths of the states ratify the amendment, it becomes part of the Constitution.

electoral college – The president and vice president of the United States are elected by the Electoral College. Each state is represented by a number of electors (delegates to the equal to the number of senators and representatives it has in Congress.

Twelfth Amendment – states that the delegates to the Electoral College shall vote separately for the offices of president and vice president of the United States. Before this amendment became law, whoever got the second highest number of electoral votes for president became the vice president.

Fifteenth Amendment – guaranteed the right to vote to all male citizens, no matter what their race.

Seventeenth Amendment – states that US senators shall be elected directly by the citizens of each state.

Nineteenth Amendment – granted women the right to vote.

Twenty-third Amendment – Under the Twenty-third Amendment, the District of Columbia (Washington DC) is entitled to have electors represent it in the Electoral College.

Twenty-fourth Amendment – makes the poll tax illegal. Its effect has been a huge increase in the number of African Americans who vote in elections and serve in public office. Before this amendment, the poll tax required voters to pay a fee to vote.

Twenty-sixth Amendment – states that all US citizens who are at least eighteen years old have the right to vote in elections.

E pluribus unum – a Latin phrase that means "out of many, one." It serves as a motto of the United States. The phrase first arose as a national motto in 1782. It was meant to suggest that out of the many states there is formed one nation. Over time, people came to identify the statement as meaning that from many different races, cultures, and backgrounds come one American people. The phrase is found on US currency, national symbols, and the country's official seal.

motto – a phrase meant to describe a nation, group, or organization.

Multiple Choice

1. B 2. C 3. A 4. C 5. D 6. B 7. C

CHAPTER 8: ECONOMIC UNDERSTANDINGS

Practice 8.1: Economic Principles and Their Impact on US History

Page 126

1. C 2. C

3. A price incentive is something that encourages consumers to buy something. The New Deal used government spending to provide incentives for people to spend money. By cutting taxes, the New Deal intended to leave businesses with more money to spend on production and citizens with more money to spend in the market. The New Deal also spent borrowed money on government programs to give citizens' jobs. By providing citizens with government jobs, the New Deal hoped to put more money back in peoples' pockets. The government hoped consumers would spend more money and help the economy move in the right direction. Roosevelt also introduced the Social Security system. It provided money to retired people and people out of work. President Roosevelt also the Federal Reserve System to give more money to banks. This made banks more secure and made them more willing to loan money. More loans meant that more people had money to buy things and businesses could stay in business.

4. Voluntary exchange between G8 countries helps maintain the economies of these nations and enables them to offer financial aid to less developed nations. NAFTA is designed to promote economic activity by allowing producers to sell their products more easily foreign markets, while allowing consumers to benefit from foreign competition. It is intended to boost the economies of all three nations. NAFTA increases production because producers can sell in more markets. It also allows consumers to spend more on more goods because competition keeps prices low. Opponents of NAFTA feel it costs US citizens their jobs. Supporters of NAFTA say that it increases production and helps the US economy. Some people criticize free trade because they believe that richer, more developed nations, often exploit (take advantage of) poorer, less developed nations by taking their resources and paying very little for labor.

5. Eli Whitney's cotton gin made cotton processing much faster and cheaper. It led to the South becoming a "cotton kingdom." New machines and factory assembly lines, like the one designed by Henry Ford for automobiles, greatly increased production and led to the US become an industrialized society. Edison's light bulb made the work day much longer and increased production by allowing factories to stay open after dark. The Bessemer Process was a new process that made manufacturing steel cheaper and allowed to railroads and cities to expand much cheaper and at a faster rate. Today, computers, the Internet, cell phones, and other forms of communications technology make production faster and more efficient than ever before.

Practice 8.2: US Economics

Page 130

1. B 2. C

3. Competition is an important part of the US economy. Competition occurs when businesses compete with one another for consumers. Since consumers are free to buy from whatever producer they want, producers have to compete to convince consumers to buy from them. Price and quality are the two main areas where producers compete. Price is how much the good or service costs. Quality is how well the product is made or the service is performed. Consumers tend to buy goods and services that are priced low and high quality. Sometimes, consumers are willing to give up a certain amount of quality in order to get a lower price. For instance, they might give up the extra comfort and features of a luxury car in order to buy a cheaper car that is less comfortable. On the other hand, sometimes people are willing to pay a higher price to get better

quality. A man who is about to propose to his girlfriend might pass on a cheaper ring in order to buy a more expensive, high-quality ring because he wants to get the best ring he can. In order to compete, businesses must price their goods and services at a level that consumers are willing to pay. Otherwise, the consumers will buy from someone else. Businesses that can't compete, must improve their quality, lower their prices, or go out of business. Competition usually keeps prices low and quality high.

4. Fiscal policy concerns how much the government taxes and spends. When the government raises taxes, it tends to decrease the amount of money in the economy. Businesses and citizens have to give more of their money to the government. Businesses have less to spend on production and employing workers, while citizens have less to spend in the market. On the other hand, when the government cuts taxes, it often boosts economic activity. Businesses and citizens have more money to spend. Monetary policy concerns the nation's money supply. If the government does not believe there is enough economic activity, the Federal Reserve will often take action to increase the money supply. The Federal Reserve loans money to banks and determines how much money banks must keep on hand rather than loaning. By lowering or raising interest rates, the Federal Reserve affects how much money banks loan. The more they loan, the more is in the economy. The more is in the economy, the more economic activity there is.

Practice 8.3: Personal Economics

Page 133

1. D 2. A

3. If people get into too much debt they run the risk of not being able to pay back the money they owe.

4. You need to save money so that you will have money for retirement, other big purchases, or to meet future financial challenges.

Chapter 8 Review

Key Terms, People, and Concepts

Pages 134 – 136

economics – the study of how governments, businesses, and people use their money.

market – where economic exchanges take place. People buy groceries, cars, computers, clothes, houses, and other items in a market. Goods and services are everything bought and sold in a market.

goods – things that can be touched, such as clothing and food are goods.

service – work that is paid for that does not produce something you can touch. Doctors and firefighters are examples of service workers. A service sometimes produces a good. A chef cooks a meal at a restaurant. Cooking the meal is a service. The meal cooked is a good.

price – the amount of money that producers are willing to sell a good or service for. In order for producers to produce a good or service, they must be able to sell it at a price that is higher than the amount it cost them to produce it.

producers – those who produce a good or service.

profit – the amount of money that producers make from the sale of a good or service. Producers want to make as much profit as possible.

consumers – those who buy a good or service.

demand – the goods and services people want and are willing to buy.

supply – the goods and services that are available that producers have produced.

opportunity cost – Whenever someone decides to spend their money on one good or service, it usually means they are giving up another good or service. The benefit of the good or service they give up is the opportunity cost.

opportunity costs of World War II – When the war began, the United States decided to stay out of the fighting. The US reasoned that war was not worth the opportunity costs of peace and economic trade. After the attack on Pearl Harbor, there were more opportunity costs. War production boosted the US economy. However, the government passed laws and encouraged people to give up buying things so that more could go to support the war effort. The satisfaction citizens would have gotten from buying things for themselves instead of sacrificing was the opportunity cost.

specialization – when one region, business, or person focuses on producing one thing. Specialization has had a lot of impact on US history. For centuries, the South specialized in cash crops like tobacco and cotton. Cotton led to a great dependence on slavery. Slavery eventually led to the Civil War. Even after the war, the South came to rely on textiles as a major industry due to its abundant cotton. In the North, large industries grew as businesses specialized in steel, oil, automobiles, and other forms of production.

Specialization also refers to individual workers. As industrialization occurred, more and more factories began to operate. In factories, workers specialized in one task. Each worker became faster and more efficient because they were responsible for just one part of the production process. Specialization tends to improve the quality of products and increase production. More goods are made in a shorter amount of time. This allows companies to sell more, make more money, provide more jobs, and pay employees higher wages. Specialization helps improve peoples' standards of living because it usually results in workers receiving higher pay and the market offering better products.

price incentive – something that encourages consumers to buy something. When a store puts shoes, clothes, or certain food items on sale, it is using a price incentive to convince consumers to buy those goods.

depression – If consumers stop spending money, businesses no longer make profits. If businesses go too long without profits, they have to fire workers or perhaps go out of business. When this happens, people lose jobs and can no longer pay for the things they need. If these conditions become bad enough they can lead to an economic period known as a depression.

Great Depression – the worst economic crisis in US history. Many people were unemployed, homeless, and very poor. The Stock Market Crash of 1929 marked the start of the Great Depression.

voluntary exchange – When producers freely choose to sell and consumers freely choose to buy. Voluntary exchange tends to help both buyers and sellers. Since consumers are free to buy what they want, their purchases reveal to producers what goods and services are in demand. This helps sellers because demand tells them what they should produce if they want to make a profit. It also helps consumers by making sure producers are only producing things consumers want or need.

trade – when countries exchange goods with one another.

imports – goods countries buy from other nations.

exports – goods countries sell to other nations.

free trade – occurs when nations trade with one another without any restrictions. The only things determining what goods are traded are supply and demand. Sometimes, trade is restricted.

tariffs – taxes on imports. Nations sometimes use tariffs to raise the price of imported goods and encourage citizens to buy products made in their own country.

sanctions – limit trade with certain countries. They are meant to punish a nation for some action or policy.

embargoes – meant to punish nations economically by refusing to trade with them at all.

G8 – an unofficial organization of industrialized nations. It includes the United States and several other countries. The G8 nations work together to maintain trade, peace, a clean environment, and address human rights questions. Voluntary exchange between G8 countries helps maintain the economies of these nations. It also enables them to offer financial aid to less developed countries.

NAFTA – North American Free Trade Agreement. It allows the United States, Canada, and Mexico to trade freely with one another. NAFTA is designed to promote economic activity in all three nations. It allows producers to sell their products more easily in foreign markets, while allowing consumers to benefit from foreign competition. Many support NAFTA as a great way to promote US economic growth. Others have criticized it because they feel it encourages US producers to move jobs to Mexico, where they can hire cheaper labor.

technology – For centuries, new technology has made production easier. Eli Whitney's cotton gin made cotton processing much faster and cheaper. Henry Ford's assembly line greatly increased production and led to the US become an industrialized society. Edison's light bulb made the work day much longer and increased production by allowing factories to stay open after dark. The Bessemer Process was a new process that made manufacturing steel cheaper and allowed railroads and cities to expand at a faster rate. Today, computers, the Internet, cell phones, and other forms of communications technology make production faster and more efficient than ever before.

private businesses – produce the goods and services that consumers buy. Private businesses range in size. Private businesses produce goods that they think they can sell for a profit. They provide what consumers need or want at a price consumers are willing to pay. Businesses also provide jobs that people depend on for income. People use their income to buy things. When businesses do well, the economy tends to grow. When businesses fail, people lose jobs, have less money to spend, buy less, and the economy can enter a down time.

banks – private businesses that specialize in loaning money. Banks are important to the economy because they allow people to buy things they normally could not afford.

interest – additional money a borrower pays a lender for the use of their money on the loan. Loans allow consumers to buy more expensive items or invest in things that they normally could not afford. They also allow banks to make money off of interest.

government's impact on the economy – The US government affects the economy in different ways. Taxes, monetary policy, and the Federal Reserve all impact the economy.

fiscal policy – how much the government taxes and spends.

tax – money citizens or businesses must pay the government. Taxes are the number one way governments raise the money they need to operate.

monetary policy – the nation's money supply.

Federal Reserve – loans money to banks and determines how much money banks must keep on hand rather than loaning. By lowering or raising interest rates, the Federal Reserve affects how much money banks loan.

competition – an important part of the US economy. Competition occurs when businesses compete with one another for consumers. Since consumers are free to buy from whatever producer they want, producers have to compete to convince consumers to buy from them. Price and quality are the two main areas where producers compete. Competition is good for consumers because it usually keeps prices low and quality high.

price – how much a good or service costs.

quality – how well a product is made or the service is performed.

labor – the work that people do.

income – the money businesses are willing to pay for labor. Income usually increases based on the amount of skill needed to perform a job. It also increases depending on how important the position is to the profitability of the company. Income is how much money a person makes.

entrepreneurs – people who start businesses. Entrepreneurs take financial risks. They spend their own money or borrowed money to start new businesses that they believe will eventually earn profits. Entrepreneurs help the US economy stay strong.

budget – a record of how you plan to spend your money. It helps keep you from spending too much. People who spend too much end up falling into debt.

debt – the amount of money that you owe. People get in debt when they spend more money than they have and are forced to borrow to pay for things.

expenses – the things people spend money on.

spending – when you give money in return for a good or service.

saving – when you take money you could spend and put it aside for a later time. People save money in different ways including: savings accounts and investing.

investing – one of the most popular ways people save money. Investing is when you allow businesses to use part of your money in return for interest or a share of their profits. People invest in a variety of ways. Many buy stocks or bonds. Others participate in mutual funds, which are made up of many companies. Still others might invest in CDs which keep their money in a special account for a set period of time.

reasons people save – people save money for different reasons. People often save for a new house, a new car, or a nice vacation. One of the most important things citizens save for is retirement.

why saving is important – Saving money is important for many reasons. People don't know what will happen in the future. They could lose their job, get hurt and be unable to work, have a huge expense that they did not plan on, or face other financial challenges. People who save money have an easier time dealing with such problems because they have money in savings that they can use to pay their bills.

Multiple Choice

1. C 2. D 3. B 4. D 5. A 6. A 7. C 8. A

Practice Test 1

Pages 137 – 150

1. A	11. B	21. A	31. C	41. B	51. B	61. B
2. A	12. A	22. C	32. A	42. B	52. D	62. D
3. C	13. B	23. D	33. A	43. B	53. A	63. C
4. B	14. D	24. A	34. D	44. C	54. B	64. B
5. A	15. C	25. B	35. C	45. B	55. B	65. A
6. D	16. B	26. B	36. C	46. C	56. B	66. A
7. B	17. B	27. B	37. B	47. D	57. C	67. C
8. D	18. C	28. A	38. B	48. C	58. A	68. B
9. A	19. B	29. C	39. A	49. A	59. C	69. C
10. B	20. A	30. C	40. A	50. A	60. D	70. A

Practice Test 2

Pages 151 – 163

1. D	11. A	21. A	31. A	41. A	51. A	61. C
2. D	12. B	22. D	32. C	42. D	52. B	62. D
3. A	13. B	23. D	33. C	43. A	53. A	63. B
4. C	14. A	24. B	34. B	44. D	54. C	64. C
5. B	15. B	25. B	35. A	45. C	55. A	65. C
6. B	16. D	26. A	36. B	46. D	56. C	66. D
7. C	17. A	27. A	37. B	47. C	57. A	67. C
8. A	18. B	28. B	38. A	48. C	58. B	68. C
9. B	19. C	29. D	39. B	49. A	59. B	69. C
10. D	20. C	30. B	40. B	50. C	60. B	70. B

CRCT

Please fill out the form completely, and return by mail or fax to American Book Company.

Purchase Order #: ____________ Date: ____________ Contact Person: ____________

School Name (and District, if any): ____________ Phone: ____________ Fax: ____________

E-mail: ____________

Credit Card #: ____________ Exp. Date: ____________ Authorized Signature: ____________

Billing Address: ____________ Shipping Address: ____________

Attn: ____________ ❑ same as billing Attn: ____________

Order Number	Product Title	Pricing* (10 books)	Qty	Pricing (30+ books)	Qty	Total Cost
GA1-M0809	Mastering the Georgia 1st Grade CRCT in Mathematics	$169.90 (1 set of 10 books)		$329.70 (1 set of 30 books)		
GA1-R0409	Mastering the Georgia 1st Grade CRCT in Reading	$169.90 (1 set of 10 books)		$329.70 (1 set of 30 books)		
GA2-M0409	Mastering the Georgia 2nd Grade CRCT in Mathematics	$169.90 (1 set of 10 books)		$329.70 (1 set of 30 books)		
GA2-R0409	Mastering the Georgia 2nd Grade CRCT in Reading	$169.90 (1 set of 10 books)		$329.70 (1 set of 30 books)		
GA2-H0409	Our State of Georgia (2nd Grade Social Studies)	$169.90 (1 set of 10 books)		$329.70 (1 set of 30 books)		
GA3-M0607	Mastering the Georgia 3rd Grade CRCT in Math	$169.90 (1 set of 10 books)		$329.70 (1 set of 30 books)		
GA3-R0607	Mastering the Georgia 3rd Grade CRCT in Reading	$169.90 (1 set of 10 books)		$329.70 (1 set of 30 books)		
GA3-S0508	Mastering the Georgia 3rd Grade CRCT in Science	$169.90 (1 set of 10 books)		$329.70 (1 set of 30 books)		
GA3-H1008	Mastering the Georgia 3rd Grade CRCT in Social Studies	$169.90 (1 set of 10 books)		$329.70 (1 set of 30 books)		
GA4-M0808	Mastering the Georgia 4th Grade CRCT in Math	$169.90 (1 set of 10 books)		$329.70 (1 set of 30 books)		
GA4-R0808	Mastering the Georgia 4th Grade CRCT in Reading	$169.90 (1 set of 10 books)		$329.70 (1 set of 30 books)		
GA4-S0708	Mastering the Georgia 4th Grade CRCT in Science	$169.90 (1 set of 10 books)		$329.70 (1 set of 30 books)		
GA4-H1008	Mastering the Georgia 4th Grade CRCT in Social Studies	$169.90 (1 set of 10 books)		$329.70 (1 set of 30 books)		
GA5-L0210	Mastering the Georgia 5th Grade CRCT in ELA	$169.90 (1 set of 10 books)		$329.70 (1 set of 30 books)		
GA5-M0806	Mastering the Georgia 5th Grade CRCT in Math	$169.90 (1 set of 10 books)		$329.70 (1 set of 30 books)		
GA5-R1206	Mastering the Georgia 5th Grade CRCT in Reading	$169.90 (1 set of 10 books)		$329.70 (1 set of 30 books)		
GA5-S1107	Mastering the Georgia 5th Grade CRCT in Science	$169.90 (1 set of 10 books)		$329.70 (1 set of 30 books)		
GA5-H0808	Mastering the Georgia 5th Grade CRCT in Social Studies	$169.90 (1 set of 10 books)		$329.70 (1 set of 30 books)		
GA5-W1008	Mastering the Georgia Grade 5 Writing Assessment	$169.90 (1 set of 10 books)		$329.70 (1 set of 30 books)		
GA6-L0508	Mastering the Georgia 6th Grade CRCT in ELA	$169.90 (1 set of 10 books)		$329.70 (1 set of 30 books)		
GA6-M0305	Mastering the Georgia 6th Grade CRCT in Math	$169.90 (1 set of 10 books)		$329.70 (1 set of 30 books)		
GA6-R0108	Mastering the Georgia 6th Grade CRCT in Reading	$169.90 (1 set of 10 books)		$329.70 (1 set of 30 books)		
GA6-S1206	Mastering the Georgia 6th Grade CRCT in Science	$169.90 (1 set of 10 books)		$329.70 (1 set of 30 books)		
GA6-H0208	Mastering the Georgia 6th Grade CRCT in Social Studies	$169.90 (1 set of 10 books)		$329.70 (1 set of 30 books)		
GA7-L0508	Mastering the Georgia 7th Grade CRCT in ELA	$169.90 (1 set of 10 books)		$329.70 (1 set of 30 books)		
GA7-M0305	Mastering the Georgia 7th Grade CRCT in Math	$169.90 (1 set of 10 books)		$329.70 (1 set of 30 books)		
GA7-R0707	Mastering the Georgia 7th Grade CRCT in Reading	$169.90 (1 set of 10 books)		$329.70 (1 set of 30 books)		
GA7-S1206	Mastering the Georgia 7th Grade CRCT in Science	$169.90 (1 set of 10 books)		$329.70 (1 set of 30 books)		
GA7-H0208	Mastering the Georgia 7th Grade CRCT in Social Studies	$169.90 (1 set of 10 books)		$329.70 (1 set of 30 books)		
GA8-L0505	Passing the Georgia 8th Grade CRCT in ELA	$169.90 (1 set of 10 books)		$329.70 (1 set of 30 books)		
GA8-MATH08	Passing the Georgia 8th Grade CRCT in Math	$169.90 (1 set of 10 books)		$329.70 (1 set of 30 books)		
GA8-R0505	Passing the Georgia 8th Grade CRCT in Reading	$169.90 (1 set of 10 books)		$329.70 (1 set of 30 books)		
GA8-S0707	Passing the Georgia 8th Grade CRCT in Science	$169.90 (1 set of 10 books)		$329.70 (1 set of 30 books)		
GA8-H0607	Passing the Georgia 8th Grade CRCT in Georgia Studies	$169.90 (1 set of 10 books)		$329.70 (1 set of 30 books)		
GA8-W0907	Passing the Georgia Grade 8 Writing Assessment	$169.90 (1 set of 10 books)		$329.70 (1 set of 30 books)		

2-15-10

*Minimum order is 1 set of 10 books of the same subject.

Subtotal	
Shipping & Handling 12%	
Total	

American Book Company • PO Box 2638 • Woodstock, GA 30188-1383
Toll Free Phone: 1-888-264-5877 • Toll-Free Fax: 1-866-827-3240
Web Site: www.americanbookcompany.com

Call Toll Free 1-888-264-5877 to ORDER and for FREE PREVIEW COPY